Restaurant and Fast Food Site Selection

JOHN C. MELANIPHY

John Wiley & Sons, Inc.

New York • Chichester • Brisbane • Toronto • Singapore

This publication is designed to provide accurate and authoritative information in regard to the subject matter covered. It is sold with the understanding that the publisher is not engaged in rendering legal, accounting, or other professional service. If legal advice or other expert assistance is required, the services of a competent professional person should be sought. *From a Declaration of Principles jointly adopted by a Committee of the American Bar Association and a Committee of Publishers.*

Library of Congress Cataloging in Publication Data:

Melaniphy, John C.
  Restaurant and fast food site selection / John C. Melaniphy.
    p. cm.
  Includes index.
  ISBN 0-471-55716-1 (cloth)
  1. Restaurants, lunch rooms, etc.—Location. 2. Fast food restaurants—Location. I. Title
  TX911-3.L62M46 1992
  647.95'068'8—dc20   91-34535

Printed and bound by Malloy Lithographing, Inc.

10 9 8 7 6 5 4 3 2 1

To Guy Hatfield, Jr.,

who, in the early 1950s, pioneered programs
of site evaluation and selection
that have affected my life.

Although he may not be widely known,
he is internationally respected.

Acknowledgments

This book is the result of 19 years of effort on my part, along with the assistance of many others. It has been so long in coming that it has often been referred to as "John's infamous book." Writing a book is a painful experience, especially when the author is in an everchanging environment and busy in a dynamic industry. Nevertheless, with the help of others, this work has finally come to fruition.

Eileen Hullihan has been an integral part of this process from the very beginning, typing, reviewing, suggesting, editing, encouraging, and, yes, even laughing. Nancy Sullivan carried out the original research of books and articles on the subject. Her tireless efforts have long been appreciated. My daughter, Patti, participated in just about everything; her help has been a godsend.

My wife, Carol, put up with my always-ready statement, "I have to work on the book." This came in very handy when yardwork was in the offing. Her help, encouragement, love, and yardwork have been essential.

My thanks and appreciation also go to Claire Thompson, my editor at John Wiley & Sons. Finally, I would like to thank my associates and clients, who over the years have listened to, challenged, and discussed my theories, axioms, and applications.

J.C.M.

Contents

Introduction

The food service business is exciting. It is an everchanging industry that has made millionaires of some and paupers of others. At the same time, society has contributed an everchanging scene, creating new opportunities and eliminating others. Today, more working women, fewer children, television addiction, the "yuppie" generation, the tendency to eat more meals away from home, the couch potato, emphasis on individual taste, the "escape from the kitchen" mind-set, and the graying of America are among the factors that have created numerous opportunities to meet general and specific market demands. Nevertheless, the food industry continues to have the highest attrition rate of any industry in the United States. Because it has been fairly easy to get into the business with a limited amount of cash, food operations have been severely undercapitalized. As a result, although the rewards are great, the risks are usually greater.

In many respects, the food service industry is overbuilt. Opportunities exist, however, for the right concepts in the proper locations, either by taking over a failed facility from the previous operator or by creating a new restaurant or fast food unit. If the proper concept, demographics, access, trade area, and competition are present, these elements greatly enhance the opportunity for success. It is important to approach the situation with open eyes, and to clearly assess the market and locational conditions, before placing capital and personal effort at risk.

This book makes available to the reader the significant factors and reliable sources of information about restaurant and fast food site selection. I have tried to provide readers with a method for assessing their situation to arrive at an informed decision. For more than 30 years, I have participated in the changes that have taken place in the restaurant and fast food industry. In studying markets and, more specifically, selecting locations, I have observed and become increasingly aware of many avoidable mistakes. Some of these errors were operational; many others, however, were locational, and such mistakes normally cannot be rectified regardless of the executive hours dedicated to achieving success. My goal in these pages is to help people in the restaurant and food service industry make wise market and locational choices. The principles and procedures that I have outlined here provide the key ingredients to successful locational selection. Those who carry out all the methods presented in this book will also find an organized way to determine their business destiny.

Having read this far, many food people may say, "I know all the answers; I have a successful business; why do I need this information?" There are *some* exceptions to my basic principles. You know: the restaurant located across the railroad tracks, behind the barn, adjacent to the river, accessible only by a gravel road, and miles from a living human being. If we studied this restaurant, we would no doubt find that its success is the result of uniqueness and personal touch. The restaurateur (and often his or her spouse) has spent the past 20 years, 7 days a week, contributing blood, sweat, and tears to create an atmosphere of good food and service, recognized by the general public. For each such establishment that has succeeded, literally thousands have failed. Experience indicates that the same restaurant in a more accessible location might have experienced success much more rapidly.

You may think you are an exception, and perhaps you are. It is more likely, however, that you are not, because competition is significant, overbuilding continues, and saturation is a reality. Leases generally run from 10 to 20 years, and new buildings usually cost between $400,000 and $2,000,000 plus, with the land ranging anywhere from $250,000 to $1,000,000 or more. Existing buildings often require extensive remodeling to be attractively competitive. As a result, the need to ensure success is absolute.

Site selection, if properly done, takes time and costs money, which will immediately discourage some people (I usually find them coming back after the mistake has occurred). Nevertheless, an effective market and site investigation will pay for itself many times over.

Utilizing the process is like using a zoom lens. You start out with uncertainty (if you are honest with yourself), but as you gather facts, (and I mean facts), areas of opportunities quickly become obvious. The more closely you focus on the investigation and its applications, the narrower and more precise the picture becomes. Some food people may choose to develop only locational criteria, whereas others may decide to develop both locational and sales estimation programs. The degree of intensity depends on the needs of each individual operator, or of the multichain company.

The principles, procedures, and general advice in this book, if followed, will minimize mistakes, will maximize sales, and with good management will help to ensure locational longevity. It is up to you. A dog location is a dog! How much time and money do you have for a "bow wow"? Read on!

Part One

The Tools

One

Principles of Restaurant and Fast Food Site Selection

S ite selection actions of many restaurateurs include "follow the leader," simply, "guts it out," or "find the best deal." Their criteria are nebulous; they seldom use analysis; and most often a "good real estate deal" influences their decision. Selecting what may or may not be a good location is often a rationalized decision. Furthermore, many entrepreneurs in the fast food business have suffered from the "McDonald's syndrome," namely, the philosophy that being in proximity to McDonald's assures success. Fast food failures that were located according to this insanity proliferate our major traffic arteries. Even McDonald's has made its share of locational mistakes.

The food industry is rife with massive egoists, who have all the answers—and some actually do. Most, however, do not! Unfortunately, ego often gets in the way of wise decisions, resulting in lost money and considerable grief. For those of you who do not believe this observation, I will be happy to describe the morgue of former "hot" restaurants and fast food operations whose days have come and gone rather too quickly. I had a client, for example, who was a successful restaurant operator. He had started a unique and successful concept. Against good advice (mine), he proceeded to build a similar restaurant with the same name in the same middle-sized community. As he might have expected, the mystique was lost; sales were cannibalized; the poor performance of one establishment drained the other, and subsequently both places closed. The food operator is now employed by another restaurant. The shame of the situation is that careful planning could easily have averted it.

The principles I describe in this book were developed over the past 30 years. I first set many of them to paper in 1971, following the "great food surge" of the latter 1960s and have continued modifying them to reflect significant changes in market conditions or locational factors. These principles force the user to engage in soul-searching, fact-finding, and logical thought processes that lead, hopefully, to realistic conclusions. Following these principles conscientiously minimizes locational error. If properly exploited, the selection process not only can maximize locational decision making, but also can help determine marketing decisions. Not all the principles are applicable to all situations. Some dinner restaurants, for example, offset the need for visibility with a unique concept or menu. On the other hand, visibility is critical to the fast food industry. Throughout the book, I have tried to point out the important different aspects of each principle, depending on the type of eating facility.

The following are my Principles of Restaurant and Fast Food Site Selection:

1. Know Your Operation
2. Determine Your Customer Profile
3. Delineate Trade Areas
4. Establish Locational Criteria
5. Analyze the Market Structure
6. Gather Factual Market Resource Data
7. Ensure Adequate Accessibility
8. Recognize the Importance of Employment
9. Identify Generative Areas
10. Clarify Attitudes, Trends, Habits, and Patterns
11. Evaluate Competitive Facilities

12. Understand Visibility and Exposure
13. Estimate Sales Potential
14. Evaluate Site Economics and Physical Characteristics

DEFINITIONS OF THE PRINCIPLES

Know Your Operation

Although this book does not discuss operations (because that is an entirely different subject), it goes without saying that you must understand your business. Moreover, knowing your operation is a prerequisite to any expansion. In fact, this is the strength of the food business. Food operators can usually recite and compare food costs, labor costs, controllables, and uncontrollables. Numbers are traded and widely discussed. Daily tallies, transactions, customer counts, meals purchased, and, hopefully, profits fill numerous notebooks. Nonetheless, as mundane as it sounds, you must truly grasp the complexities of your operation and accurately gauge your management ability before expanding. Have you done your homework? If you are entering the food industry for the first time, have you studied successful food operations, and do you feel thoroughly familiar with their techniques?

Determine Your Customer Profile

Customers are attracted to any food operation for numerous reasons. As a food operator, you should know why customers choose your facility. Also, identifying the characteristics of your most frequent customers is essential. Without such data, you are going into a firefight armed with a BB gun. I am continually amazed at the number of food executives, responsible for spending millions of dollars, who do not really know their customer profile. At least once a week, a major food operator or officer of a major food organization tells me that his or her customer is "everyone." When I ask, "How do you know that?" the usual response is, "Well, I observe," or "My managers tell me." That is absurd! Often after my staff has carried out our Customer Profile Survey Program, we find that the true profile varies considerably from the executive's opinion and, in fact, may be directly opposite of the customer that was represented to us. I cannot overemphasize the need to find out who your potential customers are, why they come to you, or why they do not come to you. The most important customer is usually the most frequent visitor, and that profile may differ considerably from the total customer distribution. *One of the primary secrets for successful site selection is targeting areas with demographics that match your "most frequent visitors" characteristics.*

Delineate Trade Areas

Numerous factors, including the following, dictate the size of trade areas: type of food facility, type of location, income, topography, competition, traffic artery, physical and psychological barriers, activity generators, consumer patterns, visibility (sometimes), and socioeconomic characteristics. Historically, restaurants have focused on a five-mile trade area, while fast food facilities have settled on a three-mile radius. In many instances, these distances are realistic; just as often, however, they are not. It is important to analyze the type of location and the extent of the trade area that might result from a new operation. In a major urban area a "special occasion" restaurant may attract customers from 15 to 20 miles away, and rural locations with the right type of restaurant can attract customers in a radius of 60 to 100 miles. Moreover, fast food facilities near major regional shopping centers often take on the trade area characteristics of the mall. In reality, trade areas are not rigidly round, square, or rectangular. Instead, they are positively influenced by the attraction of the restaurant and negatively affected by factors such as competition and physical barriers.

Establish Locational Criteria

Examples of locational criteria include the following: types of locations, traffic arteries, trade area size, speed limits, number of moving lanes, adjacent uses, traffic flow, traffic counts, ingress, egress, visibility, competition, employment, topography, demographics, ethnic characteristics, and perhaps a liquor license. These characteristics can take on many dimensions. For the individual who is starting a new restaurant operation and has no locational experience, the site attributes of other similar and successful food operations can provide very important guidelines. Multichain operators can draw on past experiences by analyzing their most successful units, average units, and perhaps less successful restaurants.

Another method is to examine the experiences of other operators and competitors. How have they fared? Where are their most successful units? Why are they the most successful restaurants? What is common to their locational success? Likewise, almost anyone can identify and observe unsuccessful or failing restaurants or fast food operations and probably should avoid their locational characteristics. *Studying the failures often is as useful as studying the most successful food operations.*

Analyze the Market Structure

Every market, whether it is a neighborhood, a small city, or a major urban area, has a structure that partially determines the extent of a trade area, the patterns that exist, and travel times. The structure includes the shape of a city or an area, the road network, barriers (physical and psychological), income, topography, zoning, sewer and water availability, ethnic and socioeconomic characteristics, and climate. Structure plays a role in directional growth patterns, employment concentrations, development, eating-out patterns, and other factors that have generally influenced past and present development. Furthermore, this same structure is likely to influence future growth in the community. Understanding market structure is essential in selecting good locations for food facilities.

Gather Factual Market Resource Data

Restaurant and fast food operators compete for eating-out or eating and drinking dollars, usually generated by the resident population, traffic, daytime working population, or some combination of these groups. Market resources include population, socioeconomic characteristics, age structure, income, eating-out expenditures, lifestyle, and household size. Through an orderly procedure, you can determine the extent of the present and future market.

How often have you heard someone say, "This is a great area. There are 50,000 people within three miles, and everybody is buying land in this area. It's a hot spot! You'd better hurry up." Do not get caught up in the hysteria, but instead do your homework. A small amount of investigation can clearly identify if an area meets your locational and market needs. Nevertheless, land purchases occur daily that are the result of hearsay, lack of information, or misinformation.

Cities are composed of homogeneous and heterogeneous areas that develop into neighborhoods because of income, social structure, employment concentrations, local schools, road patterns, transportation systems, directional growth patterns, generative facilities, and physical and psychological barriers. These elements provide the market resources necessary to support food service facilities. Market resources can be inventoried and quantified to determine the share of market that a planned restaurant or fast food operation can anticipate. It is possible to calculate demographics with a fairly high degree of accuracy and to compare them with customer characteristics. Also, expenditures can be estimated to determine eating-out potential. *It is not the number of people in the trade area, but rather who they are and what they spend that is of paramount importance.*

Ensure Adequate Accessibility

Accessibility within a metropolitan area includes the ability of motorists to move from one part of the area to another. Locationally, accessibility represents the ease with which people move into and out of an area and, more particularly, into and out of the specific location. When determining accessibility, it is necessary to consider major and minor traffic arteries, number of lanes, speed limits, turn signals, turning lanes, curb cuts, traffic backup, congestion points, and the existence of median strips. You must also study automobile or pedestrian traffic counts, traffic flow, traffic peaks and valleys, and other pertinent data. Traffic counts alone do not dictate accessibility; in fact, they are a misnomer. Total traffic counts, like the total population in an area, are only indicators. Rather the *hourly traffic counts* are the important ingredient.

Recognize the Importance of Employment

Many restaurants and most fast food operations need lunch and possibly breakfast business for success. Therefore, it is important to understand the employment patterns in a specific area. It is unnecessary to speculate about the number of employed persons, the types of jobs that they have, and their incomes; sources are available that can provide current facts and future forecasts.

Dinner restaurants are less concerned with employment. They are more interested in traffic patterns, the resident population base, income, visitors to the area, and their ability to attract repeat customers on a fairly frequent basis.

Identify Generative Areas

For most food service operators, particularly fast food and chain restaurant operators, generative locations are a must. By generative locations, I mean sites that are near major generative facilities, such as major malls, or concentrations of office, hotel, industrial, and other commercial facilities. For restaurant facilities located in a downtown area, the generative conduit may be several buildings or the downtown itself. In Orlando, Florida, Disneyworld is a major generative facility, and Newport Beach, California, has Fashion Square. Hotels in a beach area in Florida are generative, as are the casinos in Las Vegas. A university, such as Ohio State in Columbus, Ohio, or a hospital complex, such as Mayo Clinic in Rochester, Minnesota, can be generative areas. It is essential to explore the many varieties of generative facilities because they increase the frequency of visit into an area and establish people patterns. Understanding their importance can represent the difference between choosing a poor location and a great sales performer.

Clarify Attitudes, Trends, Habits, and Patterns

Consumer attitudes and trends are constantly changing. They are influenced by such variables as our ages, income, lifestyle, professions, aspirations, opportunities, societal trends, household composition and size, and our feeling of well being. Most of us, for example, are very much aware of the current emphasis on health in our diet (light beer versus the good old regular stuff, etc.). We need to be cognizant of present and future trends in considering locational opportunities.

We are all creatures of habit. Employed persons establish a travel pattern to and from work. Although it may vary occasionally, this pattern, for the most part, is easy to identify. A housewife also sets up a distinguishable pattern that may involve taking the children to and from school, shopping, running household errands, and participating in other recurring everyday events. The working mother's busy and hectic pattern also can be identified and evaluated. Most food strip centers spring up to intercept all or a portion of these patterns. Retail and food facilities along the routes to major regional shopping centers hope to divert customers.

Thus, it is essential to evaluate the patterns of people within an area. When creating a multiunit development strategy, you must understand the patterns of a metropolitan area. A misinterpretation or lack of knowledge of such habits and patterns has caused the failure of many food operations.

Evaluate Competitive Facilities

Competition can usually be divided into two types: direct and indirect—for most types of food operations. A French restaurant competes directly with other French restaurants, but indirectly with other specialty restaurants. Hardee's, McDonald's, Burger King, and Wendy's are direct competition to each other; whereas they are indirect competitors to Kentucky Fried Chicken, Taco Bell, Denny's, and Arby's (although recent additions to fast food menus are, in a sense, making them more directly competitive). Obviously, the more direct the competition, the greater is the tendency toward saturation. Conversely, the less direct the competition, the more the opportunity for market share exists. Competitive analysis frequently is inadequate. How can a person determine the sales potential of a proposed new unit without thoroughly understanding the performance of the existing competitive facilities? Unfortunately, it is impossible; nevertheless, would-be entrepreneurs attempt it every day.

Understand Visibility and Exposure

Visibility is the ability of a site, building, or sign to be seen; exposure is being seen over a long period of time. Whereas visibility creates opportunities for impulse eating, exposure gradually influences patterns and decision making. Visibility is extremely important to the fast food industry and popular-priced restaurants, because high visibility allows the consumer more time to change lanes and navigate the entrance to the eatery's parking lot. For some restaurants, lack of visibility contributes to a certain uniqueness and atmosphere, (e.g., a speakeasy located down an alley). Nevertheless, for most food operations, the better the visibility, the greater the opportunity to do business.

Estimate Sales Potential

To a degree, all restaurants and food service establishments are competing for the same eating-out food expenditure dollar. There are wide differences, however, between the dining expenditure of a family with children and those of a couple, perhaps including a husband and wife, friends, and/or business associates. Other factors can be differences in breakfast, lunch, and dinner expenditures or in the costs of casual versus formal dining. Entertainment adds a significant dimension, as does special occasion dining.

Almost all food operators estimate sales. Often, however, they have problems because of using methods that produce inaccurate results. Estimating sales is properly accomplished by evaluating all the factors that affect a restaurant or fast food facility's potential. Unfortunately, sales are often calculated using the "back-of-the-envelope" method. This famous, yet unscientific, approach, involves estimating the cost of land and building, computing the total occupancy cost, and using that figure as a basis to determine the amount of sales needed to justify making the deal. What a foolish way to approach such a significant risk! The cost of developing an accurate sales estimate is minuscule compared with the cost and mental anguish of a failing restaurant.

Evaluate Site Economics and Physical Characteristics

Site economics represent the ability of a restaurant's sales at a given location to support the cost of land, building, and equipment (or rent), while providing an acceptable profit and return on investment. There are two directions for approaching this topic. First, a careful estimate of the sales potential of a particular restaurant or fast food operation can be used to determine an acceptable cost of land and building. Second, the economics in the marketplace, such as land and construction costs, indicate the level of sales necessary to support a specific food facility. For a unit to provide an adequate return on invested capital, its sales potential must match or exceed the site economics. More and more food companies are reevaluating their goals and objectives because their per unit sales are insufficient to justify the current costs of land and building; often, they must modify their operations. Sometimes the higher costs are the result of environmental requirements, over which neither the buyer nor seller has control. In other cases, the company can cut costs by redefining its goals and objectives and targeting locations that will generate high sales, eliminating those that can no longer be economically justified in the local market.

A final principle might be added for chain restaurant and fast food operators regarding advertising and market saturation. My experience indicates that once a sufficient number of units have been added to a marketplace, advertising, customer acceptance, and awareness should have a positive overall impact on the sales of existing and new units. Although this works for well-run and successful chains, it has not worked for all food operations. Promotion is extremely important to the success of a food company, but the majority of restaurant and fast food operators need to be well located before they worry about advertising gross rating points.

SUMMARY

I have refined the above principles through many years of analysis and experience in the food industry. Unfortunately, food operators often consider these rules to be cumbersome, time consuming, and costly. Instead, they apply the *tokenism approach.* I dare say that if we could recapture all the food, labor, and controllable and uncontrollable costs that have been allocated to mismanagement, inadequate site selection techniques, and inaccurate sales estimation programs, we could pay for thorough site selection programs for every major food firm and have plenty of funds left over.

Two

Types of Restaurant and Fast Food Locations

R estaurant and fast food facilities normally fall into fairly specific locational categories, although these classifications are generally much broader for restaurants than for fast food operations. Because the owner's personality often plays a pivotal role in the success of a dinner restaurant, some successful operations can be found in secondary sites. Most such restaurants are marginal, however, and many fail.

In the fast food business, even with saturation objectives, there is little justification for secondary locations that produce mediocre results because higher sales requirements and significant competition demand more rigid location prerequisites. Whereas 16 kinds of location have been defined for the restaurant industry, only 11 of these site-types apply to the fast food industry. Although there are some exceptions to these definitions, the vast majority of food operations, whether they be fast food, coffee shops, steak houses, or fashionable and formal dinner houses, fall into these categories. *Locational classification is important because locational and market criteria can be different for each category.* For example, a fast food location near a major regional shopping center may have little dependence on close-in population resources, since its sales correlate with the mall's sales. Conversely, a location in a small commercial strip normally depends on nearby population resources. *Most large and diverse fast food chains should have 4 to 10 different criteria for different types of location.*

Many locations can also be categorized as freestanding *or* in-line. The term *freestanding* is self-explanatory; *in-line*, however, may be less familiar. An in-line location is usually found in a strip of stores in either a business area or a shopping center. It is not on a corner, but is located in an "inside" position. Both freestanding and in-line sites will be explored later in this book. The following sections describe the various types of locations. (They are not listed in any special order.)

MAJOR TRAFFIC ARTERIES

In general, a major traffic artery is one that usually carries more than 15,000 cars in a 24-hour period. In many major metropolitan areas, a major traffic artery is a street that carries more than 20,000 cars during the same 24-hour period. These locations usually develop because a high concentration of traffic moves through the area. Often, the major artery enjoys significant intersecting streets. Numerous food facilities, both fast food and dinner houses, are concentrated along such traffic arteries. In some cases, however, individually owned dinner houses have sought this type of location, though usually away from concentrations of other food facilities. For the most part, fast food units, given proper demographics, income, generative concentrations, and eating-out food expenditures, flourish here. Dinner houses also, depending on the socioeconomic level they serve, generally have good results. Examples include Ogden Avenue in west suburban Chicagoland, Rockville Pike in the Washington, D.C., area, Westheimer Avenue in Houston, and Ventura Boulevard in Los Angeles.

NEAR SHOPPING CENTERS AND COMMERCIAL CONCENTRATIONS

The strongest concentration of activities in suburbia is usually in proximity to major malls and other major commercial facilities. In fact, the most significant suburban generator is almost always a major mall, although other entities, such as office buildings often coexist. The high frequency of travel to and from such areas, encourages many food facilities to locate nearby. While this kind of location is desirable, it does not ensure success, because other considerations, such as competition, demographic characteristics, and ingress and egress, must be right. Areas of this nature do offer a much higher likelihood for success when they are located on a major traffic artery with good access.

MAJOR MULTIPLE-USE GENERATIVE CONCENTRATIONS

These concentrations vary from regional shopping centers to major office developments to hotels, industrial parks, and mixed-use developments. Originally found in downtown areas, today, this type of location is almost always in the suburbs. Recently, some new ones have been developed in the city, outside of downtown areas. Many food operations are either in the developments or in proximity to them.

DENSE-URBAN AREAS

A dense-urban location (outside of downtown) is generally in the central city or in older suburban communities with significant density of population. Such a location will often have 200,000 plus persons within a three-mile radius. Until recently, the most sought-after locations were in newly developing suburban areas, but excessive competition and the slowdown in suburban sprawl have shifted the locational emphasis of many restaurants back to the city. Gentrifying "yuppie" and "dink" (dual-income-no-kids) neighborhoods offer especially desirable opportunities. Many fast food operators have found a gold mine in locations on major traffic arteries within the dense-urban environment. The "Lettuce Entertain You" group in Chicago has been especially successful developing varying restaurant concepts, often with limited parking, oriented toward young (and older) professionals in gentrified Chicago neighborhoods. Competitively priced dinner houses have also enjoyed a renaissance in these areas. More of this type of activity is likely during the next five years.

HIGHWAY INTERCHANGES

Highway locations are principally oriented toward the U.S. interstate and highway system. To a lesser extent, this is also true in Canada. Food facilities are located on accessible highways, near major interchanges of limited access expressways, or on service roads adjacent to major freeways. Accessible highway locations usually attract customers from a wide area, particularly in rural areas. This is especially important since *driving time is more important than distance*. Although highway locations generally serve a very wide area, both fast food operations and dinner house facilities usually have a lower frequency of customer visit. It is not unusual, for example, to find a fast food operation with a trade area of 10 to 15 miles, or a restaurant with a 40-mile trade area (sometimes even much larger) because of its proximity to an interstate system.

A highway location can be risky for a fast food operation. It is essential to select the right interchange and to provide adequate ingress and egress. The risk can be reduced if there is an employment concentration or a major residential area nearby. An interchange in an area with a large employment concentration will have a positive impact on lunch business, again assuming acceptable ingress and egress to the site. At a heavily trafficked interchange location with an adequate backup residential population, a popularly priced dinner house featuring good food will often be successful. Naturally, the basic market resources must be sufficient. Interstate locations in rural areas, oriented specifically to the traffic on the highway, require special locational considerations, including driving times, truck stops, tourist attractions, distance between stops, service station concentrations, hotel and motel locations, time extensions between major cities, and nearby employment concentrations.

For the most part, restaurants in tollroad service centers have played to mixed reviews. Recently, many have been taken over by well-known fast food operators. On heavily traveled sections of tollroads, such eateries usually do quite well; but where traffic is light, the results have been disappointing. Restaurants at tollway interchanges have also had uneven success. Dinner houses have generally done reasonably well, but toll costs have adversely affected popular-priced restaurants, especially fast food facilities.

DOWNTOWN LOCATIONS

Downtown areas are continuing to change; most of them, however, have declined as major retail centers. Fewer shoppers are oriented toward downtown, and evening and weekend dining has diminished significantly, although revitalization has reversed this situation in a few major urban areas.

My studies indicate that women, more often than men, influence the restaurant selection decision. Because most women avoid visiting downtown areas unless they work there, their orientation is directed toward more familiar areas, rather than toward downtown restaurant facilities that may present traffic and parking hassles, and security problems, especially in the evening. Furthermore, suburban housing is considerably distant from the downtown area, and suburbia has a fine selection of good restaurants.

The perception of crime in the downtown areas has had an important effect; people simply do not feel safe in most downtowns at night. As a result, more and more such areas are deserted after dark, resulting in a decline in dinner houses. Most restaurants in downtowns must live off a very strong lunch and light, if any, breakfast and dinner business. This paradox has led to a rise in the number of fast food operations, which are "picking up the slack" heretofore met by full-service restaurants. While occupancy costs are high, sales potential in an adequate location is also high. It is no longer unusual to find a fast food operation within a downtown area capturing in excess of $2,000,000 in sales. These fast food facilities are oriented toward the daytime working population. The potential market depends almost wholly on the number of people working or visiting the downtown area daily. In a smaller number of downtown areas, a true improvement is occurring and dinner houses are flourishing. However, caution is the watchword.

Numerous downtown redevelopment projects are planned or underway across the country. Some represent opportunities for full-service restaurant operations; others lack the dynamics to attract nighttime business. Each development must be carefully evaluated to determine its individual potential. For example, Water Tower Place in Chicago has been successful for full-service restaurants and fast food facilities. Conversely, Horton Plaza in San Diego, a major downtown redevelopment project, has not been able to attract enough evening customers to its restaurant facilities, although the complex is successful.

OLDER BUSINESS DISTRICTS IN LARGER CITIES AND SUBURBAN DOWNTOWN AREAS

Shopping centers and malls have adversely affected most older business districts and many suburban downtown areas. As a result, their importance has declined significantly, unless they are a public transportation point or have a commuter train station. A number of large, older, commercial business districts in major midwest and northeastern cities offer considerable opportunity for moderately priced restaurants, family-oriented facilities, sandwich shops, pizza parlors, coffee shops, and fast food operations. Some fine dinner houses exist in these areas. However, interest has diminished because of the high cost of real estate and the moderate sales results.

MAJOR MALLS AND SHOPPING CENTERS

Successful major malls provide concentrations of pedestrian traffic within the mall areas and therefore present locational opportunities. Enclosed malls usually offer greater potential because they protect against inclement weather. This has been especially true for fast food operators who have discovered the possibility of high sales within such areas. The critical factor in determining whether to enter a major mall is the dynamics of the mall itself: age of the customers; sales productivity (per square foot); and, most important, the placement within the mall. It is quite possible to be in the right mall, but in the wrong location.

Perhaps the most successful restaurants in malls have been theme restaurants, such as Houlihan's or Ruby Tuesday's. However, more often than not, they have visibility, signage, and an outside entrance to control their own environment. Some dinner houses have been developed in major regional shopping centers; however, the degree of success has been quite varied. No correlation exists between the amount of sales generated by a mall and the sales that a dinner house in the mall can expect. More often, the restaurant is better off in a nearby location where it can control its own destiny and is not subject to the high costs of mall occupancy.

Food courts in major malls are affected by the mall's sales productivity, the location of the food court, competition in the food court, the types of food units to be included, the number of seats available, and seating type and turnover. (In many cases, seating and turnover are insufficient.) Well-planned food courts with a carefully selected group of fast food operations have done very well. Mall developers like food courts because they can generate more rents and percentage rentals in smaller space. Furthermore, if properly executed, the food court becomes a minigenerator, creating traffic for nearby retailers in the mall.

UNIVERSITY AREAS

Primarily concentrated in resident universities or college areas and towns, this market is usually oriented mainly toward fast food operations, theme facilities, coffee shops, popularly priced sit-down restaurants, and watering holes. Expensive dinner houses have experienced varied results. Large student bodies, who have a strong orientation toward fast food menus, usually generate a lucrative market for such an operation if the unit is adequately positioned. A one-half block locational mistake can spell disaster. Again, it is absolutely essential to know your market. Some fast food operations have located units in student unions, with mixed results, because of high labor turnover and poor profits. Theme restaurants and "fern bars" have usually fared well when properly located, based on awareness of the existing competitors and the local "watering hole" traditions. Old patterns are sometimes difficult to change.

HOTELS, RESORTS, AND VACATION AREAS

Full-service restaurants and some fast food operations have developed near hotel concentrations, resorts, and vacation areas. Such facilities are directed at a specific market and hence are affected by changes in that market. The following questions need to be answered: Are there sufficient visitors generated by the hotel facilities to create a market for additional food facilities outside the hotels themselves? What is the quality and quantity of the food facilities provided within the hotels and resorts? In various parts of Florida and in places like Las Vegas, large concentrations of visitors to hotel facilities have created markets for both dinner houses and fast food operations. However, they have gone through both good times and bad. Again, it is essential to understand the characteristics and extent of the market that you are attempting to serve. It is also important to be aware of the seasonal nature of some resort locations. Can the new restaurant or fast food facility operate profitably on fewer than 12 months annually?

INDUSTRIAL AREAS

Restaurants and bars and grills are often found in industrial areas. Occasionally, a fast food facility is located inside or at the primary entrance/exit to a major industrial area or park. Such food facilities commonly are daytime and early evening operations. Lunch is normally the primary meal, followed by the after-work crowd. In areas with multiple shifts, some restaurants are open around the clock. Because industrial areas often appear dark and unappealing to the average consumer, they tend to have a specialized clientele. Good food with an expanding reputation can result in a popular restaurant, but the location and the operation must attract the basic customer first, if the facility is to develop broader appeal.

RESIDENTIAL AREAS

Usually the worst type of location in a suburban area, residential sites require truly generative restaurants. There are situations where such facilities have fared well and will continue to fare well, but, they are exceptions. This location is more appropriate for a family-oriented dinner house operation, and even then it is risky. While an area with limited competition, a dense residential population, and some employment represents the best opportunity, the road to high sales is usually a long one.

Consistently successful restaurants are found in dense residential concentrations, such as Chicago's near north side, or Manhattan, where there are high concentrations of population within relatively short distances. This kind of location can be good for fast food operations, given adequate site selection. Also, areas such as the dense parts of northern New Jersey, where it is difficult to find adequate sites, can offer promising opportunities. However, suburban residential areas with lower densities rarely provide acceptable sites. Residential locations usually pose great dangers for fast food operations and may also be quite risky for most restaurants. Remember, in such locations, the food operation must be totally generative, which is much more difficult than most "ego trippers" realize.

COUNTRYSIDE, CROSSROAD, AND HIGHWAY LOCATIONS

These locations are usually either between two cities or reasonably-sized towns, or between a city and a major recreational area. The business is often seasonal. Such locations usually start slowly and build in sales over time. The owner puts in long hours, knows his or her customers, provides good food, and offers perceived value. Without the sense of superior food and value, this type of restaurant usually is short-lived. To maximize a highway location, the use of billboards is necessary: first, to get the driver and passengers thinking about eating; and second, to reinforce their desire as the vehicle approaches the interchange or intersection.

UNIQUE DESTINATION LOCATIONS

Throughout the world, there are some (limited) unique restaurant facilities that have created a location. *They are few and far between!* Nevertheless, because of their novel menu, atmosphere, entertainment, service, physical design, or other important elements, they are capable of attracting customers who would normally ignore such locations. These high-risk sites require expert management, but for those who do know what they are doing and do it well, the rewards are immense. These restaurants are very difficult to duplicate without eliminating the appeal of their uniqueness. Examples include: Anthony's in Boston, Bern's in Tampa, the Hilltop Steak House in Saugus, Massachusetts, the Tavern on the Green in New York City, and the Kapok Tree in Clearwater, Florida. Unique destination locations are almost always for restaurants rather than fast food facilities, which rarely can generate adequate sales on this type of site.

SMALL TOWNS

Small towns and rural areas in North America that have unusually high food expenditure patterns form a separate locational category. This pattern occurs not so much because of the eating-out habits of the resident population, but rather because the location is positioned between two major cities, and people stop there while traveling to and from these urban areas. A classic example is Barstow, California, located between Los Angeles and Las Vegas, Nevada. Additionally, the more successful restaurants are usually located in or near a town accessed by a major highway or interstate; the traffic count is a critical factor.

SPECIAL LOCATIONS

A wide variety of situations can create special locations. Among the possibilities are tourist, seasonal, scenic, water-oriented, and unique amusement-oriented restaurants, as well as clubs, dinner playhouses, comedy clubs, penthouse restaurants, boats, and food facilities and kiosks in airports, railroad stations, and some bus terminals. Special locations include Faneuil Hall in Boston, the French Quarter in New Orleans, Ghirardelli Square in San Francisco, and other tourist attractions.

Another type of special location is oriented to the "funky" group between 18 and 35 years of age (although some of us "older types" think we are funky and act and dress to show it). These facilities need large numbers of people to succeed. Their businesses are often affected by changes in the economic cycle. Examples in this group are Division Street and Lincoln Avenue in Chicago, "the Flats" in Cleveland, or the Aurora suburb of Denver. Here, a significant number of eating and drinking places of all sizes, shapes, and types have appeared to meet the influx of this age group. These food facilities can be both highly successful and very risky because the customers change their preferences over a relatively short time span. Thus, a restaurant's business can decline from a capacity crowd to a low degree of activity almost overnight. Since the patrons are extremely fickle and their tastes and desires are highly variable, operations must be viewed on a short-term basis. Staying ahead and surviving changes in customer preferences requires shifts in concepts and emphasis approximately every five years. The operator should look at such an area very carefully before making a commitment.

Other special locations include resort areas, where the activity is highly seasonal. Cape Cod, Fire Island, Ocean City, Vail, Aspen, the Wisconsin Dells, Lake Tahoe, Hilton Head, Virginia Beach, Jacksonville Beach, Daytona Beach, and similar areas experience a high influx of people for relatively short periods. They require special food operations that often are not open all year round. These locations have to be considered on an individual basis.

SUMMARY

The type of location dictates the appropriate criteria for determining whether to enter a market area and, if so, what kind of site to select. The careful consideration of various locations, particularly for chain operations, can maximize sales, profits, and return on investment. It is essential to study both success *and failure* by type of location.

Three

Customer Profile

By the time most of you finish this book you may tire of reading about the importance of understanding your customer profile and, more importantly, the characteristics of your most frequent visitor. It is impossible to overemphasize these factors, however, because they provide a clear indication of the demographic needs for additional locations. This chapter explains how to determine a profile of customer characteristics. Parts of this process may seem academic, but even if you have in the past hired a local survey firm to conduct customer interviews, you should fully understand what you have been asking for, versus what you have received. It may be that you have been getting "half a loaf."

One of the greatest weaknesses of the restaurant industry is that many restaurateurs do not fully know their customer. Simply reading the *Crest Reports** or other studies regarding customer trends and characteristics is not sufficient when evaluating individual locations. *Crest Reports* are excellent for tracking consumer trends over time. However, we have found that specific customer profiles have differed significantly from the Crest data. Therefore, it is necessary to determine your own customer profile.

It is important to differentiate between the terms *marketing* and *market*. Marketing is the selling or promotion of products, whereas market is the arena in which the seller competes. Many food operators have carried out extensive marketing research related to

---

Crest Reports are published monthly by GNR Crest.

28

product, price, awareness, menu acceptance, advertising, service, and employee assistance. Often, however, the data do not cover vital customer characteristics, such as age, income, and frequency of visit, as well as other market factors including competition and driving time. Therefore, marketing research is generally of little value with respect to market research. Sometimes, the two aspects are combined, but to meet the objectives of both market and marketing endeavors, it is usually necessary to compromise and neither group is truly satisfied. Instead, it is better to separate them and generate the necessary data for each endeavor.

Developing a customer profile takes time and costs money. It would be foolish to say that it does not. Nevertheless, if done correctly, it will be some of the best money you ever spent. The results will provide a clear picture of your customers—their ages, incomes, occupations, their reasons for visiting your facility, and their frequency of visit. The profile will also reveal customer likes, dislikes, and suggestions for improvement, and will define your competitors.

There are both simple and complex ways to glean this information. For the multiple-unit operator, the complex methods are generally more meaningful. The single operator usually finds that the simple method provides sufficient information for conducting his or her business and for considering the expansion to an additional unit. Some firms rely heavily on the *Crest Reports*, which reflect changes for various types of food categories. These data can be very helpful in charting an overall course but must be used cautiously with individual markets, and more particularly, with individual locations. Through hundreds of interviewing programs in specific restaurant and fast food operations, we have found that there is a wide disparity between national or regional statistics and those that are developed for individual restaurant facilities. The sample size and the objectives of the larger programs make this gap completely understandable. Fine-tuned locational selection requires honed tools that can detect the variations in customer profile by trade areas and type of location. The rest of this chapter presents the steps in this process.

DEFINE YOUR OBJECTIVES

The first step in determining a customer profile is to define your objectives for a specific type of restaurant or fast food facility. This profile may be for one of various *dayparts*, that is, an eating time segment for a particular restaurant, and may represent one or several meals (breakfast, lunch, dinner, late evening snacks). For example, a Denny's type restaurant operation, open around the clock, is concerned with the primary dayparts (breakfast, lunch, and dinner), as well as late evening and perhaps the entire night. Furthermore, multiple-unit operators must consider geographic differences, varying types of locations, different-sized units, sales levels, profit performance, and perhaps some aspects of management. Enough units must be selected and surveyed to identify adequate customer characteristics, trade area, and most frequent visitor data.

A sample set of objectives for site development, considering both multiple-unit operators and individual restaurateurs, might be as follows:

1. Multi-unit operator only: Determination of the locational, market, and site characteristics of high-volume units versus mediocre or low-volume units.

2. Multi-unit operator only: Selection of cross-section of units for determining customer characteristics.

3. Determination of customer characteristics, especially for most frequent visitor, that can be applied to future locations.

4. Identification of predominant customer characteristics.

5. Establishment of number of units to be opened over a given time period, based on available resources.

6. Budgeting of financial resources required for new unit development.

7. Determination of an operator for a new unit.

8. Establishment of sale(s) goals.

9. Determination of maximum outlay for rent or the purchase of land and building.

10. Estimation of leasehold improvements.

11. Determination of financing.

12. Selection of site(s) for new unit or units.

13. Market determination of how much business the new unit or units can achieve.

14. Estimate of potential profit.

Each multi-unit or individual operator must define his or her objectives and then gather the facts to test their viability.

NECESSARY INGREDIENTS

The initial process of determining a customer profile involves obtaining a customer sample and analyzing existing units or competitor's units.

Obtaining A Customer Sample

The objective of interviewing customers is to develop a sample that represents the majority of a restaurant's customers stratified by day-part. Restaurateurs who do not keep customer counts can use daily sales to achieve a valid sample. If sales are under $3,000,000, interviewing customers during a fairly normal week over a four- or five-day period will normally provide an adequate sample. The days selected should be the four or five busiest days. Certain restaurants, such as special occasion places, may require interviewing over a longer period of time, since repeat customers visit the facility so infrequently.

Rather than going berserk trying to calculate a representative sample, take your problem to a professional interviewing firm. If that is too costly, the statistics professor or instructor at a local college or university should be able to figure out your sample size needs rather quickly and may even suggest developing the sample as a class project. That is acceptable, and inexpensive, as long as someone with some experience in the food service business supervises the project and evaluates the results.

Once you have established a set of objectives, whether it be for a single unit or for 200 additional locations, avoid surprises by committing everything to paper. Furthermore, as the process progresses, be prepared to revise some of the objectives.

Analyzing Your Existing Units or Your Competitor's Units

The following steps for selecting the units to survey are admittedly oriented toward multi-unit operators. Nevertheless, if you are an individual operator, you can learn a great deal from what competitors have done. Watch for their mistakes and avoid them. Also, many factors in the analysis of multi-unit operations apply equally to individual establishments.

1. Evaluate the performance of all existing units. Using sales as a measure, list all the locations in descending order, regardless of geography. Once sorted in descending order, the high sales volume units versus the low or mediocre sales volume units usually stand out dramatically. The question then is why are the high-volume units doing so well? (And, conversely, why are the mediocre units doing so poorly?) What do they have in common, and what are their differences?

2. Reshuffle the list of units geographically and then by sales in descending order to see if there are any basic geographic differences in respect to sales performance.

3. Review the units by individual cities and towns. Why, for example, does a unit in, say, St. Louis or Atlanta do so well; whereas a similar unit in Boston or Las Vegas does so poorly?

4. Analyze the units by type of location. This delineation often shows that one kind of location results in greater sales than another. Should new units be concentrated in the type of location that generated the highest annual sales?

5. Evaluate the management in both the high and the low sales volume units.

The preceding steps force the individual doing the analysis to ask: Why? Some of the answers will be obvious. Most importantly, however, the list provides a structure for selecting a sample of restaurants or fast food operations.

The small operator, with less than 10 units, might find it wise to interview in all of them, or at least those that appear to be representative. That may seem extravagant; however, small operators cannot sustain the loss of a unit. Therefore, the data are often far more important to small businesses than to large ones. *Large operators can hide mistakes; small operators fail because of those mistakes.* If cost is a significant factor, then conduct a customer profile analysis of the one, two, or three best units, since they are what you would like to duplicate in the future.

TYPES OF INTERVIEWS

Five basic types of interviews are used in the food industry: personal, telephone, card, mail, and focus.

Personal Interviews

Personal interviews are surveys that are conducted "face to face." In my opinion, they are the best kind to use in the restaurant and fast food business they are conducted under controlled circumstances. Unfortunately, they are also the most expensive when outside people conduct them. The advantages are that the interviewer can directly observe the interviewee while running through the necessary questions and can ask the questions immediately after the customer has experienced the facility. We recommend interviewing customers as they leave the establishment, which does not disrupt the existing operation. In some cases that requires a bit of ingenuity since the entrance may be narrow, and it is desirable to avoid creating traffic congestion and/or an uncomfortable interviewee.

In some restaurants I have noticed interviewers roaming around the tables and trying to interview people while they eat. I am strongly opposed to that procedure because it disturbs people during their meal. While they may not object to the interruption, it does influence their opinions. It is much better to interview customers as they are leaving the facility, thereby not disrupting their dining experience.

Telephone Interviews

There are times when it is inappropriate to interview people who are leaving a restaurant. This is especially true with fine dining restaurants, where having completed a large meal, people are less inclined to stop and answer a number of questions. Furthermore, if the facility is a "watering hole," interviewing the customers can become an arduous chore. In such cases, it is far smarter to establish a guest book or mailing list and ask people to provide their name, address, and phone number. That information can then be used to develop the sample. Customers are called at a later date and queried regarding their eating-out patterns, their socioeconomic characteristics, and their opinions, about the specific restaurant.

One of the problems with telephone interviews is that respondents can terminate the survey simply by hanging up. Interestingly, that does not happen as often as you might think. Nevertheless, some sensitive issues, such as income and age, must be handled carefully. They are usually placed as the final questions so that, if the respondent abruptly ends the interview, at least all of the other information has been obtained.

Telephone interviews need to be conducted during the evening (avoid Monday night from September through December because of football) and on weekends. During the day, the phone is likely to be answered by the elderly, who may be unaware of the dining out patterns and habits of the rest of the family.

Interview Cards

Interview cards are *not* comment or suggestion cards. Some fast food and restaurant operators use comment cards to determine their customers' level of satisfaction. This approach is unrealistic because such cards are filled out by people who are either extremely happy or unhappy. Since the silent majority seldom responds, the cards are not representative. Interview cards are forms that the host or hostess usually distributes when customers enter the restaurant. The customers fill out the cards sometime during their meal and place them in the survey box near the main exit. It is important to allow customers to place the completed forms in an acceptable "survey box" rather than to give it to a restaurant employee, which may create some feeling of intimidation.

Interview cards are not as controlled as personal interviews or telephone interviews. To allow for error deviation, a larger number of interview cards is usually required, and some cards must be discarded because of nonsensical answers. Interview cards, however, represent an inexpensive way of determining a customer profile because they do not involve any direct interviewing costs. In one survey that my staff conducted, we used personal interviews in 24 units of a chain restaurant, while using interview cards simultaneously in another 24 units. We found that the interview cards were not quite as reliable as the personal interviews, especially for the age and income questions.

Mail Interviews

Some food service operators cannot realistically interview their customers because of their fast service and extremely quick customer turnover. This is also true of people going through drive-thru or double drive-thru facilities. In those instances, it may be necessary to provide a questionnaire and return envelope along with each filled order. The customers are then asked to fill out the questionnaire and mail it back at their convenience.

Mail questionnaires have a low response rate, usually ranging between 9% and about 12%. Therefore, to get a reliable sample, it is necessary to pass out a considerable number of questionnaires. Some food operators provide a discount coupon or some giveaway for filling out the questionnaire, but I have found that this is unnecessary and usually does not significantly increase the number of responses. In fact, it often introduces bias into the questionnaire, since the respondent is inclined to answer positively. If a sample size requires 300 completed interviews, given a 10% return or mail back, it is necessary to distribute 3,000 questionnaires. In fact, a restaurant or fast food operation with a low frequency of visit must distribute an even larger number to get an adequate sample. It could require the distribution of 4,000 or more questionnaires to get a sample of 300.

For drive-thru operations, a combination program may be in order. First, an interviewer might be stationed near the ordering point. After the customer has placed the order, the interviewer asks four or five critical questions while the vehicle proceeds to the pickup window (this system requires highly agile and athletic interviewers). Since the interviewer's objective is to avoid slowing down the line, (but it will), he or she can ask only a limited number of questions. At the final point the server distributes a mail-back questionnaire and return envelope to be filled out and mailed back at the customer's convenience. Thus, one part of the program is controlled and the other part is uncontrolled.

Focus Interviews

In recent years, focus interviews have become popular in the restaurant and fast food industry. A focus interview is an interview of 10 to 15 people with specific backgrounds and socioeconomic characteristics, usually in a room designed for this particular purpose. The objective of a focus interview program is usually to gain insight into the preferences and habits of a segment of the population. The selected people generally engage in a structured conversation, and are sometimes aware of the objectives. A specific objective may be to gain information regarding the restaurant's acceptability, menu, quality of food, quantity of food, advertising, pricing, and other important issues.

Unfortunately, the results from focus interviews are being used as a final conclusion, when, in fact, they are simply the beginning point. Focus interviews are most effectively used to help design a questionnaire and to gain insight into some of people's perceptions. They are not suitable for developing a customer profile, since the sample size is too small to draw such conclusions. In fact, a well-developed customer profile can pinpoint the specific characteristics to select for a focus interview. Although focus interviews are important and have their place, only limited conclusions can be drawn. This is even true if there are three, four, or five focus groups, and a trend of commonality begins to emerge. While such an interview provides an indication, it needs to be tested in a more realistic sampling environment.

IMPORTANT CONSIDERATIONS

Prior to commencing with a customer profile program, it is important to recognize some significant elements. They are discussed in the following sections.

Frequency of Customer Visit

Identifying customer frequency is a critical factor. For restaurant and fast food units that have a high frequency of visit (and most do), identifying the most frequent visitors and isolating their characteristics provides the basis for identifying future locational opportunities. Next, you can review the resident population of prospective trade areas, identify the ones with the closest match to your customer characteristics, and ensure the opportunity for success.

Travel Time

The travel time of customers is more important than distance. In fact, most customers have no concept of distance but do have a strong concept of time. Many food operations have been able to identify time patterns for frequent daypart visitors by accurately defining trade areas by daypart, as well as the trade areas overall. For those restaurants that are primarily walk-in, the orientation is walking time rather than driving time, yet the characteristics will hold similar weight.

Customer Age

Age is one of the most sensitive demographic characteristics in the food service business. Recognizing this fact prior to commencing a customer profile program is essential. Furthermore, it is important to know not simply the average age of your customers, but rather the distribution of age (20 to 25, 26 to 30, 31 to 35 years and so on). In looking at new locations, comparing the resident population data can identify the extent to which the population falls within the appropriate age categories, thus ensuring a greater probability of success.

Income

Income is usually the second most sensitive characteristic. Although age and income may vary in their degree of value, rarely do we find a situation where other factors are more important.

Competition

Most restaurateurs believe they know their competition. It is rather interesting at times to present a restaurateur or fast food operator with the results of an interviewing program showing his or her true competitors. The interviewers usually ask customers what other restaurants they patronize frequently. A restaurateur who has correctly identified competitors can be shocked and disheartened to discover that customers frequent the competitor's units more often than his or her own establishment. It is important to identify this frequency ratio.

The Primary Reason for Eating at Your Food Establishment

The primary reason people eat at a specific restaurant or fast food establishment repeatedly is *good food*. Rarely is there a more significant response. While atmosphere does play a role in different types of facilities, good food will normally be the highest response. At lunchtime in the fast food business, good food and fast service are usually the highest responses. Nevertheless, good food almost always remains the primary reason. Atmosphere may be lovely, but in the long run, it will not prevail in sustaining a restaurant's success.

Interestingly, several years ago, price was rarely important in determining where customers would go. Recently, however, price, especially in terms of value, has become an important response. This change is related to current economic conditions. Usually if the food is good, price is less influential than the average restaurateur believes. Food people agonize over raising prices, when often customer interviews reveal a lack of price sensitivity; as a result, price increases would not create any significant adverse downside effect. This finding is especially true when there is a strong orientation to the good food of the restaurant and a high rate of frequency of visit. However, when areas become overbuilt with fast food units, price becomes a factor in the competition to build traffic. The $0.99 hamburger becomes the $0.59 one, and so forth.

Party Size

The importance of party size varies by type of facility. There are strong variations within the food industry. McDonald's, for example, often enjoys a larger party size than does Wendy's or Burger King, primarily because of attracting young children and families. Party sizes vary all across the board. Special occasion restaurants generally have large parties (four or more) because the dining experience is a celebration. A more typical restaurant will usually have a party size of two during the week, with more fours on the weekend. Regardless of the kind of restaurant, each restaurateur and fast food operator should know his or her customer party size and whether it is a sensitive or significant item.

Satisfaction Level

Sales to a restaurant operator, are the indicator of customer satisfaction. Nevertheless, when interviewing customers, it is important to find out their likes and dislikes, and their suggestions for improving the restaurant, thus encouraging them to come more often. For well-run and highly regarded restaurants, the primary response to "What do you like most about our restaurant?" is usually food related, such as "good food," "quality of food," "ambience," and "presentation." Because I have performed evaluations for so many years, I can usually look at interview results without knowing the name of the restaurant or fast food operation and tell whether individual units are healthy or sick. If the primary reason for visiting the establishment is some factor other than good food, usually a problem prevails.

We usually ask if there is anything that the customer dislikes about a restaurant. That question may seem negative to some, but as long as it is asked in a positive context, (*dislike*, rather than *do not like*) it is not offensive. Interestingly, in well-run restaurants, the customers will respond that they dislike "nothing," or if there is a significant waiting time, what they dislike most is quite naturally "waiting." If there are significant dislikes, such as "rudeness," "price," "slow service," and "bad food," the customers will so indicate.

It has always been my belief that interviewers should encourage suggestions to resolve negative issues: "What can the restaurant do to encourage you to come more often?" or, "What can we do to improve?" Again, for successful facilities, "nothing" will be the primary response, but even in well-run and highly accepted restaurants, there may be some suggestions. One that we see quite often is "bigger plates at the salad bar." Well, as most of you know, it is your intention to keep small plates at the salad bar in order to minimize the amount of salad that is consumed. Therefore, it is necessary to distinguish between helpful and less useful responses to both the "dislike" and the "improve" questions.

Origin of the Trip

Asking customers "Where were you prior to your visit here today?" helps to develop a clear picture of the trade area and, more specifically, its primary portion (where the most frequent visitors originate). This question would be followed by "In what city or town is that?" and "What are the closest crossing streets to your place of work or residence?" The objective is to pinpoint by frequency of visit, the specific location where the trip to the restaurant originated. Usually we plot these responses on maps (either manually or electronically), color coded by frequency. Thus, the user can clearly see the extent of the trade area and, more importantly, its primary portion (the location of the most frequent visitors) versus its secondary portion (less frequent visitors). Furthermore, if computer processed, the data can be coded to the questionnaire and customer characteristics can then be reviewed by smaller portions or subparts of the trade area.

Some companies mount a map on a stand and use it when interviewing customers. The interviewer asks the respondent to indicate approximately where he or she lives or works. This eliminates the plotting since the "grid number" or "zone" is recorded by the interviewer. I have found, however, that many people cannot read a map, and therefore, unless the interviewer truly knows the neighborhood, the process wastes important customer interviewing time. Instead, we achieve greater accuracy by having people who know the area plot the information in the office.

THE INTERVIEW PROGRAM

Interview forms are developed for different situations and varying types of food operations. How much time it takes to complete the interviewing process influences their design and the number of questions to be included. Quite surprisingly, people will often be cooperative for longer periods than most of us realize, for either personal or telephone interviews. If the interview form flows in a logical pattern so that the interviewer and the interviewee establish a rapport, time becomes a less important factor; skilled interviewers know how to get answers from customers without offending them. Moreover, when the interview is over, a good interviewer profusely thanks the respondent for "helping us to understand your needs and to serve you better."

We carried out an interview program in a city in New York State during the month of November, when the chilly winds and blowing snow created numerous obstacles. November is certainly not an ideal month in which to interview. However, some important decisions had to be made, and so November it was. The entrance was so small that the interviewers had to intercept the customers and interview them outside after they had left the restaurant. The operator wanted to ask more questions than I care to mention. As a result, the pretest of the form indicated that it took 28 minutes to complete the survey. Amazingly, the customers did not object or complain, so the program was implemented and more than 500 customers answered the entire interview. There were only five refusals. Those are hardy people in New York. I do not recommend going to this extreme; however, it shows that if the interview is handled smoothly, people will respond.

The Appendix of this book has questionnaires as well as a telephone survey, for various restaurant and fast food operations, including a fast food facility, a coffee shop, a dinner house, and a theme restaurant. These examples are not necessarily the whole answer to any particular food service operator's problems or opportunities, but they are guidelines for designing a questionnaire. There are, in fact, literally hundreds of kinds of questionnaires that can accomplish interview objectives. Nevertheless, I think these samples will be helpful.

In addition to the factors discussed in the preceding sections, a number of other considerations go into the design of a questionnaire. For example, a lead-in statement is necessary to explain the purpose of the questions. The interviewer might say, "We are conducting a survey of our customers here at [your restaurant or fast food name]. Would you mind answering a few questions for us." The following items should also be determined:

Date
Location of the Unit
Daypart or time of day or evening
Frequency of visit
Travel time
Origination of the trip
Place of residence
Place of employment
Competitive facilities frequently patronized
Primary reason for visiting the restaurant
Features especially liked about restaurant
Features especially disliked about restaurant
Suggestions for improvements
Age of the respondent
Marital status
Occupation of the respondent
Spouse's occupation
Party size
Household income
Sex
Ethnic characteristics

Numerous other questions could be included. Often, there is a *rating* of items such as food quality, food quantity, drinks, service, price/value, atmosphere, cleanliness, waiter or waitress, and host or hostess. Some of the questionnaires in the Appendix have categories of response. For example, under "frequency of visit," there are a number of response categories, allowing the interviewer simply to check the appropriate answer. Such techniques speed up the process. Categories can be determined by pretesting the questionnaires to gain an understanding of the likely responses.

Open-ended questions (which require a written answer) are the slowest to handle and, thus, tend to make the respondent impatient. The more questions that can be categorized, the faster the process goes. Also, tabulation is easier and less expensive. Regardless, the important objective is to obtain an accurate customer profile; if that requires open-ended questions, then they should be utilized. Shortcuts significantly reduce the amount of information that will ultimately be available and later can cause "gnashing of teeth," when the user realizes that expediency in the interviewing process has resulted in the omission of vitally needed information.

Most medium- and large-size cities (and some small towns) have market research firms that conduct interview programs for all types of facilities. They can assist you in designing a questionnaire and certainly in carrying it out. Most of them also have the capability of tabulating the information, should you require that service. There is usually an hourly charge plus a supervision fee. Ask for a cost estimate prior to commencing the operation.

Pretest of the Survey Form

Prior to conducting an interview program, it is *essential* to pretest the interview form with some of your customers. A pretest is designed to determine whether respondents can understand the questions; how smoothly the questionnaire unfolds; how many minutes it takes to conduct the interview; and whether the questions generate adequate answers. This trial run will also indicate whether the interview form is too long or is taking too much time, the level of the respondents' irritation, and any problems with the interviewer's location. A professional interviewer experienced in coping with some of the problems should conduct the pretest. The interviews should not interrupt the normal flow of activity within the restaurant, but should be positioned on-site either outside or in a vestibule away from the hostess's desk. This approach allows the interviewer to intercept people as they leave the facility.

Answers to the pretest may suggest some ways to improve the interview form. If there are internal questions within your organization regarding what to ask or not to ask, you might develop several variations of the forms. Using these assorted pretests will help you determine which one works the best and which questions are pertinent.

Interviewer Instructions

Clear and concise interviewer instructions are essential. For a single-unit operator carrying out an interview program, informal directions are acceptable. For larger programs, I recommend written instructions that the interviewer can refer to when questions arise. Suitable instructions will address the specific attire, time, place, position, demeanor, introduction to the restaurant manager, and approach to the customers. These instructions will also tell the interviewer what to do when a customer refuses to participate, what to do when an interview is terminated before completion, when to take breaks, how to record answers, which questions to probe, how to handle groups, what to do with the completed interview forms, and who to contact in the event of a problem. Uniformity of administering the program is important. Adequate instructions eliminate the need for the interviewer to make any decisions.

Conduct of the Survey Program

The next step is to conduct the interview program. It is important to position interviewers so that they will not interfere with the normal flow of business in the restaurant but still can intercept the customers as they leave the facility. Although weather may preclude the possibility, the interviewers normally should stand outside where there may be more room and where they will cause little or no interference.

Our experience has shown us that customers are more receptive to women, preferably middle-aged women, who tend to relate well to a wide group of people. Experienced interviewers are a great asset; they know, for example, how to engage the customer and commence the questions, while gradually steering the customer out of the traffic flow. The person being interviewed, if correctly positioned, cannot read the interview form, which is on a clipboard that the interviewer holds. Every time the respondent tries to look at the form, the professional interviewer will shift slightly, making that a much more difficult possibility. The interviewer is not necessarily trying to hide the form from the interviewee, but rather wants to keep the pace of things moving along without interruption.

TABULATING THE DATA

There are two basic ways to tabulate the interview results. The first is the simple "hash mark" approach. The second involves computer processing the results. The simple approach requires merely taking a large columnar sheet, recording a hash mark for each response, and placing a slash diagonally across the previous four for every fifth tally. Table 3.1 depicts the hash mark approach, which can be as accurate as a computerized tally.

Not long ago, I was involved in a lawsuit involving a food operation and a city. It seems that the city had cut off part of a fast food unit's access, and as a result, the food operator filed a lawsuit against the city. The food operator had limited resources; so when he came to me, I suggested the simple approach. I designed five questions and placed the questions in the back of a spiral notebook. We hired two college students to interview his customers asking the five questions, which could quickly be memorized. Thus, the responses were simply recorded one, two, three, four, five in the notebook, eliminating the need for a questionnaire. The data were subsequently tabulated on columnar sheets using hash marks. When we ended up in court and I testified, the opposition's

TABLE 3.1

Hash Mark Tabulation: Customer Visits to Charlie's

Frequency	Number of Responses
First visit	⊓Ⅎ⅃ ⊓Ⅎ⅃ III
Daily	⊓Ⅎ⅃ ⊓Ⅎ⅃ ⊓Ⅎ⅃ III
Twice a week	⊓Ⅎ⅃ ⊓Ⅎ⅃ ⊓Ⅎ⅃
Once a week	⊓Ⅎ⅃ ⊓Ⅎ⅃ ⊓Ⅎ⅃ ⊓Ⅎ⅃ ⊓Ⅎ⅃ ⊓Ⅎ⅃ II
Every two weeks	⊓Ⅎ⅃ ⊓Ⅎ⅃ ⊓Ⅎ⅃ III
Every three weeks	⊓Ⅎ⅃ II
Once a month	⊓Ⅎ⅃ ⊓Ⅎ⅃ ⊓Ⅎ⅃ ⊓Ⅎ⅃ ⊓Ⅎ⅃ ⊓Ⅎ⅃ ⊓Ⅎ⅃ ⊓Ⅎ⅃ ⊓Ⅎ⅃ ⊓Ⅎ⅃ ⊓Ⅎ⅃ ⊓Ⅎ⅃ I
Every two months	⊓Ⅎ⅃ ⊓Ⅎ⅃ ⊓Ⅎ⅃ III
Every three months	⊓Ⅎ⅃ II
Every six months	⊓Ⅎ⅃ ⊓Ⅎ⅃ II
Once a year	⊓Ⅎ⅃

attorney tried to make a significant issue of the noncomputerized tabulations, implying that the data were inaccurate. When I took out the columnar sheets and laid them before the judge, he became fascinated; in fact, these were the only results that he truly understood, since computer printouts overwhelmed him. There is a place for both simplicity and sophistication. Needless to say, my client won the case.

The preceding example is not presented to imply that I do not endorse computer processing. Quite the contrary, almost everything that we do is computer processed because of the need for multiple cross-tabulations and because of the volume of data to be handled. Moreover, once in the computer, the data can be viewed in various ways, enabling us to test the sensitivity of the various profile elements. Tables 3.2, 3.3, and 3.4 depict alternative methods for presenting computerized data. In a simple frequency distribution the responses are usually listed in descending order, based upon overall responses. Table 3.2 depicts a frequency distribution based on the question, "How often do you eat here at Charlie's?" but in this case, so that the user can study the frequency more easily, the responses are not listed in order of highest response. This kind of presentation is probably the easiest for the layperson to understand. Notice how frequently the customers patronize this unit. At least 37.9% of the customers visit the unit once a week or more. It is equally important

TABLE 3.2

Frequency Distribution: Customer Visits to Charlie's

Frequency	Percent
First visit	6.3
Daily	8.7
Twice a week	7.3
Once a week	15.6
Every two weeks	8.7
Every three weeks	3.4
Once a month	29.6
Every two months	8.7
Every three months	3.5
Every six months	5.8
Once a year	2.4
Total	100.0

TABLE 3.3

Profile Matrix Program
Your Primary Reason for Coming to Charlie's Today

	Total	Frequency of Visit				Prior to Visit			Age								Income (000s)				
		Once a Week Plus	1, 2, or 3 Times a Month	1, 2, or 6 Times a Year	First Visit	Home	Work	Shopping	Under 21	21–25	26–30	31–35	36–40	41–45	46–50	Over 50	Under 24.9	$25–34.9	$35–49.9	$50–74.9	Over $75
Total Respondents	579	57	176	84	209	285	167	33	14	64	148	102	107	47	36	56	74	100	163	75	137
Percent	100.0	100.0	100.0	100.0	100.0	100.0	100.0	100.0	100.0	100.0	100.0	100.0	100.0	100.0	100.0	100.0	100.0	100.0	100.0	100.0	100.0
Good food/unique	391	42	147	57	104	210	110	22	10	41	107	71	66	31	23	37	52	60	121	54	86
Percent	67.5	73.7	83.5	67.9	49.8	73.7	65.9	66.7	71.4	64.1	72.3	69.6	61.7	66.0	63.9	66.1	70.3	60.0	74.2	72.0	62.8
Recommended	59	1	3	6	48	30	8	1	1	7	11	10	10	7	4	9	9	11	13	7	18
Percent	10.2	1.8	1.7	7.1	23.0	10.5	4.8	3.0	7.1	10.9	7.4	9.8	9.3	14.9	11.1	16.1	12.2	11.0	8.0	9.3	13.1
Meet friends	25	4	6	3	8	9	12	2	—	1	6	8	4	1	2	3	—	7	7	2	9
Percent	4.3	7.0	3.4	3.6	3.8	3.2	7.2	6.1	—	1.6	4.1	7.8	3.7	2.1	5.6	5.4	—	7.0	4.3	2.7	6.6
Atmosphere	20	1	6	3	8	5	8	1	—	4	5	3	5	1	1	1	1	5	5	2	7
Percent	3.5	1.8	3.4	3.6	3.8	1.8	4.8	3.0	—	6.3	3.4	2.9	4.7	2.1	2.8	1.8	1.4	5.0	3.1	2.7	5.1
Good drinks	8	—	1	3	3	1	3	2	—	1	3	1	3	—	—	—	1	2	3	1	1
Percent	1.4	—	0.6	3.6	1.4	0.4	1.8	6.1	—	1.6	2.0	1.0	2.8	—	—	—	1.4	2.0	1.8	1.3	0.7
Convenient	6	1	1	3	1	2	2	2	—	—	1	1	2	1	—	1	1	1	—	—	2
Percent	1.0	1.8	0.6	3.6	0.5	0.7	1.2	6.1	—	—	0.7	1.0	1.9	2.1	—	1.8	1.4	1.0	—	—	1.5
Good service	2	1	1	—	—	1	—	—	—	—	1	—	—	1	—	—	—	1	—	—	—
Percent	0.3	1.8	0.6	—	—	0.4	—	—	—	—	0.7	—	—	2.1	—	—	—	1.0	—	—	—
Informal	1	—	—	1	—	1	—	—	—	—	—	—	1	—	—	—	—	—	—	—	—
Percent	0.2	—	—	1.2	—	0.4	—	—	—	—	—	—	0.9	—	—	—	—	—	—	—	—
Oyster bar	1	—	—	—	1	—	—	—	—	—	—	—	—	—	—	—	—	—	—	—	1
Percent	0.2	—	—	—	0.5	—	—	—	—	—	—	—	—	—	—	—	—	—	—	—	0.7
Other	66	7	11	8	36	26	24	3	3	10	14	7	16	5	6	5	10	12	14	9	13
Percent	11.4	12.3	6.3	9.5	17.2	9.1	14.4	9.1	21.4	15.6	9.5	6.9	15.0	10.6	16.7	8.9	13.5	12.0	8.6	12.0	9.5

that 73.3% of the customers visit the unit at least once a month or more. This is a truly unique unit.

Table 3.3 shows a more sophisticated approach. Here, a number of items have been included in the banner, or column headings, extending left to right across the top of the table. The banner contains columns entitled Total, Frequency of Visit (four columns), Location Prior to Visit (three columns), Age (eight columns), and Income (five columns). This table represents a "Profile Matrix Program." The left side of the matrix reflects the possible responses to the question, "What was your primary reason for coming to Charlie's today?" Table 3.3 reads down, so that the user can analyze the response to the question on the left as to frequency, prior location, age, and income. (Notice the impact of "good food/unique.") There is a similar table for each survey question. The advantage of the program is that it allows for the cross-tabulation of every question by the items in the banner which makes determining customer profiles far easier. It is not essential to use this type of presentation. However, for someone who makes frequent evaluations, the Profile Matrix Program provides a clear picture and, more importantly, saves time.

For multi-unit operators, this format can allow for the structuring of the data presentation by individual units. For example, the banner could list anywhere from 16 to 34 unit numbers or names. One has the ability of looking at each response relative to the responses obtained at that unit. Table 3.4 depicts a nine-unit example and shows how this arrangement simplifies the evaluation of customer profiles by unit. For comparative purposes, the last three columns represent a summary of 20 other units.

ANALYSIS OF THE DATA

Analysis and interpretation of the data are extremely important; the accuracy of the data, however, has greater significance. If the data are flawed, then the conclusions that the user draws from the analysis may also be flawed.

The following points should receive particular attention:

- Study carefully the answers to the question, "How often do you eat here at [name of your restaurant] Restaurant?"
- Is there a point where the percentage of customer frequency drops appreciably? For example, do most of the customers

TABLE 3.4

Tabulated Results of Personal Interviews
Conducted in Nine Selected Restaurants
(Numbers Are Percentages)

	A			B			C			D			E		
	Lunch	Dinner	Total	Lunch	Dinner	Total	Lunch	Dinner	Total	Lunch	Dinner	Total	Lunch	Dinner	Total
1. Number of persons in the respondent's party															
One	1.7	3.4	5.1	5.8	2.5	8.3	8.0	3.6	11.7	5.4	1.8	7.2	9.8	0.8	10.7
Two	24.4	25.0	49.4	16.7	30.1	46.8	11.7	29.2	40.9	12.6	25.7	38.3	16.4	19.7	36.1
Three	6.3	9.1	15.3	3.8	12.8	16.7	3.6	12.4	16.1	3.6	13.2	16.8	4.9	15.6	20.5
Four	5.7	7.4	13.3	1.9	14.1	16.0	1.5	10.2	11.7	2.4	9.6	12.0	0.8	14.8	15.6
Five	1.7	5.1	6.8	1.3	4.5	5.8	—	6.6	6.6	1.2	9.0	10.2	—	9.8	9.8
2. Origin of the respondent's visit for lunch or dinner															
Lunch—Work	10.2			4.5			10.2			8.6			15.6		
Lunch—Home	31.8			26.3			17.5			18.6			18.9		
Lunch—Total	42.0		42.0	30.8		30.8	27.7		27.7	27.1		27.1	34.4		34.4
Dinner—Work		8.0			5.1			5.1			0.8			7.4	
Dinner—Home		45.5			64.1			67.2			71.9			58.2	
Dinner—Total		58.0	58.0		69.2	69.2		72.3	72.3		72.7	72.7		65.6	65.6
Total			100.0			100.0			100.0			100.0			100.0
3. Respondents visiting for the first time															
Yes	3.4	11.9	15.3	5.1	7.7	12.8	3.6	13.9	17.5	3.0	8.4	11.4	4.9	20.5	25.4
No	38.6	46.1	84.7	24.4	60.9	85.3	24.1	57.7	81.8	24.0	64.7	88.6	28.7	45.1	73.8
4. Frequency of visits															
More than once a week	6.8	10.2	17.0	3.8	3.2	7.1	6.6	9.5	16.1	11.3	5.4	16.8	10.7	4.1	14.8
Once a week	9.1	8.0	17.0	6.4	12.2	18.6	7.3	14.6	21.9	9.0	19.8	28.7	9.0	15.6	24.6
Once every two weeks	3.4	5.7	9.1	3.8	8.3	12.2	4.4	10.2	14.6	1.2	16.7	18.0	3.3	9.8	13.1
Once a month	6.3	6.8	13.1	7.1	13.5	20.5	2.2	12.4	14.6	1.8	16.8	18.6	3.3	4.1	7.4
Once every two months	4.0	7.4	11.4	2.6	10.9	13.5	2.2	12.4	14.6	0.6	2.4	3.0	2.5	10.7	13.1
Once every six months	8.5	6.3	14.8	0.6	4.5	5.1	2.9	4.4	7.3	—	—	—	—	0.8	0.8
Once a year	1.1	—	1.1	0.6	0.6	1.3	—	—	—	—	0.6	0.6	—	—	—
Other	—	—	—	—	—	—	—	—	—	—	—	—	—	—	—
5. Respondents who plan to shop on the date of interview															
Yes	14.8	17.0	31.8	14.1	20.5	34.6	6.6	17.5	24.1	6.6	4.8	11.4	6.6	13.1	19.7
No	26.7	40.0	66.5	14.7	48.7	63.5	21.2	54.7	75.9	19.8	68.3	88.0	24.6	50.8	75.4
6. Respondents who patronize other eating places															
Yes	22.2	23.3	45.4	22.0	35.1	57.1	21.9	44.5	66.4	12.5	17.4	29.9	29.5	57.4	86.9
No	20.0	34.7	54.5	9.0	33.9	42.9	5.8	27.8	33.6	14.4	55.7	70.1	4.9	8.2	13.1
7. Respondents' families who patronize other eating places															
Yes	28.4	33.0	61.4	17.9	53.2	71.2	23.4	61.3	84.7	13.2	56.3	69.5	18.8	38.5	57.4
No	13.6	25.0	38.6	12.8	16.0	28.8	4.4	10.9	15.3	13.8	16.8	30.5	15.6	27.0	42.6

	F			G			H			I			Composite 9 Stores			20 Stores		
	Lunch	Dinner	Total	Lunch	Dinner	Total	Lunch	Dinner	Total	Lunch	Dinner	Total	Lunch	Dinner	Total	Lunch	Dinner	Total
	6.8	1.7	8.5	6.0	1.2	7.2	4.9	0.7	5.6	2.6	4.5	7.1	5.4	2.4	7.8	3.9	2.6	6.5
	19.9	20.5	40.3	18.8	15.9	34.7	18.3	21.1	39.4	16.7	30.1	46.8	17.4	24.7	42.1	18.0	19.0	37.0
	6.8	10.2	17.0	6.0	10.1	16.1	63.4	9.9	16.3	1.3	12.8	14.1	4.6	11.8	16.4	9.2	8.6	17.8
	4.0	9.1	13.1	8.7	10.1	18.8	7.0	12.0	19.0	3.2	10.3	13.5	3.7	10.7	14.4	7.0	8.8	15.8
	2.8	8.5	11.4	0.6	7.2	8.8	3.5	4.2	7.7	1.3	4.5	5.8	1.5	6.5	8.1	3.4	4.4	7.8
	5.7			23.3			6.3			5.1			8.8			11.3		
	36.9			18.8			38.7			21.2			26.2			37.9		
	42.6		42.6	42.0		42.0	45.3		45.3	26.3		26.3	35.0		35.0	49.2		49.2
		2.8			1.4			5.8			6.4			4.8			7.1	
		54.5			56.5			47.9			67.3			60.2			43.7	
		57.4	57.4		58.0	58.0		53.7	53.7		73.7	73.7		65.0	65.0		50.8	50.8
			100.0			100.0			100.0			100.0			100.0			100.0
	2.3	5.1	7.4	—	8.7	8.7	-21.1	33.1	54.2	6.4	17.3	23.7	5.7	13.8	19.5	7.0	7.5	14.5
	40.3	52.3	92.6	40.5	47.8	88.4	23.2	21.1	44.4	19.9	56.4	76.3	29.0	50.8	79.8	41.4	42.8	84.2
	12.5	4.0	16.5	18.8	2.9	21.7	3.5	2.1	5.6	3.2	25.6	5.8	8.0	5.1	13.1	6.2	4.6	10.8
	8.0	9.7	17.6	17.4	8.7	26.1	4.9	3.5	4.9	7.1	10.9	17.9	8.2	11.5	19.5	7.1	6.7	13.8
	9.1	10.2	19.3	4.3	23.2	27.5	3.5	3.5	3.5	0.6	6.4	7.1	3.8	9.7	13.5	6.0	7.3	13.3
	4.0	10.8	14.8	—	10.1	10.1	3.5	2.1	3.5	1.9	11.5	13.5	3.6	10.0	13.6	8.0	9.2	17.2
	4.5	9.1	13.6	—	5.8	5.8	9.2	10.6	9.2	2.5	8.3	10.9	3.3	8.6	11.9	3.2	3.2	6.4
	2.3	5.1	7.4	—	—	—	—	—	—	3.2	9.6	12.8	2.2	3.8	6.0	6.4	6.7	13.1
	—	1.7	1.7	1.4	—	1.4	—	—	—	1.3	5.8	7.1	0.5	1.1	1.5	2.1	2.2	4.3
	—	—	—	2.9	—	2.9	—	—	—	—	—	—	0.5	1.2	1.8	5.9	6.1	12.1
	18.2	16.5	34.7	10.1	5.8	15.9	16.9	9.2	26.1	16.7	19.2	35.9	12.7	14.3	27.0	14.6	15.3	29.9
	24.4	39.2	63.6	31.9	5.1	82.6	26.1	42.3	68.3	9.6	53.2	62.8	21.4	49.5	70.9	31.3	33.2	64.5
	28.4	23.8	52.3	14.5	27.5	42.0	40.8	52.8	93.7	24.4	67.9	92.3	24.6	38.3	62.9			
	14.2	33.5	47.7	27.5	30.4	58.0	4.9	1.4	6.3	1.9	5.8	7.7	10.5	26.6	37.1			
	15.9	17.0	33.0	8.7	2.9	11.6	26.1	37.3	63.4	11.5	28.8	40.4	18.8	38.1	56.9			
	26.7	40.3	67.0	33.3	55.0	88.4	19.8	16.9	36.6	14.7	44.9	59.6	16.4	26.7	43.1			

come once a week or, say, once a month? These responses will indicate the most frequent visitors.

- Isolate the most frequent visitors and look at their responses, in contrast to the total sample.
- The origin of designation of the customers should be plotted on maps and color coded both by daypart and frequency. Colored circles or dots might be used for people whose trip originated at home, whereas colored triangles or squares could be used for people who traveled from work or from shopping.

Figure 3.1 depicts a customer distribution for an entire sample. Operators who are considering how close to build units in relation to one other, really need to look at a similar representation of the most frequent visitor customer pattern, since it reflects the trade area orientation to a specific unit. Moreover, it is necessary to evaluate carefully the customer profile of the most frequent visitors and how it varies from the total profile. Usually there is a considerable difference. Thus, simply relying on the total interview results to develop a customer profile may create a misleading pattern.

CUSTOMER PROFILES

Presented on the following pages are customer profiles of a multi-unit fast food operation, a fine dining restaurant, a regional pizza chain, and a theme restaurant and bar. While they do represent actual food chains and individual operators, you should not assume that they are compatible with your particular food operation. Each facility is different and has its own idiosyncrasies.

Customer Profile: Multi-Unit Fast Food Operation

The profile, based on a sample of more than 100 units is as follows:

- Of the customers, 90% come to unit from within three miles.
- Average driving time is eight minutes.
- Good food and fast service are the two primary reasons for coming to unit.
- More than 80% of trips originate at home.
- Approximately 75% of customers are between 25 and 35 years old; median age is 32 years.

FIGURE 3.1

Customer Distribution*

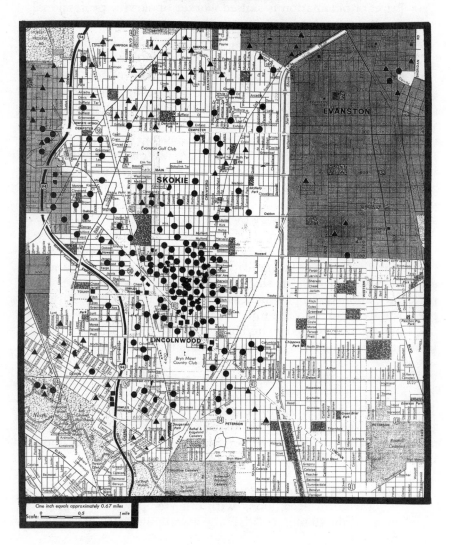

*Black dots, most frequent customers; triangles, less frequent customers; squares, customers who visit less than once a month.

- Average household income is $32,000; more than 72% of customers have incomes between $27,000 and $40,000.
- Primary occupation is skilled worker or service professional.
- Family size is 2.9 persons.
- Most customers do not bring children.

Note the significance of age and income in this profile: 75% of the customers are in the 25- to 35-year-old age group, and 72% of the customers are in the $27,000 to $40,000 income category. Armed with this information, it is simple to identify markets within a metropolitan area that have a preponderance of the same characteristics. Where these age and income factors can be duplicated in large numbers and a decent location can be found with adequate access, the site should represent a high-volume opportunity for this particular operation. Again, this is a *specific* fast food chain and should not be used in any way by any other company.

Another point to recognize is that while the customers show a family size of 2.9 persons, they come without their children. As a result, family size is not a significant factor. Another important consideration is that 80% of the customers originate at home. Thus, proximity to major employment is not a significant factor. Although the customers come to the unit because of good food and fast service, when responses are isolated by daypart, the fast service is significant at lunchtime but is almost nonexistent at the dinner hour.

Customer Profile: Fine Dining Restaurant

This restaurant was found to be *income sensitive;* namely, the higher the income, the greater the opportunity to capture high sales. The check average was $27 for dinner and about $18 for lunch, and annual sales exceed $4,000,000:

- Overall trade area is metropolitanwide. However, for lunch the downtown area, along with other employment concentrations within 10 minutes' driving or walking distance, makes up trade area.
- Average household income is more than $75,000 annually.
- More than 65% of customers are married; 75% of married customers have spouses who are employed.
- Customers are predominantly between 25 and 45 years old (74%); average age is 38 years.

- More than 45% of customers visit the restaurant at least once a month; first-time visitors amount to 30% of total. More than 82% of those interviewed at lunch indicated that they would come back another time for dinner.
- More than 75% of lunch customers come from their place of work in less than 10 minutes. An additional 20% come from home. About 38% walk to restaurant for lunch.
- Good food is primary reason for eating here. Also, facility is a good meeting place to see friends, business associates, and visitors to city.
- Customers dislike occasional long waits for a table.

As you may have deduced, this restaurant is unique, and highly regarded, and is working to become an institution.

Customer Profile: Regional Pizza Chain

This chain had a strong frequency of visit, as well as a healthy number of first-time visitors:

- Approximately 65% of customers visit unit once a month or more; 14% are first-time visitors.
- More than 67% of customers are between 25 and 44 years old, with an average of 34 years. Approximately 37% are in 25- to 34-year-old group, while an additional 30% are in 34- to 44-year-old group.
- Customers have average household income of $37,500. More than 50% belong to $25,000 to $35,000 income category.
- Good food and fast service are primary reasons for lunching at these units. At dinner, good food is primary reason.
- Approximately 60% of customers reside within three miles; 40% come from farther away.
- While the average driving time is 11 minutes, more than 45% of customers drove from home in 10 minutes or less. Overall, 60% travel less than 10 minutes. Also, 20% of customers work within a 9-minute driving time. Overall trade area reflects that 60% of customers reside within three miles, and 40% reside beyond. (Rather than simply using this total, operator must look at each location and isolate what actually occurs.)
- Of total customers, 60% come without children; 40% bring some children.

- Approximately 75% of customers decide to eat at the particular pizza operation within two hours of visit. (This is a good reason for visibility and exposure. Customers need to see or remember restaurant, or receive stimulation from some form of advertising within that two-hour period.)
- Customer occupations include skilled blue-collar work, lower level management, and office work.
- About 15% of customers only eat out at this facility.

Customer Profile: Theme Restaurant and Bar

The theme restaurant and bar customer profile reflects the young nature of the customers and their high frequency of visit:

- About 55% of customers are between 21 and 35 years old. Moreover, 70% are single.
- Average income is about $37,000. Customers are heavily concentrated in $25,000 to $45,000 income categories.
- Lunch customers originate from work, while evening customers come primarily from home. Cocktail hour customers originate from work.
- Customers mainly are employed in white-collar professions.
- Primary reason for visiting restaurant is good food and atmosphere.
- Average driving time is 11 minutes.
- More than 75% of customers come at least once a month.

SUMMARY

An accurate customer profile is essential to pick winners. This knowledge will help maximize sales and minimize the competitive hazard. Multi-unit operators should consider developing a new profile every two to three years to track shifting customer characteristics, competitive orientation, dining-out frequency, and other factors.

The cost of a mistake can make the cost of developing a customer profile seem as pleasurable as if the money were being spent for a weekend on the French Riviera. In other words, it is a lot cheaper to do it now than to "eat the mistake" and pay the price. Talk to somebody who has had to bite the bankruptcy bullet and I am sure that you will receive the same advice. Now is the time!

Four

Trade Areas

Trade areas are geographic areas that generate a measurable amount of sales. They come in numerous shapes and sizes. Most food operators like to think of them in terms of mile radii, when, in fact, they are neither round, square, nor rectangular but are shaped by forces of attraction and proscription. This chapter focuses on trade areas, their importance, how to determine them, and what influences them.

Trade areas are never exactly the same, although they may share many traits. It is surprising but true that commonality is more often found in dinner house trade areas than in fast food operations. The distance and size of trade areas for fast food operations vary by type of location, but are usually quite pat for any *specific type*. Conversely, a dinner house trade area may be very similar from one market to another, particularly in terms of distance, attraction, or driving time; the location is a less important factor.

For decades, theorists and practitioners have attempted to define trade areas; perhaps the most famous definition is that of William J. Reilly. In 1929, Reilly wrote a thesis at the University of Texas, creating what is known as the "Law of Retail Gravitation" (commonly referred to as "Reilly's Law"). The law determines the size of a trade area based on the size of the community and the distance between two locations. Often, population or square footage of competitors or seats in competitive restaurant facilities are substituted for the population. Perhaps the most significant thing about Reilly's Law is that it *rarely* works. Thus, whereas it is a theoretical tool for attempting

55

to define a trade area, it is really not a very practical tool in the reality of competitive business. There are many more variables than the formula takes into account.

There are many ways to define trade areas. Whether it be miles, minutes, census tracts, zip codes, neighborhoods, cities, metropolitan areas, squares, circles, rectangles, amoebas, or blobs, trade areas are supposed to reflect the area from which a restaurant or fast food operation generates its customer activity. By my definition, a trade area is the area from which a unit can expect to capture approximately 85% of its business. Why 85%? Because it is often difficult, impractical, and too costly to develop data that cover the remaining 15%. For example, many destination dinner houses attract out-of-town customers; as a result, the 15% may cover the United States and to attempt to account for it is impractical. Additionally, a fast food operation in proximity to a regional shopping center may generate, say, 10% to 15% of its business from farther than 10 miles. Trade areas are essentially established to evaluate the area from which an operation can expect to capture a *measurable* amount of business. Actually, for most restaurants and fast food operations, the important part of a trade area is that portion from which the most frequent visitors originate. This area is often referred to as the *primary trade area* and usually represents the area where a majority of a particular unit's sales originate.

I will examine those factors that determine trade area sizes and shapes and will discuss methods for determining a specific trade area as well as the important elements it contains. For an individual attempting to establish a trade area, who does not now operate a restaurant or fast food operation, there are ways to use a potential competitor's facility to assist in defining a trade area. There are many variables, but I have found over time that they can be isolated and that there are typical trade areas for specific kinds of food operations depending on their location. Thus, although other factors play a role, the type of location is often the most sensitive item in the determination of trade area size.

TRADE AREA SHAPES

Trade areas are a function of the unit's ability to attract customers from a geographic area in relation to topography, physical and psychological barriers, accessibility, driving time, competition, population characteristics, expenditure resources, visibility, and type of location. Therefore, in comparing restaurants or fast food operations, often dissimilar trade areas will be apparent. Only after studying the geography and type of location is it possible to see the patterns that do exist and the importance of establishing the primary trade area as the basis for assessing a unit's success.

Topography

Topography plays a definite role in trade area shape. Mountains, hills, valleys, lakes, rivers, and other impediments affect road development and thus the ability of people to get from one area to another. Moreover, topography combined with weather (snow, ice, rain, and fog) has a strong impact on trade area shape. If consumers cannot traverse a hill, such as those found in Duluth, Minnesota, during the winter, they will find alternative places to go, which will certainly affect trade area shape.

Barriers

Physical barriers inhibit traffic movement. In addition to those mentioned under Topography, there are railroad crossings, bridges, cemeteries, industrial parks, sizable office complexes, large military installations, airports, and other impediments to consumer movement. Psychological barriers can be ethnic differences, income variations, high crime, noisy or unsightly areas, congestion, expressways (even though it is possible to pass freely over or under them), large parks, and other psychological impediments that affect the decision-making process in selecting a meal away from home.

Competition

Competition plays a critical role in the shape of a trade area. The more direct the competition, the greater the impact that it will have, and conversely, the more indirect the competition, the less impact it will have. Competition must be appraised both qualitatively and quantitatively to assess the impact that it might have on the shape and size of a trade area. Figure 4.1 depicts a trade area for a dinner house. Note the major competitors (black circles with numbers) that have influenced the trade area as well as the road

FIGURE 4.1

Primary Trade Area for a Dinner House*

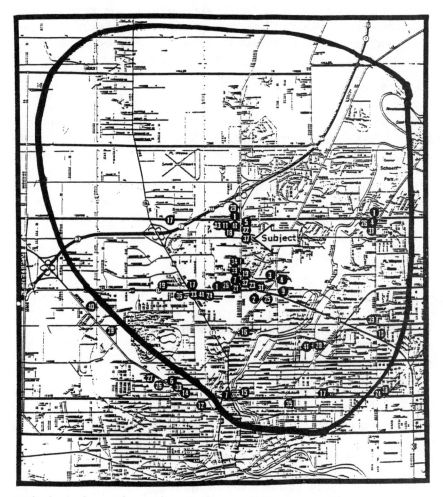

* Black circles with numbers indicate major competitors.

patterns that have had an equal impact on the area's shape. The primary trade area represents about 65% of the unit's sales.

Road Patterns

Road patterns, like competition, prove to be one of the most significant factors affecting the shape of trade areas. Access is critical; the better the access in one or more directions, the more extensive the trade area, all other things being equal. Inadequate access adversely affects the trade area, especially in the direction from which access is limited. Traffic flow affects the extent of a trade area and its relationship to road patterns.

Ethnic Characteristics

Ethnic characteristics may have an impact on the shape of trade areas. This is particularly true when an ethnic group is not attracted to a particular type of restaurant and excludes itself from the restaurant's customer base.

Income Differences

Income differences can have a considerable impact on a trade area's shape. A dinner house serving persons with an average income exceeding $45,000 will not attract many customers from an area where incomes are, say, $20,000, and a fast food operator whose customers are predominantly in the $20,000 to $25,000 income category may not include, as part of its trade area, persons in the $40,000 to $50,000 income category.

Population Density

Population density can affect a trade area because of traffic backup, the lack of parking spaces, and unacceptable travel times. Thus, for some, the greater the population density, generally, the smaller the trade area. The exception is the unique fine dining restaurant, which tends to draw from a wide area, especially on weekends. However, when evaluated on the basis of frequent customers, that trade area diminishes significantly, showing the effect of density.

TRADE AREA SIZE

The size of a trade area is affected by the type of location and type of food facility. Other influential factors include the road network, congestion, driving time, population density, and uniqueness.

Road Network

The number of roads or expressways leading to a particular location, along with the number of lanes provided and the speed limit, affects the size of a trade area.

Congestion

The greater the amount of congestion, the more the trade area is usually proscribed, assuming that the congestion occurs when the restaurant would normally generate its traffic. Unfortunately, often the perception of traffic congestion will cause the consumers to avoid a particular area even though at the time of dining, congestion may not be a factor.

Driving Time

As previously indicated, driving time to and from an area is far more significant than the distance that people are willing to travel. Often, proximity to a high-speed, limited access expressway substantially increases the size of the trade area because customers can travel greater distances in less time. A customer driving to a particular location via an expressway will usually cover a significantly greater distance than a customer driving a local traffic artery for the same amount of time. Figure 4.2 shows a driving time map reflecting a 5- and 10-minute driving time from a restaurant location. Notice how the area to the east (the right), which is a more congested section, is shorter than the area to the west. Also, note the distance that can be achieved to the south (bottom of the map). Less congestion and an additional traffic lane are the reasons.

Population Density and Community Size

In the western and northwestern United States, the low population density and long distances between cities accustom people to

FIGURE 4.2

Driving Time Analysis

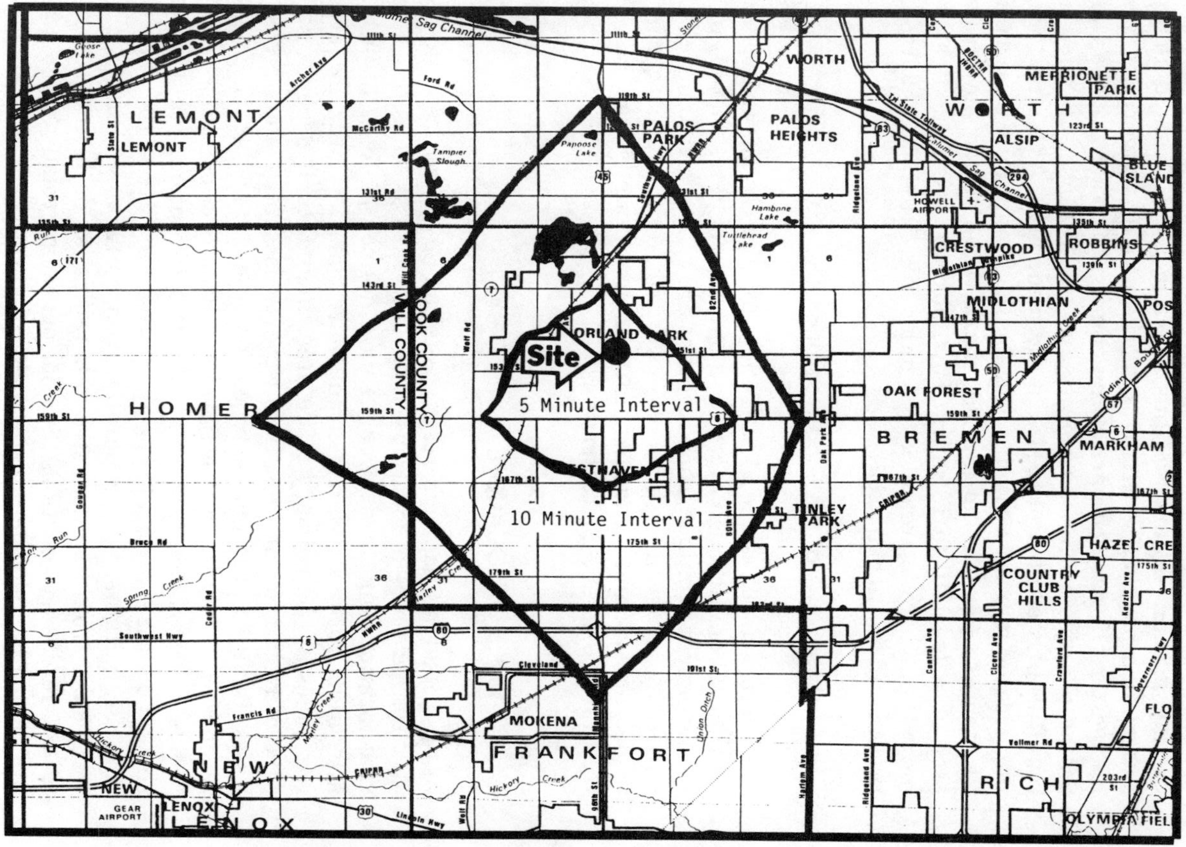

driving greater distances. Thus, food facilities located in these states often have larger trade areas than their counterparts in the midwestern or eastern part of the country. Throughout the United States, the size of the community and the distances to other communities play a role in the size of the trade area. A fast food operation located in a western city or a smaller community elsewhere in the country (away from a major market) will often have a trade area of at least 10 to 15 miles. This, of course, is in contrast to a more typical trade area of 2 to 3 miles in a densely populated portion of a major urban area.

Uniqueness of the Food Operation

The more unusual the food operation, usually the larger the size of its trade area. Although every food operator believes that his or her establishment is unique, such facilities are exceptions. Uniqueness is only truly achieved with success over time and is apparent in the trade area size and the average driving times found in an analysis of the unit's customer characteristics.

TYPES OF LOCATIONS

As described in Chapter 2, restaurants can be categorized into about 16 different types of locations. Over the years of evaluating restaurant locations and trade areas, I have noticed patterns in business attraction. Historically, restaurants have considered the area within five miles as the primary trade area. In reality, it depends on the type of restaurant and location. Nevertheless, for comparative purposes, Table 4.1 presents the types of restaurant by the percentage of business that normally is generated within and beyond a five-mile radius. Every restaurant is a potential exception, but this table shows how the locational type can have an impact on the trade area size. Restaurants near generative concentrations usually achieve more sales from beyond a five-mile radius, as do highway or interstate interchange locations. Special occasion restaurants generally are or should be located near a major highway, since they have a low frequency of visit and, therefore, need a large population base. This factor can be offset by a large concentration of tourists or visitors, such as in Orlando, Florida.

TABLE 4.1

Sales Often Generated Beyond Five Miles

	Sales Range (%)	
Restaurants	Within Five Miles	Beyond Five Miles
Major traffic artery	50–60	40–50
Near major mall	40–50	50–60
Multi-use generative center	40–50	50–60
Dense urban area	70–80	20–30
Highway interchange	40–50	50–60
Downtown locations-unique	60–70	30–40
Older business districts	70–80	20–30
Within a mall	50–60	40–50
University areas	75–85	15–25
Special locations	N/A	N/A
Hotel/resort area	70–80	20–30
Industrial areas	80–90	10–20
Residential areas	80–90	10–20
Countryside, crossroads, highway	40–50	50–60
Unique destination	30–40	60–80
Small towns	50–60	40–50

Fast food operations usually fall into about eleven locational types. Table 4.2 lists the various types of fast food location and the percentage of business normally captured within a three-mile radius. A three-mile radius has been used for consistency in comparison but is not sacrosanct. It is, however, the standard most commonly used in the fast food industry, for better or for worse. In some cases it is applicable, and in many other cases it is not appropriate.

Note that there are considerable differences in the percentage of business attracted to a particular location from beyond the three-mile radius. Moreover, there is some distortion for a typical fast food operator during the lunch hour because of business attracted from employment concentrations. Also, locations near a major mall more often will take on the larger trade area characteristics of the mall. It is not uncommon to find that more than 80% of the business attracted to a fast food operation in proximity to a major regional

TABLE 4.2

Sales Often Generated Beyond Three Miles

Fast Food Units	Sales Range (%)	
	Within Three Miles	Beyond Three Miles
Suburban highway	60–70	30–40
Suburban commercial area	65–75	25–35
Dense urban area	80–90	10–20
Near a major mall	30–40	60–70
Highway interchange	50–60	40–50
Older business district	70–80	20–30
Industrial areas	65–75	25–35
University area	80–90	10–20
Small town	40–50	50–60
Residential areas	80–90	10–20
Downtown areas	90–100	1–10

shopping center comes from *beyond* three miles. This is also true of a location near a major highway interchange in a highly automobile-oriented community such as San Diego or Houston. Conversely, dense-urban locations tend to generate between 80 and 90% of their business *within* a three-mile radius. This is also true of university areas where, in fact, the figure may be as high as 90%. The remaining 10% represents people moving through the area, transients, and extremes that are difficult to quantify. Small towns often will generate customers from a 10, 15, or perhaps a 20-mile radius on an unusually high frequency basis. Perhaps the opposite extreme is a downtown location whose trade area may extend but two blocks.

OTHER CONSIDERATIONS

Special Occasion Restaurants

Special occasion restaurants generally have a low frequency of visit but an extremely wide trade area. They also normally experience high average driving times. For example, it is not unusual for a special occasion restaurant such as a Japanese steak house, a

Polynesian restaurant, or a tourist attraction to have a customer who comes to the unit once every six months, drives an average of 45 to 60 minutes, and comes with a party of four or six. To propagate itself, this type of facility should be situated in a location that is accessible to a large number of people.

Special Setting and Atmosphere

Throughout the world, numerous restaurants are situated on lakes, rivers, oceans, marinas, mountains, ranches, farms, towers, golf courses, and other sites with a special appeal. That appeal only works if the operation provides good food in a unique atmosphere.

Value

Trade areas in some parts of the country are significantly influenced by meal values. This is truer for some types of food operations than for others. For example, Florida consumers are very price conscious. While there are numerous successful high-priced dinner houses in Florida (usually tourist-oriented), there are many more moderately priced food operations playing on the value aspect of customer attraction. Restaurant facilities in Florida with a competitive price–value relationship have generally fared better. Additionally, they must be prepared to cater to an older population base whose frequency is much greater than that of the general population. In fact, in some cases, the significant value–price relationship has actually offset secondary locations and solidified success. Since the residents of many of the Florida communities are extremely price conscious, they are willing and prepared to travel to out-of-the-way places to capitalize on the value. Often, the cost of capitalizing on the value is greater than the value received. Nevertheless, often the perception is more important than the reality.

Singles and Childless Young Married Couples

Restaurant–bar operations catering to this group have varying trade areas. The "themers," or "fern bars," or sports bars as they are often called, generate trade areas of different sizes and shapes, depending on the amount of competition. Sometimes they are simply "watering holes" with little ambience other than reasonably priced drinks in a convenient location. Their trade areas can be quite large, depending on the part of the country they are in and the extent to which they attract young singles. Tougher enforcement of drunk driving laws has significantly reduced trade area sizes, and in many instances, forced a change in emphasis from bar to food facility. This trend will continue.

TRADE AREA DETERMINATION

For the existing operator, trade area determination is rather simple; utilize customer survey data. An important element of that analysis is to plot customers on maps, differentiating between those whose trip originates at home and those whose trip may originate from work, shopping, or some other place. Customers are also segmented by meal or daypart. For example, a restaurant near a hotel row may have, as its customer distribution, the hotels and motels that proliferate the area. In contrast, a food unit in an industrial area may have, as its primary trade area, those industrial plants in the immediate vicinity. Furthermore, many fast food and restaurant facilities usually draw the majority of their customers from residential areas. As a result, the trade areas reflect the residential areas of these customers as well as the socioeconomic characteristics of both the customers and the areas of attraction. Therefore, existing operators should first plot their customers on maps by *frequency of visit* and then by *daypart* (breakfast, lunch, dinner, late evening). Dinner house operations should also follow this procedure to fully understand the trade area differences (and they do exist) between lunch and dinner customers. For example, lunch customers may originate from nearby office complexes, whereas dinner customers originate from home.

A good base map is necessary for an accurate job. For a fast food operation, this generally means a good street map. For example, if your unit were located in the Sharpstown area in Houston, Texas, it would be necessary to have a good base map showing the southwest sector of the Houston Metropolitan Area; and if you had a dinner house on Long Island, New York, you would need a good map of Long Island.

The next step involves plotting your customers' points of origin and frequency of visit with color dots that represent frequency of visit and daypart. Color pins can also be used; however, the map must be handled carefully because the pins can easily be knocked off and their location can be difficult to retrace. I prefer color dots because they stand out and easily clarify the primary and secondary portions of the trade area, as well as differences between lunch and dinner, and work, home, and shopping.

If the questionnaire asks for the respondent's zip code, then it is easy to "zero" in on the area in which the respondent lives. Often in narrow trade areas, the dots will build up close to the unit, making it difficult to find the streets. An alternative is to use a clear acetate overlay or tracing paper. I also strongly recommend that one individual do the plotting because that person will become increasingly familiar with the map and the streets, thus simplifying the task. When completed, the map will reflect the unit's customer attraction. The colors of frequency will define the primary trade area, whereas less frequent visitors will be located in the secondary area. However, to fully appreciate the map's capabilities, it is necessary to add several additional elements. This can best be done by placing the new elements on another sheet of clear acetate.

Some computer firms are providing customer distribution by grids. This is fine as long as the symbols in the various grids reflect frequency of customer visit. Moreover, new computer programs such as "MapInfo" (1-800-FAST-MAP) or "Streets on a Disk," (805-529-1717) provide a way to tabulate locations by addresses directly onto a computer map using the Census Bureau's Tiger map system. As the systems are improved and the graphics gain better definition, this procedure will become the norm rather than the exception. Until then, the old systems continue to work well, even if they are somewhat tedious.

The first items to place on the map are your direct and indirect competitors. Note the location of the competitors in relation to your location and the customers' dots. Also, note whether competition is affecting your trading area and, if so, in what direction. This is especially important relative to the location of high frequency visitors. Next, take a standout color such as red and, on an overlay or on the map, outline with a felt pen the major traffic arteries, particularly noting the artery that provides access to your existing location. Next, look at the road patterns in relation to the competition; now add the physical or psychological barriers that may be playing a role in your trade area delineation. For example, rivers, streams, airports, major industrial parks, lakes, and, in some cases, major interstate highways can become physical or even psychological barriers. Note them in black as barriers and their relationship to your site and the distribution of your customers. Now add the major activity areas such as regional shopping centers, major office parks, and major industrial areas. There may be other types of generative or activity areas that should be noted. Again, look at these factors in relation to the distribution of your customers.

Next, consider the socioeconomic characteristics of the people who reside within the various areas of your trade area and its environs. For example, is there a sector, say to the north, where few customers originate? Does competition exist in that sector? Is it in the normal flow of traffic? Does the normal pattern of people who reside in that area fit your facility, or are their socioeconomic characteristics appreciably different from those of your customers? If so, perhaps that is why there are few customers from that particular area. You might shade those residential areas in green that have the most compatible socioeconomic characteristics. Are these the areas where most of your customers originate?

After further review of the trade area, you may also wish to superimpose a "driving time analysis" on another overlay. Driving time analysis is simply the time required to drive specific distances on access arteries during normal traffic at normal speeds. For example, if your customers are driving to the unit in an average time of 12 minutes, you may wish to duplicate on the map what your customers are telling you. This information may indicate to you that your trade area is smaller in one direction because of traffic congestion and the amount of time required to travel to and from that particular direction.

Other items to put on overlays may include hotels, resorts, funeral homes, cemeteries, stadiums, baseball parks, racetracks, and airports. It is only necessary to identify what may have some impact and to look at it in light of your customer distribution, the road patterns, and other pertinent factors. Following this procedure cannot help but provide a greater understanding of your trade area and the reasons it has taken its particular shape.

For downtown locations, the process is done by blocks rather than miles, but the approach is the same. Moreover, two trade areas will emerge for some downtown restaurants. Lunch may have a trade area of less than a mile, whereas the dinner trade area may cover the metropolitan area or a major part of it.

ENTRANTS INTO THE FOOD INDUSTRY

The prospective restaurateur, who cannot study current customers, may use the procedures in this chapter to evaluate competitors' trade areas or to evaluate the type of restaurant facility being contemplated. For example, if you are considering the development of a Mexican restaurant in a particular city, you may wish to evaluate a similar Mexican restaurant. Identifying the customer characteristics and trade area profile will provide a much clearer understanding not only of the customer characteristics but also the type of trade area that can be anticipated. The methods for carrying out such an evaluation were described in Chapter 3 and are applicable here.

There are several different ways to identify the trade areas of competitive facilities. Some are relatively simple, while others are time consuming and somewhat costly.

Review of Vehicle Stickers

In suburban locations with three or more communities in the general vicinity, a review of vehicle stickers for the cars parked in the competitive restaurant's lot will generally provide a picture of the direction in which the patrons are coming. This is simple to do, does not attract much attention, and will, in many instances, provide at least a directional picture of activity.

License Plate Study

A license plate study inventories the plates on the cars in the competitor's parking lot over several days, by daypart. For example, a fast food operator might record license plates for the lunch and dinner hours for three or four of the busiest days, such as Thursday through Sunday. A dinner house operator might take several weekends and record the license plates for the dinner hour for Friday through Sunday, or perhaps Thursday through Saturday, depending on the peaks of activity.

Next, it is necessary to procure the names and addresses of the persons to whom the cars are registered from the State Department of Vehicle Registration (or whatever the agency is called in the operator's state). In most states, there is a charge for this service that ranges from nominal to expensive. Nevertheless, if it is reasonable, it can represent a quick way of finding out who the customers are and where they are coming from. In some locales, the local automobile association may have the automobile registrations. For the higher priced dinner house, registrations can become a problem because of the number of leased vehicles registered to businesses. Nevertheless, the process can provide a rough picture of the trade area. Once an operator has secured the data, the best way to represent the trade area is to plot the addresses on a map.

License Plate Study and Telephone Interview Program

After securing the names and addresses of the people who visit the respective restaurant facility, the operator can obtain their telephone numbers from a telephone directory and call them regarding their visit to the restaurant, frequency of visits to other food operations, what they liked, what they disliked, and other pertinent factors. (See Chapter 3 for a discussion of interviews and questionnaires.)

Interviewing Competitor's Customers as They Leave the Premises

This is an excellent way to find out where the competitor's customers originate. However, as you might expect, the competitor usually doesn't appreciate it. Therefore, this is usually a short-lived endeavor. Generally, he or she will call the police and have you thrown off the property. If your establishment is to be in a different city, where it poses no threat to the competitor, perhaps you can make a deal by suggesting that you will provide the interview results free in return for getting a "handle" on the distances that customers are coming from and some characteristics of those customers. Again, the types of questions to ask are discussed in Chapter 3.

Passing Out Mail-Back Questionnaires

Another trick that sometimes works is passing out a questionnaire with a return envelope to diners as they leave the property. Often, it necessitates standing on the curb or in the street so as to be on public rather than private property. The diners are asked to fill out the form at their leisure and return it. Mail questionnaires have a low response rate (9% to 12% normally) so that a large number must be distributed to get an adequate sample size. In some cases, this will also offend the owner or operator, who will, in turn, call the police and perhaps create some harassment. Occasionally, it is worth the effort.

Other Alternatives

Some people in the food business have found it beneficial to pass out coupons to the competitor's customers as they leave the premises, with some type of an incentive for filling out a questionnaire. I am sure that there are many other little ploys that can be useful in different situations. Basically, it is important to know the extent to which you can anticipate generating customers. This will help in planning the restaurant and, more importantly, in identifying the markets that you can expect to capture. While the procedures may seem complicated in some respects, the benefits to be derived are greater by far than the effort required.

SUMMARY

Understanding your trade area—and your competitors'—is extremely important in site selection. This knowledge can save many mistakes and certainly helps to define the strengths of competitors. The trade area outlines the area from which you can expect to generate business. Also, demographic, income, and employment data will be developed within the trade area to determine the potential market. Thus, accurately defining the trade area has a significant impact on the overall potential, and subsequently on the sales of a specific location.

Five

Locational Criteria

W hether an operation is a multi-unit chain, a single restaurant, or a fast food unit, practical and usable locational criteria are necessary. The multi-unit chain operator can study the various units and differentiate good locations from bad by isolating the locational characteristics that are common to the units with high sales. The individual operator can identify successful competitors in the marketplace and compare locational characteristics. It is also helpful to examine the characteristics of restaurant or fast food facilities that have failed. Later on in this book, I will provide some site selection guidelines that may be helpful in identifying possible locations. Nevertheless, each individual should look at his or her market to see what role location has played in the success of certain restaurants and the failure of others.

It is obvious that the multi-unit operator does have an advantage in this situation. Since most multi-unit operators have some "below par" units, this exercise will provide insight into locational differences. Sometimes, however, it is difficult to identify specifically whether management, product, or location is the problem with a particular unit. Nevertheless, the operator can compare it with a very good unit and identify the differences. At times, the difficulty is a combination of poor ingress and egress or perhaps visibility, instead of being a single major element, but more often, poor location is the overall problem. The following sections describe elements normally analyzed in developing locational criteria.

GEOGRAPHY

To the multi-unit operator, geography is important because customers in different parts of the country display differences in eating-
out expenditures and habits. The first thrust, then should be an
analysis of the sales performance of the existing units based on their
distribution into geographic areas. Are there differences? If so, why?

SALES SIZE AND TRENDS

The sales size and performance trends are extremely important. Often, the best starting point is to rank the unit sales in descending
order and to study both ends of the range. What are the characteristics of the units at the top of the list, and why are other units at the
bottom of the list? Such an exercise will begin to provide clues. Is
location a factor in success?

CITY OR MARKET AREA SIZE

The size of the city or market area is not necessarily a reason for a
unit being at the top or bottom of the list, but it may have a notice-
able effect. Often the problem in sales performance is not the efforts
of people nor the location, but rather the community's size, which is
too small to justify the initial development of a unit. Ranking the
units by size of community provides additional clues into the locational profile.

TYPE OF LOCATION

Rearranging the units by type of location and comparing sales performance will provide additional clues as to the differences between
the good and the poor units.

ACCESSIBILITY

Although accessibility means many things to many people, it always
represents two primary elements: road capability and adequate ingress and egress. First, the roads in the general vicinity must be able

to move adequate numbers of people to and from the location. In the case of a generative restaurant, the restaurateur's interest is not necessarily in the total numbers of cars that pass the location on a 24-hour basis, but rather, the ability of his customers to get to and from his location when they wish to dine. The second factor—ingress and egress—refers to the ability of customers to get into and out of a specific location. This aspect of accessibility relates to elements such as speed limits, traffic lights, traffic backup, number of lanes, median strips, and left-hand turn lanes, and other factors.

The fast food operator may wish to rank the units in descending order on the basis of traffic counts, first listing the traffic counts by location; next by peak traffic times; and finally by low traffic times. This breakdown will provide a clear picture of the actual traffic passing the location during the hours that the facility is open, especially during its peak hours. These figures should be provided for all prospective locations.

TOPOGRAPHY

In many parts of the country, topography is a significant factor. Thus, it is necessary to classify whether the locations are on hills, curves, in low spots, between two hills, inaccessible from parts of the trade area, and so on. Topography may be so extreme that most locations are "compromise sites"; that is, they are sites because they have been dug out of, say, a mountainside and are the only locations available.

VISIBILITY

An essential element to the fast food operator and most restaurateurs, visibility represents both the amount of time and the distance that the consumer can see the facility or its sign from various directions. For highway locations, visibility is critical. For the in-line location, or perhaps a downtown location, walking visibility becomes the strategic factor. In either case, good visibility provides the opportunity to intercept or influence consumer decisions. Visibility should be cataloged, at least in minimum terms, such as "both directions unlimited," "both directions limited," or "one direction unlimited," on the Site Location Inventory Form (see Appendix).

There are many so-called rules and axioms regarding visibility. Some say a unit must be visible for 400 feet, others say 300, 200, 100, or even 50 feet. In my experience, it is difficult to quantify a specific distance other than "unlimited" because of road shapes, adjacent uses, large signs, speed limits, traffic volumes, and other factors. Instead, time of visibility is the most important factor. For example, at 45 miles per hour an automobile is traveling 66 feet per second. In five seconds the vehicle will travel 330 feet. For the average driver with normal distractions, this is unlimited visibility, assuming that either the sign or building are visible. Other visibility definitions may be found in Chapter 12. *As a general rule, go for maximum visibility when selecting a location.* Also, in the fast food business, the better the visibility, the easier it is for potential customers to see a sign or building and change lanes to get to the entrance.

ADJACENT USES

Adjacent uses should be identified and analyzed. For example: Are the facilities in proximity to a regional shopping center, or are they in a strip commercial area? Are the locations in or near office or industrial concentrations, a highway interchange, or on a major limited-access roadway? Nearby uses are very important. Since few fast food operations are generative; they must be in the normal pattern or in proximity to generative facilities, which create traffic.

In studying adjacent uses, keep in mind that major regional shopping centers located in developing suburban areas with little or no employment concentrations are predominantly oriented toward women. A food facility whose primary customers are men will often find it difficult to capture its usual share of business. Furthermore, unless the facility enjoys a certain uniqueness, evening sales in proximity to a new regional shopping center in a "pioneer" location (a fringe area location) are also difficult to capture.

COMPETITION

Competition is critical to any food operation. Direct competition (e.g., McDonald's versus Burger King) represents a similar food type and price range. Thus, in the same general price level, a steak-oriented restaurant is directly competitive with another steak-oriented restaurant, a French restaurant is competitive with other French restaurants, and a theme restaurant is competitive with other theme restaurants. Indirect competition competes for the same dollar, but less directly. For example, Arby's is competing with McDonald's and Burger King for the same eating-out dollar, and Red Lobster is competing for the same dollar as Sizzler. In these cases, however, the price range and food type are dissimilar enough to have a more indirect effect. An inventory of the direct and indirect competitive facilities to each existing unit should be completed and reviewed in light of their comparative sales performance.

DEMOGRAPHICS

There are basic differences in customer attraction, especially by age of the customer. Contrary to popular belief, all persons eating out are not necessarily prospective customers to all facilities. For example, McDonald's has presold the children to such an extent that teenagers are very definitely McDonald's market. While Burger King would like to think that this is also their situation, we find a lower rate of attraction in those age groups, with Burger King serving a slightly older market. Wendy's usually appeals to even older customers. Therefore, while each corporation is in the hamburger business, there are enough differences in product and presentation to attract different aspects of the market. As part of a locational profile, it is necessary to know not only who your customer is, but also how many people are in the trade area and their age and income structure.

SUMMARY

Analyzing locational criteria will eventually result in a quantification that reflects the ingredients in a good location as well as the factors that should be avoided. Learn from your surroundings, your competitors, and others.

Part Two

Application

Six

Market Structure

Every area, whether it be a neighborhood, city, metropolitan area, or region, has a structure. Understanding that structure can clarify market actions and make site selection much easier.

SHAPE OF THE CITY OR METROPOLITAN AREA

The shape of a market, a city, or a metropolitan area is often over-looked when considering locational opportunities. Shape is extremely important. Consider for a moment, Chicago, Milwaukee, Detroit, Cleveland, Buffalo, Los Angeles, Toronto, and Miami. They are fan-shaped cities. Their principal arteries extend from the downtown area in a radial fashion, and growth has occurred along the primary radial arteries. Food facilities have been developed on the major arteries to intercept or, in some cases, to generate customers. In northeastern and midwestern cities, public transportation has played a role in the market's structural growth. In contrast, Indianapolis has a square shape and has had the opportunity to grow in almost every direction. Birmingham, Alabama, is a rectangular city, located between two mountain ranges. The city initially grew between the two barriers and eventually extended itself over the mountain range to the south.

Mountain ranges have channeled the growth, the shape, and the size of many western cities. In fact, physical restrictions have thwarted the directional growth of some cities. This is true of both Phoenix and Tucson, Arizona. Lincoln, Nebraska, had a moratorium on water and sewer connections beyond 84th Street, which effectively limited the potential for growth in the eastern sector. As a result, growth has been forced to move to the north and south and, to some extent, to the west.

Why is the shape of a city important? It has true significance only when considering the development of several or more units within an area. The shape will then help determine the number of units and the direction in which they can be placed. Often, one community shape will provide the opportunity to develop more units in a marketplace than another. For example, a fan-shaped city will usually allow the placement of more units on intercepting arteries that radiate from the central core than, say, a square-shaped city. Population deployment can make it impossible to serve everyone adequately because of the population deployment within the various geographic sectors and possibly an inadequate number of people in one or more directions.

TOPOGRAPHY

Topography has a strong influence on the structure of the market. Prior to the completion of the interstate system in Atlanta, Georgia, a person could stand on a hill and look across to another area, yet be unable to get there conveniently. At that time, markets were limited to corridors, since lateral movement was almost impossible. With the completion of the interstate system and, more particularly, the circumferential around Atlanta, shopping habits and eating-out patterns changed significantly. People could now travel conveniently from one part of the market area to the other without driving in toward town and back out again. Improved access also played a major role in changing employment concentrations in the Atlanta area.

Topography also affects markets such as Duluth, Minnesota, where in the wintertime it becomes nearly impossible to drive up and down the bluff because the elevations change drastically and are covered by snow and ice. It is common for locations on hills to be adversely affected by wet pavement, ice, or snow. Additionally, topography affects the size of a trade area, and in some cases can eliminate the possibility of developing a unit, even though the market appears to have enough people. Nevertheless, it is impossible for those people to get to the location because of physical problems.

BARRIERS

There are two primary types of barriers: physical and psychological. Physical barriers include lakes, rivers, cemeteries, parks, airports, dams, hills, railroad crossings, mountains, ravines, canyons, valleys, airports, and large industrial areas that prevent consumers from moving conveniently from one area to another.

Psychological barriers are no less common, but somewhat more subtle. Psychological barriers are "mental walls" that consumers establish in ignoring one area for another. Psychological barriers include ugly, dilapidated areas, high crime areas, areas of heavy truck traffic, highly congested areas, major expressways, or heavy industrial areas. Major expressways can actually be more of a psychological barrier than a physical barrier because in most cases underpasses and overpasses provide access from one side to another. Numerous other psychological barriers exist in different communities. Think for a moment, in your own community, is there a "wrong side of the tracks" that you avoid? Is there a major bottleneck intersection that creates traffic delays and, as a result, you along with others, take shortcuts to avoid that particular area? Are there railroad grade crossings that create a physical (when the trains come through) or psychological (the threat of trains) barrier? Can you think of some others that affect your own personal patterns? How do you think that they affect others?

Figure 6.1 is a map of Seattle, Washington. This city is interesting because it provides extreme physical barriers and, to some extent, psychological barriers. Note that Seattle is a series of peninsulas connected by bridges, and thus, activities in one sector may differ appreciably from those in another. Whereas, traffic can traverse the bridges from one area to another, especially to and from work, the patterns change considerably when it comes to shopping and eating out. For fast food facilities and typical restaurants, the patterns are affected even more. The fine dining restaurant, however, featuring good food, ambience, and atmosphere can breach physical, and sometimes even psychological barriers—*if the restaurant is unique enough.* Is yours?

STREET AND ROAD PATTERNS

Throughout a community, street and road patterns play a major role in the movement of people and the establishment of trade areas. The

FIGURE 6.1

Map of Seattle, Washington

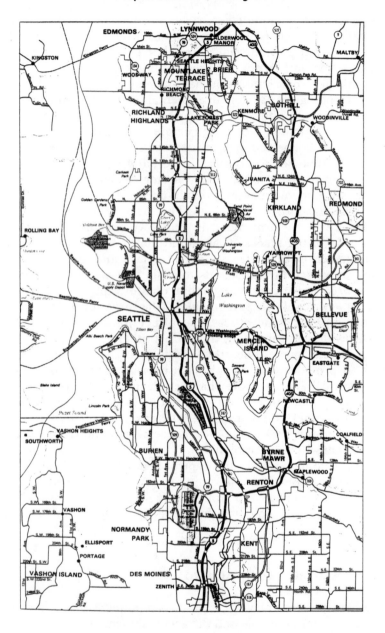

completion of the interstate system eliminated many impediments and created new problems. People's travel patterns changed because the roads provided a system for driving from one sector of the community to another, supposedly faster. The growth of most cities has occurred along their major arteries. Studying the history of a city will quickly indicate the importance of road patterns in establishing growth trends and determining why certain facilities are located where they are.

ETHNIC CHARACTERISTICS

Although ethnic concentrations affect the structure of the market, many of them have changed drastically during the past 50 years. Some have dispersed, whereas others have become more pronounced. For example, the old Italian, German, Irish, Jewish, and Polish neighborhoods in our central cities have shifted appreciably and, in many instances, no longer exist in a single concentration. Conversely, the black and Hispanic populations have generally remained concentrated, though expanded, within sectors of our metropolitan areas. Thus, they are more easily identifiable and can represent significant markets or significant problems depending on the income structure of a particular facility.

Ethnic characteristics can play a significant role in an establishment's success. For example, first, and often second, generation foreign-born persons generally do not eat in fast food operations; therefore, areas with such population concentrations are a poor choice for that kind of business. Conversely, chicken and fish fast food operations usually capture high sales in black neighborhoods, especially if the units are located in proximity to a major health service, drugstore, supermarket, or liquor store. Jewish communities have a strong orientation toward food services, but they consume little liquor; therefore, "watering hole" facilities generally do not fare well in those areas.

INCOME

Income certainly is a major factor in a community. We all tend to gravitate toward people of similar socioeconomic standing; in fact, we tend to upgrade our situation so that our children will have better opportunities than we had. Thus, income affects the overall structure of a community and the attitudes of its residents.

Consider your own city. First, where do the highest income residents live, in contrast with the lowest income residents? Next, where are the middle-income residents? Now, consider factors such as physical and psychological barriers, road patterns, and ethnic characteristics. Do they affect the areas of income concentration within your city? Almost certainly, they do. Furthermore, if you begin to record these various characteristics on a map, the structure becomes quite obvious. More importantly, you should now understand why these patterns exist.

EMPLOYMENT BASE

Major employment concentrations affect the structure of a market. Employment should be differentiated by heavy industry, light industry, distribution facilities, white-collar concentrations, and retail or service employment. Now think of employment in terms of income. Where do people live in relation to the employment concentrations? Is there some relationship to income? Once again, a clear picture begins to emerge. Blue-collar workers will tend to live in proximity to major heavy industry. In contrast, white-collar workers will be concentrated near suburban office concentrations. In cities that have excellent public transportation to and from the suburban sectors, white-collar concentrations will develop along major rail lines leading to and from the central city. In Chicago, for example, heavy industries, such as steel mills and automobile manufacturing plants, have historically been allocated on the south side of the city. Thus, the southern sector has had a much greater concentration of blue-collar, skilled, semiskilled, and unskilled workers. Because of Chicago's excellent commuter transportation, persons employed in the downtown area live in proximity to the major rail lines extending to both city and suburban neighborhoods.

The creation of O'Hare International Airport and the interstate system has had a major impact on industrial parks, office development, commercial construction, and residential development in northwest suburban Chicago. Within the past 10 years, the suburban sector of Chicago has added more than 50 million square feet of new industrial space, the majority of which is located in the Elk Grove Village area. Thus, O'Hare, which employs more than 35,000 people, and the Elk Grove industrial complex, together have become the second largest employment center in the Chicago Metropolitan Area. Downtown remains number one in employment. Therefore, in determining a community's structure, it is helpful to understand the employment base—its location, its concentration, and its type.

LAND USE LOCATIONS

The map concept is useful in determining land use. Elements to identify on the map include income, road patterns, physical and psychological barriers, employment concentrations, and commercial concentrations. The next step is to consider where new industry is locating, where new shopping centers are planned or where they exist, what roads are being changed or upgraded, what expressways will *not* be built, and where traffic concentrations exist versus lightly traveled roads. All these factors contribute to the structure of the market.

COMPETITION (OVERVIEW)

After establishing the general structure of the market, it is useful to consider the competitive aspects. Where are the fine dinner houses located relative to more moderately priced restaurants? Where are the fast food operations concentrated and why? Where do they appear to be successful; where do they appear to have failed? Several conclusions will be obvious. The fine dining houses will generally be in areas that either are, or were, in high income areas. Sometimes, however, better restaurants have been located in industrial areas for 20 or 30 years and, have developed a regional reputation because of good food and the proprietor's perseverance. Thus, people will continue to go back to the "old neighborhood" to dine because of the uniqueness and good food. Nevertheless, most competitive facilities will fall into the general income ranges of the people that they ordinarily serve.

Evaluating fast-food concentrations can be confusing because of the "follow the leader" syndrome that occurred in the 1960s and early 1970s, when one restaurateur followed the other to disaster. Thus, many areas that were inferior locations in the latter 1960s, today, because of their maturity, have become highly desirable. Others, however, have not, and will not, achieve success. The fast food business is *not* a "follow the leader" game, particularly, in relation to successful operations and the rising cost of real estate and buildings.

GROWTH PATTERNS

Evaluating the direction of a city or community's growth provides numerous clues about the evolving market structure. It is especially critical to find out whether major expressway access exists, where industry has relocated and new industry has developed, where office concentrations are, where new regional shopping centers have risen, where high schools or colleges have been constructed, and where sewer and water service is available. Taking the time to review all these elements on a map will suggest answers to pertinent market structure questions.

This knowledge will be a revelation for some, provide a better understanding for others, and, for still others, will reinforce their understanding of the importance of market structure and locational needs.

Seven

Fieldwork Procedures

Fieldwork is exactly as the phrase implies—work carried out in the field, that is, in a particular city, community, or neighborhood under consideration. *There is no substitute for fieldwork.* It is impossible to carry out market studies and site selection in the office; there are too many intangibles that become apparent only by visiting the city, the area, and the site. Before reaching any conclusions, the investigator must walk the land, collecting and evaluating the data in a logical framework. Fieldwork for a single site *normally* requires 7 to 10 days, and fieldwork for an entire metropolitan area, including a multisite development strategy, can take from 2 to 8 weeks, depending on the size of the market. Remember, also, that the first time through this new procedure will require more time. Once understood, fieldwork becomes increasingly easier since the researcher learns what to look for and does not waste time gathering unproductive data. Doing fieldwork is like using a fine camera. You start out with a wide angle and as you gather and evaluate more information, the lens zooms in, and the target or the answer becomes obvious.

DATA GATHERING

The first step is to contact local agencies for data. The Fieldwork Checklist that appears at the end of this chapter, suggests a number of potential sources of information. It is necessary to keep in mind, however, that there is a wide variation in both the availability of data and its reliability. Therefore, in carrying out fieldwork, you must ask many people the same questions to see how often you receive similar answers. Some issues are controversial and so there will not be a definite conclusion, merely multiple opinions. It is often necessary to sift through all the opinions and make some judgment regarding their reliability. For example, the path of a planned highway may not yet be established, and many bureaucrats and politicians will have differing opinions regarding the proposed locations. To evaluate all the opinions and "guestimate" the probable route, the investigation often must simulate changes in the market. As a general rule, most proposed highways will be delayed at least 10 years, and many will not be constructed because of a lack of federal and state funding.

The various agencies on the checklist appear in the order in which they are usually contacted. The user should adapt the procedure as needed, to obtain reliable data for a specific restaurant or fast food operation. Additional adjustments may also be necessary, depending on how the contacts respond as the project proceeds. The following sections describe the agencies that, on a continuing basis, provide most of the data.

The Chamber of Commerce

The Chamber of Commerce is usually visited first, primarily because of its contacts. The Chamber of Commerce consists of businesspersons and concerned citizens who work as a group to promote and improve their city or metropolitan area. Their principal objective is to "sell" the present and future benefits of the city to anybody who will listen. Thus, the Chamber of Commerce tends to distribute "upbeat" data concerning the community, emphasizing its assets and eliminating negative aspects. This is their job, and they do it well! Furthermore, much of the data furnished by chambers of commerce is often from annual publications such as the *Sales and Marketing Management Survey of Buying Power* and the *Editor's and*

Publishers Market Guide. Both of these publications will be discussed later in this chapter. R. L. Polk and R. R. Donnelley also gather data, providing varying degrees of intensity for numerous cities. Usually only the larger chambers of commerce actually develop their own data.

It is important to keep in mind that most chambers of commerce are very downtown oriented; that is, the largest number of members are often concentrated in the downtown area and, as a result, their primary efforts and considerations are toward that sector. The main reason for contacting the Chamber of Commerce is its contacts. Key members are usually involved in almost every facet of city improvement programs and projects and, as a result, are sensitive not only to the issues, but also to the people who are most knowledgeable.

Chambers of commerce are generally in or near the downtown area. We generally arrive unannounced (although appointments can be helpful in larger cities). We ask to speak with someone, preferably the director of research or the director of the Chamber, regarding the current status of the community. Usually the receptionist wants to place everyone into categories, such as industry, demographics, convention facilities, and office, residential, or commercial buildings. To maximize the information that you can obtain, try to avoid immediate categorization. In larger chambers of commerce, it may be necessary to identify your interest in commercial development, but this can be disadvantageous because many chamber staff people automatically assume that they know what you need, and often they do not. Also, some fast food operations and restaurants are "dirty words" to many communities. They do not want any additional food facilities. Using the approach that you are "an investor" seeking opportunity within the community can be an effective tactic to avoid this problem.

In your opening request to the Chamber of Commerce official, you might state: "I am reviewing investment opportunities within your area, and I am most interested in population growth, directional growth patterns, employment concentrations, areas of new industrial development, major and minor shopping complexes, income, school enrollments, major arteries, major planned improvements in either the thoroughfare plan or expressways, and the overall idea of what the area will look like over the next 10 years." This will provide enough opening ammunition to get the Chamber spokesperson going. You will want to ask further questions regarding specifics. It is also necessary to obtain a good map, and this can generally be supplied by the Chamber of Commerce. Do not be afraid to write or draw on the maps.

When dealing with population data, identify its source, and ask for any population projections that have been made, or find out where they might be obtained. The Chamber representative may refer you to another source. If so, ask for the name of a specific individual.

Be as explicit as possible in requesting such information as the following from the Chamber of Commerce:

- *Population Trends, Projections, Age Structure, and Ethnic Concentrations.* Most of this information will be census data prepared and published by the United States Department of Commerce, Bureau of the Census, at the beginning of each decade (e.g., 1960, 1970, 1980, 1990).
- *Data from Special Census.* These are censuses that have been carried out by the city, the county, the state, the Census Bureau, or any other governmental or private agency since the last official census.
- *Migration Trends within the Area.* These include not only in-migration and out-migration of people, but also neighborhood trends, such as ethnic change, age variations, new developments, and areas of deterioration and blight.
- *Average Family Income and Household Income.* Ask about the availability and validity of data by small areas within the city or metropolitan area. Average family income includes income earned by family members living under the same roof. Household income includes income earned by all members living in a household. They need not be related. Thus, household income can be both larger and smaller. Sometimes the additional persons are retired, and therefore have little income. Other times the reverse is true. The information is available from the official census, but the data in some cases have changed considerably because of inflation and recessions. Chambers of commerce normally provide data from *Sales and Marketing Management Survey of Buying Power.* They may know of other sources as well. Take down the name of the source and perhaps have the Chamber representative pave the way by calling the agency and introducing you.

- *Data from Other Agencies.* Ask about the strength of the research done by the utility companies, the telephone company, the local universities, the Planning Department, the Urban Redevelopment Department, the Regional Transportation Authority, and any other agencies. Also, request the names of the individuals who are responsible for the research so that when you go to the agency, you have the name of a specific person and can use the name of the contact at the Chamber of Commerce as an entree.
- *Area Employers.* Almost all chambers of commerce have a list of major employers, with the number of their employees, and can tell you the locations of new industrial development.
- *Other Research Sources.* The Chamber spokesperson should also be able to describe the research activities of the newspapers, banks, hospital planning councils, urban revitalization authorities, and other governmental and private agencies that develop data about the future of the area. Request permission to use the Chamber representative's name in contacting people. This is almost always granted.

Planning Agencies

Major cities may have more than one planning agency. For example, there may be a planning department for the city itself, a county planning department, and perhaps an overall regional planning authority. If so, it essential to see each group. Smaller communities may have only one group and very small cities may lack a full-time planner. In that case, it may be necessary to track down the chairman of the Planning Commission to obtain data. Usually, larger planning agencies can supply published data. In small towns, it is often necessary to handcopy some of the data because printed data are unavailable. Moreover, planning insights may be recounted orally.

Planning agencies, by their very nature, must carry out numerous studies to develop economic data needed for both current and long-range planning decisions. As a result, they conduct population evaluations, make population projections, and consider the impact of change. They can provide population analyses with projections, hopefully, by census tracts or some subdivision of the city or metropolitan area.

Income analyses reflecting the changes that have occurred since the last census are generally obtainable. Sometimes income forecasts have been prepared; more often, however, they have not. Nevertheless, discussions with the planner regarding shifting neighborhood patterns and prospective changes in income can be most beneficial.

Planning agencies usually evaluate employment concentrations and employment trends and make meaningful data available. The extent to which employment data are useful depends somewhat on the problem's complexity. Often it is necessary to secure more definitive data along with wage and salary scales from the state's Department of Employment (known by various names; the data-gathering phase will provide the pertinent form of address). This department maintains statistics, follows through on the government Affirmative Action labor policies, and generally is responsible for unemployment funds.

Employment concentrations are especially important in considering various types of restaurant and fast food operations. Operators of restaurants that require a strong luncheon business obviously need to know the locations and sizes of employment concentrations. Often the planning agency has data for the number of people employed, by type of employment, in both industrial areas and office concentrations. Where the square footage of office space data are available, but employment is not, a simple computation will provide fairly good parameters regarding the number of people employed in the various complexes (see Chapter 13).

A restaurateur featuring fine dining might wish to delve deeper into the types of employment located in the various concentrations, particularly the number of executives, who are inclined to frequent better dining facilities in the luncheon hour. Conversely, the fast food or reasonably priced restaurant operator would be interested in the total number of people, exclusive of those diners who tend to frequent higher priced restaurants. This is simply another way of getting at a specific market for which a food operator is competing.

Data for industrial concentrations can be plotted on a map to reflect more adequately where they are, and their relative numbers of employees. The planning agency representative can also explain where new industrial developments are planned and where they are actually taking place. Every community throughout the United States is attempting to secure new industry, but very few are, in fact, capturing major new facilities. Most movement is relocation from the city to suburbia. For the restaurateur, the shifting patterns of industrial locations and office concentrations within the metropolitan area are what matter.

Commercial concentrations, particularly in suburban sectors, are perhaps the most important consideration for many average food operations. These concentrations include shopping centers of all sizes and varieties and, most particularly, regional shopping centers with strong concentrations of high sales volume retailers. Commercial complexes are important because they generate frequent traffic, in fact, usually the most frequent traffic of all the suburban uses. The planning agency has had to plan for the development of new shopping centers of all sizes, shapes, and forms. Therefore, they should have data regarding, not only where the existing major competitors are, but also where future centers are planned. Often these data include the name of the shopping center, the number of stores, square footage, the names of the principal department stores, the number of parking spaces, and the estimated annual sales. At this point, you might also ask about good restaurants or the location of food concentrations.

Military bases are sometimes an important consideration in market evaluation. The planning agency can normally tell you about development near the base, as well as its longevity. Total civilian and military employment, both past and present with forecasts of the future, can be important to the restaurateur or fast-fooder who is considering a location in proximity to a major military installation. When in doubt about data, call the base commandant.

Unusual traffic generators must be considered. For example, Disney World, in Orlando, Florida, and Disneyland, in Anaheim, California, produce an unusual amount of traffic, thus creating opportunities for food facilities. The planning agency can provide initial information regarding placement of the activity, impact of the development, number of visitors, traffic flow, traffic counts, problem areas, and commercial concentrations in proximity to the major generator. Also, ask whom to see for more information.

Traffic planning should be investigated. The planning agency must necessarily study the past and present, and forecast the future, with respect to existing and proposed traffic arteries, street capacities, curb cuts, and capital spending for improvements. Customarily, such planning is done on at least a five-year basis. The data collected from the planning agency will probably need to be verified with the city, county, state, and federal highway departments, as discussed later in this chapter.

Major colleges and institutions such as medical complexes, large governmental installations, and others can be catalysts for restaurant and fast food activity. Many have populations the size of a small city, whereas others generate activities commensurate with downtown areas. The planning agency members can usually identify these major institutions and provide some indication of the total enrollment, employment, and/or visitors.

Building permit activity data can be useful. Most planning departments maintain building permit statistics, since they need to evaluate them regarding changes occurring within the city or metropolitan area. Nevertheless, it may be necessary to go to the Building Department to gain the specific data. These statistics are valuable in identifying the locations of residential and commercial development activities, and in evaluating increases in dwelling units within an area and the total potential population. You should be aware that a building permit does not always result in a new dwelling unit. Ask!

Aerial photographs, which can show helpful overviews of the area, are often available from larger planning agencies. If not, the agency should be able to indicate where to obtain the best reproductions. Flood maps, reflecting the 100-year flood plain, should also be obtained. Inquire about flood-prone areas and what is being done about any problems. Finally, ask about sewer problems, where they are, how often they occur, and what is being done to correct the situation. These may seem to be unimportant items; however, if you have ever had a restaurant located in a flood area, you are painfully aware of the difficulties.

The planning agency is a useful source to gain information regarding what has happened in the past, what the current situation is, and what is likely in the future. By asking numerous questions, reviewing the data, and referring to other sources, it is possible to gain considerable insight into the community and the posture of the city.

City and County Building and Zoning Department(s)

There are usually separate city and county building and zoning agencies, each with its own regulations, building codes, and ordinances. Obtain copies of all needed ordinances. The zoning map will sometimes have the flood plains clearly marked; if not, procure and review a flood plain map so as to avoid problem areas. If you discuss your plans with the appropriate officials regarding permit procedure, hearings, Health Department requirements, Environmental Protection Agency requirements, and fire zones, you should get a fairly good idea of how the community may react to your facility. Questions regarding the prominent zoning attorneys within the community are always worthwhile, because zoning can become a serious obstacle in many municipalities.

City, County, and State Traffic or Highway Departments

To carry out a study of the entire metropolitan area or of a site that is affected by city, county, and state traffic, it is necessary to visit the city, county, and state highway departments. Conversely, the restaurateur seeking an individual location within a specific area may only need to see the appropriate agency governing that area. In either case, traffic departments can supply the following information:

- *Road Improvement Plans.* Plans for street improvements, new roads, upgrading, and other capital expenditures are generally developed for a one- to five-year term. If a plan or map is not available, the agency representative should draw any changes on your map and indicate expected completion dates.
- *Traffic Counts.* Although traffic counts can often be purchased, it is sometimes necessary to ask the highway department to extract data for specific intersections. Nevertheless, most cities carry out 24-hour traffic counts over various periods of a year. These counts are averaged out to reflect the normal traffic that can be expected on an artery over a 24-hour period (some traffic counts cover shorter times, such as 12 hours). Cyclical variations are also often averaged out, or two counts are provided, one at the high point, and the other at the low point. Highway engineers generally can provide insight into the increased traffic that may be expected on the major arteries. Eventually, as you begin to zero in on specific areas, you should approach the highway department regarding *hourly* traffic counts that will reflect the peaks (high points) and valleys (low points) of traffic. When possible, secure traffic count maps for the current year and for several preceding years. These maps will indicate the changes that have occurred.
- *Traffic Flow.* If possible, secure a "traffic flow" map, which depicts the size of traffic volume by the width of the road (see Figure 9.2). The portions of the roadway that appear widest carry the most traffic, and conversely, those roads that are depicted as the narrowest carry the least traffic. To aid in understanding area

patterns, smart investigators also record major generators, employment concentrations, and other significant factors on this map.

Liquor Commission

Where liquor is a factor, obviously the liquor rules and regulations as well as the availability of a liquor license are paramount. Therefore, it is necessary to stop at the liquor commission (or whatever it is called in the area), to find out the necessary information. Often for a dinner house, the availability of a liquor license will determine which area is possible. Such a site may not be good enough to support a restaurant.

Newspapers

In some major cities, newspapers do significant consumer research, shopping center analysis, and eating-out research. In most communities, however, newspapers are a rather poor source of information. It is, therefore, necessary to contact the newspaper, ask for its research bureau, and discuss with the appropriate personnel what material is available. Also, newspaper circulation coverage data and rates should be obtained if you contemplate newspaper advertising. The restaurant critic is another possible contact; however, we have found that most of them can offer only superficial information and have limited recall unless they are being fed.

Public Transportation Authority

Because federal financing mandates a regional approach, many medium and large cities today have a regional public transportation authority. Facilities that need public transportation, or food facilities that are located in downtown areas, are affected by public transportation. Information regarding bus routes, rail schedules, and the number of people embarking and disembarking at specific locations can be vital in evaluating potential opportunities within a city.

United States Department of Commerce

In most major and medium-sized cities throughout the United States, the United States Department of Commerce has field offices that sell census publications. They also usually have a library where visitors can review the various census publications and make copies of necessary items.

Redevelopment Agency

Restaurateurs and fast food operators developing units in the central city, will find it worthwhile to contact the Redevelopment Agency. The primary reason for this contact is to obtain any studies that the agency has completed on the central city. These reports typically consider age, income, ethnic characteristics, population and population change, and the present and future direction of the various areas within the city. This information can be particularly beneficial if you are interested in any of those areas, but it can also provide insight into the changes that are anticipated within the city or the metropolitan area.

State Department of Revenue (Sales Tax Receipts)

This agency is known by a variety of names. Essentially, the Department of Revenue is responsible for collecting the sales taxes imposed by most states (and some cities). The data that are generally compiled—reflecting collections for cities, incorporated areas, and counties—include the category "Eating and Drinking Places." Some states break it out by those with alcoholic beverages and those without. Nevertheless, existing operations should acquire the data for several years' operating experience, as well as the most current 12-month period, in order to study any fluctuations in sales tax receipts. These data reflect the changes that have taken place in eating and drinking expenditures. It should be noted that in the Eating and Drinking Places category, the sales tax receipts and the sales are generally understated. Occasional food operators have been known to "skim" their receipts; thus, the reported taxes are typically less than those that are actually collected.

Telephone Company

The telephone company, like the utility companies, must plan for new installations throughout an area. Therefore, they must consider all the demographic factors that might affect where and to what extent growth will occur. The phone company generally has a research person in small communities, up to a department in large service areas, whose job is to make these evaluations. They are generally a very useful source in determining where new residential as well as commercial and industrial telephone connections, will occur.

Gas and Electric Companies

Sometimes the gas and electric companies are a combined operation; in other cases, they are individual utilities. Whatever the arrangement, their research people should be contacted since they also have had to research changes that will occur within the metropolitan area and consider their needs for meter connections on a long-term basis. All the data from the various utility companies can be compared, along with the forecasts made by the other agencies, such as the Planning Department, to see where they agree and disagree. Subsequently, you can go back and discuss the discrepancies with each of them to determine the most likely future scenarios. Keep in mind that the electric utilities with nuclear facilities are under pressure from regulatory agencies, and have become sensitive to giving out information. The data have been used against them, so they are very cautious. You must thoroughly explain your reasons for wanting their help.

State Department of Labor

Good employment data, as well as wage rates, can be secured from the state department of labor, (the name of which varies considerably). Nevertheless, the state agency is responsible for employment statistics, unemployment data, and assisting people in their job hunts. In some cases, it is also responsible for unemployment compensation. This is another source that reflects the vitality of the community, the types of jobs, and the employment classifications that have grown versus those that have declined.

Convention and Visitors' Bureau

Normally a part of the Chamber of Commerce, the Convention and Visitor's Bureau is a separate entity in some cities. Convention and visitors' bureau data can be beneficial, particularly if you are looking in Orlando, Florida; Las Vegas, Nevada; Williamsburg, Virginia; and other places that attract many tourists or convention activities. This factor often distorts eating and drinking expenditures;

therefore, it is necessary to look at the market in terms of income and expenditure dynamics, which will be described in Chapter 14.

Military Installations

The best source for civilian and military employment information on military installations is generally the base commandant or the public relations officer. They should be contacted directly for current data. Occasionally, the data are classified. Nevertheless, by discussing the likely employment figures with all the various organizations mentioned in this chapter, it is possible to develop a reasonable picture of the current employment levels versus past levels and perhaps future ones.

Hospital Planning Organizations

Hospital planning councils can serve as excellent sources for forecasted data. They generally are responsible for determining the number of hospital beds that a community will require and, to do so, must forecast population by relatively small areas. These organizations will usually be found only in larger cities.

School Enrollment

School enrollment figures and projections can be beneficial when considering small areas, particularly since the changes that the School Board anticipates in enrollment for specific schools can serve as a measure of changes in population. The data also provide insight into children's ages.

United States Postal Service

In very small communities where planning agencies are unavailable and it is difficult to get current information, the U.S. Post Office Department can be an important source. Each postmaster is responsible for preparing population figures for his or her respective area annually and forwarding them to the Postmaster General. Therefore, the local postmaster can often provide statistics for residential deliveries by each mail carrier's delivery route. Thus, the information is in relatively small segments and can be helpful. Residential deliveries generally understate the number of households; therefore, the data base, although essentially correct, requires some adjustment. To understand the data, it may also be necessary to draw the various delivery routes on a map.

Financial Institutions

Larger financial institutions in some cities have been developing data and, in fact, in some cases are actually carrying out studies for their clients. Usually, the Chamber of Commerce will know if any banks or savings and loans are conducting research and who you should see.

SUMMARY

Although there are other agencies, both public and private, the preceding sections describe the most accessible ones. The objective is to develop a network of relevant information by asking numerous questions and by being skeptical. Study the data and determine what is pertinent to you. A pattern will emerge indicating your best course of action. Be persistent!

FIELDWORK CHECKLIST

The following checklist provides guidelines and information about data sources. Except for the Chamber of Commerce (which should be visited first, for obvious reasons), contacts can be approached in any order that suits your individual needs.

Chamber of Commerce

The Chamber of Commerce is an excellent place to begin field research. In larger communities, try to make an appointment to meet with the director of research or with the Chamber's director or president. If the Chamber of Commerce does not have the information you need, Chamber personnel may know where you can find it. The following data are usually available:

____ Maps—metropolitan area, region, county, city

____ Population trends and projections (at least 10 years in each direction)

____ Households and household size

____ Per capita and household income trends and projections (at least 10 years in each direction)

____ Restaurant Directory or Yellow Pages

____ Identification of new growth corridors

____ Regional malls and shopping centers

____ Retain sales information (Note source of information, e.g. *Census of Retail Trade* or *Sales and Marketing Management.*)

____ Major newspapers

____ Major employers by name, location, and number of employees

____ Commercial developers

____ Office building and office park inventory by location and size

____ Industrial park inventory (location and size)

____ Major commercial banks and savings and loans

____ Leading real estate brokers

____ Major commercial corridors

____ Identification of low, middle, and upper income areas

____ Information on area's economic history (What is the mainstay of the area's economy? How well is it diversified? How reliable is it on particular goods or services?)

_____ Area flood maps (When did the last big flood occur? Which areas were hardest hit?)

_____ Major streets and expressways, new roads, freeways, toll roads, upgradings, and important improvements

_____ Local, county, and state policies regarding direct access to properties on major traffic arteries—left-hand turn lanes, deceleration lanes, traffic signals, medians, and other traffic control items

_____ Local tax rates

_____ Sewer and water data

_____ Utility costs

_____ Names and locations of knowledgeable people who can help answer your questions

Planning Agencies

Most communities have two planning agencies; some have three. The local planning agency deals only with the host city in which you are interested. The second agency is typically a county organization and will have information on both the central city and its suburban area. The third agency, where it exists, is a regional planning organization. Although some redundancy is likely, in that you will be requesting from the planning agencies, ostensibly, the same information that you obtained from the Chamber of Commerce, the effort is worthwhile because often these groups will have entirely different estimates of the same variables (such as population projections). Once you obtain all the data, you will need to determine which information is the most accurate. You should ask for the following:

_____ The 1990 Census data

_____ Population trends and projections

_____ Household and household size—trends and projections

_____ Age cohort trends and projections

_____ Race trends and projections

_____ Census tract maps and base maps

_____ The most recent average daily traffic counts on all primary arteries and changes in secondary arteries

_____ A listing of all planned and proposed changes in road alignment

_____ Names of major employers indicating location and number of employees

_____ Locations of significant commercial, industrial, retail, and residential concentrations with sizes, square feet, and employees

_____ Zoning maps and regulations

_____ Building codes

_____ Aerial photographs

_____ Flood maps and areas of continuing problems; steps that are being taken to eliminate problems

_____ Significant planned real estate developments—retail, residential, industrial, and commercial

_____ Retail sales estimates

_____ Directional growth patterns and the causes or rationale behind these particular patterns

_____ Name, location, and size of major institutions (armed forces, universities, hospitals, and government complexes)

_____ Residential building permit data going back at least five to eight years. (All building permits _do not_ result in new housing. Some units are not built.)

_____ Layout of the city's central business district (CBD) with pedestrian counts, name and sizes of major office buildings (existing and proposed), size and location of department stores

_____ Sanitary sewer and water availabilities and problem areas, especially related to sewers (Ask about combined flooding and sewer problems.)

_____ Public transit ridership counts

Department of Employment Security—State

Find out who assembles regional employment and unemployment data and personally visit the agency to obtain these data. Try to get trends that cover at least a 5- to 10-year period. Ask for totals for civilian employment and unemployment and also for employment by individual Standard Industrial Classifications (SIC); usually there are eight major categories. If the agency publishes a monthly labor newsletter, collect at least the previous 12 months' publications. Find out if the current data are by place of residence, or by place of employment, since some states have changed the method of tabulation from time to time. Oftentimes, the total civilian labor force and unemployment are by place of employment rather than by the community where the employed reside.

News Media

Visit the leading newspapers and speak with someone in their marketing or research department. These people typically prepare annual reports that contain pertinent information on their market areas, such as population trends, major shopping centers, and patterns of the resident base. The reports are usually available free of charge.

Often newspapers have restaurant reviewers on staff. Meet with this person and, if possible, obtain a list of competitive restaurants. For example, if yours will be a family restaurant, then you should obtain a list of all family restaurants so that you can visit the existing competitors in the trade area.

Highway Department: State, County, and City

____ Planned improvements
____ New roads or expressways
____ Policy on median strips
____ Traffic flow maps
____ Traffic counts (year)
____ Long-range plans

Telephone Company

Request data on telephone connections. Also obtain both the White and Yellow Pages for the central city and its surrounding suburban areas.

Utility Companies

Contact the research department for the following:

____ Growth projections
____ Electric residential connections
____ Gas meters
____ Planned utility extensions
____ Utility rates

Department of Revenue—State Sales Tax Collection

Obtain sales tax data, both for the current month as well as for the previous 12-month period, if available. Also, obtain annual sales tax data indicating at least five-year trends. When getting these data, find out the tax rates. They may vary for different items, but you need to know what the rates are so that you can convert them to sales dollars. Convert sale taxes to eating and drinking sales by dividing the sales taxes by the tax rate.

Convention and Visitors Bureau

Get statistics and trends indicating whether conventions are primarily local, state, regional, or national, and whether or not they are seasonal. Find out the number of people by year, by convention, if possible, and their estimated expenditures. Note any trends. Find out where conventioneers stay, where they go, and where conventions are usually held.

Industrial Development Commission

This agency (which may have slightly varying names) attempts to attract new industry to the state and to individual communities. Ask for the following:

____ Population growth
____ New jobs
____ New industries
____ Industrial concentrations

Field Reconnaissance

The field review, (which is initiated after the completion of research activities) should include the following tasks:

1. Drive all primary and secondary roads. Use a tape recorder to note everything you see, paying particular attention to the location of significant commercial concentrations, shopping centers, malls, office buildings, institutions, traffic signals, speed limits, number of moving lanes, and the character of the neighborhoods.

2. At the end of each day, summarize your recorded notes onto base maps of the area.

3. Visit all the appropriate shopping centers and malls in the region. Meet with mall managers and obtain the following:

_____ List of tenant stores and anchors

_____ Sales performance of centers and their anchors

_____ Size of centers

_____ Date opened

_____ Who owns the centers

_____ What changes, if any, are planned

_____ Hours of operation

_____ Trade area from which they are drawing

Restaurant Inventory

This is perhaps the most critical and time-consuming part of field-work. Using the map on which you have recorded much of your data, record all the facilities that will be competitive with your restaurant or fast food unit. Then for each restaurant, obtain the following (Restaurant and Fast Food Competitive Inventory forms are provided in Chapter 11):

_____ Name

_____ Location

_____ Size, in terms of seating capacity and square feet. (If there is a bar, note number of seats at bar.)

_____ Hours of operation

_____ Whether facility has a drive-through window (If so, estimate percentage of business served through window.)

_____ Number of parking spaces

_____ Copy of menu

_____ Average check size and number of table turns per day (To determine average check size and number of table turns per day, visit these restaurants during breakfast (if served), lunch, and dinner. Speaking with waiters, waitresses, and managers, will help you estimate the number of persons served by daypart and their average check.)

_____ Sales generated by bar (If liquor is served, speak with restaurant staff and/or try to estimate percentage of sales generated by bar. Talk to suppliers regarding order volumes and activity levels.)

Major Employment Concentrations

_____ Office development
    _____ Size (square feet)
    _____ Employees (total number)
    _____ Types of companies
    _____ Food facilities in buildings
    _____ Amount of time for lunch
    _____ Amenities
_____ Industrial concentration
    _____ Type
    _____ Employees (total number)
    _____ Food facilities currently used
    _____ Amount of time for lunch

Driving Time

Do a driving time analysis for each direct competitor you identify. This analysis will entail driving for 15-20 minutes in all four directions (north, south, east, and west) at varying times of the day. Note mileage covered, speed limit, locations reached at five-minute intervals, and time of day. Either mark the information on your map or record it. Evaluate the periods when traffic is heavier.

Visibility of Competitive Restaurants and Potential Sites

From what distance can you see the restaurant and how long can you see it? For a fast food unit, can you see it far enough away to change lanes easily so as to enter the property?

Accessibility

Study traffic counts, traffic flow, and major commercial concentrations. Note overall access. Where are congestion points? Note median strips, traffic backups, traffic signals, speed limit, number of lanes, speed of flowing traffic, left-hand turn lanes, and other significant accessibility factors.

Real Estate Community

Identify who makes the most deals. Speak with real estate brokers to get a feel for land and building values and availability at a variety of areas.

Land and Building Values

Meet with at least two certified real estate appraisers to get a feel for land and building values in the region. Also talk with experienced real estate brokers about values.

Identifying Potential Areas for Your Facilities

_____   Match your customer profile to market
_____   Identify concentrations
_____   Tentatively select locations

After completing the research and reconnaissance steps, you should know the city you are investigating as well as, if not better than, anyone else in the community. In addition, take _plenty of photographs_ of anything that you feel may have some significance later in the site selection process. Just as you can never ask too many questions, you can never take too many pictures of the city and the surrounding area that you are investigating.

Videotaping is a new technique that is gaining popularity. This approach, while somewhat time consuming and costly, allows for both a video and audio presentation of the results. Also, it is immediate! I have found this technique especially helpful in presenting the results of a site selection program, when the board of a company is in another part of the country or has never seen the area. It does not have to be a professional presentation with music and announcers. Rather, the simplest presentation can be an effective way to communicate the market area, the competition, the access, and the site under consideration.

Eight

The Meaning of Demographics

The analysis of the demographics of a location is an essential element in site selection. Unfortunately, demographics are often misunderstood; sometimes misinterpreted; and, equally as often, ignored. It is important to get one fact straight right from the start. *Total population figures by themselves are meaningless.* What is significant is the number of people in the individual *age* and *income* categories. There also may be other demographic factors that can only be determined by fully understanding a specific customer profile.

Demographics may seem boring, but knowledgeable food people appreciate their meaning and implications. This chapter explains where the data originate, how the information is developed, who updates the demographics, how to get the necessary data, and what the information really means. There is also a review of the demographic computer services, which now provide most of the demographic data used in site analysis.

Demography is the statistical study of people and their characteristics. The results are called *demographics* and may include statistics about population, age, income, employment, housing, racial characteristics, family structure, household structure, place of residence, geographic mobility, and many other factors. Since 1790, the United States has collected data, in varying degrees, through the Department of Commerce, Bureau of the Census. The most recent census was conducted in 1990 and will be available in detail in 1992 and 1993.

The following pages briefly describe the various census publications and explain how to obtain them. Most food people today use the various computer demographic data companies, which provide data in numerous forms for any site in the United States. I will discuss this approach later in the chapter, after presenting basic facts about census data. Everyone who is choosing or evaluating locations should know the sources of pertinent data and how to verify the numbers. *Simply because the information originates from a computer and is derived from census data does not guarantee its accuracy.*

CENSUS PUBLICATIONS

The U.S. Census of Population and Housing is conducted by the census bureau in every year ending in "0". Thus, every decade there is a census designed to count people, housing, their respective characteristics, and changes from the previous decade. Additional census activities occur in other years, including the Census of Business (every five years—usually in years ending in "2" and "7"). The Census of Business counts retail and service establishments, along with retail sales by specific categories. While census data are used for thousands of reasons, your primary purpose is to determine if a new location or area under consideration has adequate population resources and characteristics to justify the creation of a new unit.

The latest Census of Population and Housing was taken in 1990 and the next will be in 2000. The 1990 census will be available in print, microfiche, computer tape, and computer disk at varying times by 1994. The 10-year census is available for each state, as well as the District of Columbia, Puerto Rico, the Virgin Islands, Guam, American Samoa, and the Trust Territory of the Pacific Islands. A summary for the United States is also available.

The 1990 Census

The printed reports for 1990 are expected to include the following:

- *1990 CPH-1: Summary of Population and Housing.* These publications, available for each state, contain population and housing counts for counties, standard consolidated statistical areas

(SCSAs), standard metropolitan statistical areas (SMSAs), and urbanized areas. There are some additional counts for urban and rural areas. Reports are expected to be available in 1992.

- *1990 CPH-2: Population and Housing Unit Counts.* The report provides total population and housing unit counts for 1990 and previous censuses. Data are included for states, counties, cities, towns, and other components. State reports will be available in 1991 and 1992.

- *1990 CPH-3: Population and Housing Characteristics for Census Tracts and Block Numbering Areas.* A report will be provided for each Metropolitan Statistical Areas (MSA) and Primary Metropolitan Statistical Areas (PMSA). Census tracts are small units of a metropolitan or city area providing detailed population and housing data. The individual tracts are many different shapes and sizes because they were added to the census over the years. Block statistics or block numbering areas are published for MSA/PMSAs and provide population and housing data on a block-by-block basis. To be included, the MSA/PMSA must have a 1990 population of more than 10,000 people. Figure 8.1 depicts a section of the Nashville census tracts.

- *1990 CP-1: General Population Characteristics.* This series provides detailed statistics on age, sex, race, marital status, and household characteristics. Tentative release date is 1992.

- *1990 CP-1-1B: General Population Characteristics for Metropolitan Statistical Areas (MSAs).* This contains population data for MSAs. The publications should be available in late 1992.

- *1990 CP-2: Social and Economic Characteristics.* A book for each state contains data on population, race, income, education, labor force, family composition, geographic mobility, occupation of employed persons, and several other items. These data are provided for the state, counties, urban, and rural places, CSAs, MSAs, urbanized areas, and places with more than 2,500 people. The books should be available in 1992.

- *1990 CP-2-1B: Social and Economic Characteristics for Metropolitan Statistical Areas.* These reports will be available in 1993. They will provide age, income, employment, race, age, and other important data.

- *1990 CH-1: General Housing Characteristics.* Detailed statistics on housing units, including value, rent, number of rooms, tenure,

FIGURE 8.1
Census Tract Map, Nashville, Tennessee

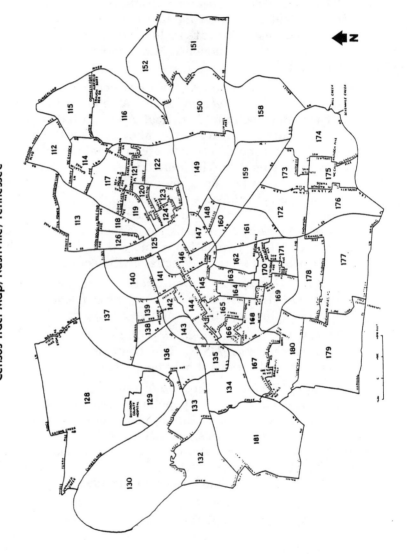

vacancy, and occupancy by owner. The reports for individual states will be available in 1992.

- *1990 CH-1-1B: General Housing Characteristics for Metropolitan Statistical Areas.* This report for MSAs contains housing data and will be available in 1992.
- *1990 CH-2: Detailed Housing Characteristics.* A detailed report for each state contains detailed housing data for places with more than 2,500 inhabitants.
- *1990 CH-2-1B: Detailed Housing Characteristics for Metropolitan Areas.* Detailed data for MSAs will be available in 1993.

If you have questions regarding the census data, contact either the Census Bureau in Washington, DC (301-763-4100), or the Department of Commerce office in any major city.

Current Population Reports

Current population reports are provided by the Census Bureau in the intervening years between decennial censuses. They usually are as follows:

- *P-20: Population Characteristics.* There are approximately 15 reports annually, covering detailed elements of the population, usually for the entire United States.
- *P-23: Special Studies.* A few reports are issued annually regarding aging, family, households, birth rates, and other factors.
- *P-25: Population Estimates and Projections.* The Census Bureau provides monthly estimates of the U.S. population, as well as annual population projections for states, counties, cities, and some towns. The projections include age, births, deaths, migration, income, and other data.
- *P-27: Farm Population.* In concert with the Department of Agriculture, the Census Bureau provides annual reports regarding the population living on farms. Also, the data include age, race, employment, and selected other characteristics.
- *P-28: Special Census.* Special censuses are conducted for communities requesting the service. The cities and towns pay a part of the cost. These censuses are usually required to certify population changes that can result in greater funds from the state or from some federal programs. Special censuses can be

very helpful, especially for communities that have enjoyed considerable growth.

- *P-60: Consumer Income.* These reports include estimates of income by various demographic and socioeconomic characteristics.

Upon publication, all the preceding reports are available from the Department of Commerce, Bureau of the Census, Census Bureau's Data User Services Division, Customer Services, Washington, DC 20233. Also, throughout the United States, the Department of Commerce has field offices where census data can sometimes be purchased in the government bookshop; or available data can be studied in the Department's library in the local office. Unfortunately, many items must be ordered from Washington because most specific reports are not carried in the local offices' inventory. Copies of specific pages that you may need can usually be made in the Department's library.

In Canada, the census is conducted every five years. The latest census, conducted by Statistics Canada, is for 1991. Results of the 1991 census will not be available until sometime in 1992 and 1993. The Canadian census follows many of the outputs provided by the United States.

DEMOGRAPHIC COMPUTER SERVICES

As I pointed out at the beginning of this chapter, most people do not understand demographic data and especially do not want to be bothered with the census books and the updating process. To capitalize on this need, a number of computer service firms purchased the census computer tapes in 1980 and 1990 and developed retrieval programs. Additionally, they have created system programs for forecasting population, household, age, and income projections. These programs provide a method to obtain data for specific sites in the United States. Canada also has such a service. The data can be compiled for just about any configuration, as long as you adequately indicate what you want. However, the most frequently used configuration is mile radii. Orders can be placed over the telephone, and the data can be sent to you by mail, air express, or facsimile; if you have a computer with a modem, the data can be transmitted directly to your computer.

Computer demographic firms are numerous. Many of them provide retail expenditure data forecasts, lifestyle estimates, and numerous other forecasts based on the 1990 Census of Population and the 1987 Census of Business. The following is a representative list of demographic firms:

United States	*Telephone Number*
Urban Decisions Systems	800-633-9568
Equifax-National Decisions Systems	800-866-6510
Claritas/NPDC	800-627-2345
CACI, Inc.	800-292-2224
Donnelley Marketing Information Services	800-866-2255
R.L. Polk & Co.	313-393-4786

Canada	
Compusearch	416-348-9180

Although the demographic services are convenient and generally inexpensive, they are not without flaws. First, the basic data are from the 1980 and 1990 census tapes. If there is an error in the tape data, that error is often carried over into the data that you receive. Second, the projections are not necessarily correct simply because they were generated by a computer. Unfortunately, more than 90% of the users rarely check the data for accuracy. The methods used for forecasting the data to the current year are often not quite what the buyer is led to believe. I have evaluated the data and projections from just about every company, and have found that they all have strong and weak points. If there is a single commonality, it is that they all have some difficulty in supplying detailed methods for projections in specific areas. Also, when the data are obviously in error, challenges often meet with silence.

Knowing where data is available to check the numbers provided by the demographic computer service firms provides a simple check-and-balance system. I ask my people to take the census tract map of the area under study, draw on the trade area, and check the number of census tracts included. Moreover, ask yourself: *Do I believe the numbers?* This is especially important in communities where growth has been significant, or where growth has slowed or the population is declining. In those areas, the forecasts may be too high or too low. Simply, be aware!

Demographic computer service firms provide an excellent service. However, since their data serve as the "backbone" for decision making, it is important to be sure that "you receive what you think that you are buying."

IMPORTANCE AND MEANING OF DEMOGRAPHIC DATA

As I indicated earlier, the most important consideration regarding population is not the total number, but, rather, the characteristics of the population. In fact, I cringe when I hear people tell me that they must have 50,000 or 75,000 people within three miles or 100,000 persons within five miles. *Again, what matters is not the total number, but rather the characteristics of those people.* For example, if you draw a three-mile circle (radius) around most locations in St. Petersburg, Florida, you will probably have at least 50,000 people. However, you also will quickly find that the average age of the population is between 48 and 50 years. St. Petersburg has a large retired population, and when they do eat out, they tend to be extremely price conscious. Thus, although the total population may meet locational criteria, they may all be the wrong age. A more realistic way of expressing population needs is to determine how many people you should have in the appropriate age and income categories.

Another common example is an area with a very young population, with many children under 10 years of age (see Table 8.1). These families do not eat out at restaurants as frequently as the general population because of the need for babysitters or, simply, the cost of eating out. There may be 50,000 people within three miles; when they eat out as a family, however, they are influenced by what the children want. Normally, they eat at a very limited number of restaurants and fast food operations (primarily McDonald's). Thus, the total number of people is deceiving, especially if your targeted customer is between 30 and 40 years of age. The *total* number of people is sufficient; however, the number of people in the appropriate age category (30 to 40 years of age) is insufficient. In the next several years, a large number of people will advance into the 30-to-40-years category. However, until that happens, business may be slow.

Another example of misleading information relates to income. It is necessary to look to the actual distribution of households by income categories, rather than the average or median household income. It is not unusual to have a "split" income distribution; a

TABLE 8.1

Age Distribution, Three-Mile Radius—1990

Age Category (in Years)*	Population	Percent
0–10	9,060	15.1
11–20	6,990	11.7
21–30	13,080	21.9
31–40	5,090	8.5
41–50	9,320	15.6
51–60	12,980	21.7
65+	3,340	5.6
Total	59,860	100.0

*Average age is 35 years.

Source: Census of Population, 1990.

large concentration of households may have incomes, say, between $20,000 and $25,000, and another group may have incomes of $40,000 to $50,000. The average will then be $33,000; the split, however, may result in too few households in your specific income category. When this happens, your operation will usually be either a loser or a low producer. Table 8.2 depicts this kind of income distribution. In more than 30 years of evaluating and selecting locations, I have found *age and income* to be the most sensitive demographic elements in identifying the right opportunities.

Here is a more specific example. Say that the location, at Main Street and Kennedy Avenue (in any city in the United States), is for a potential fast food location, and a three-mile trade area is appropriate. The fieldwork has been completed, and customer interviews indicate the following age characteristics for the most frequent visitors:

Age (Years)	Percent
18–24	45
25–34	42
Total	87

Thus, 87% of the most frequent visitors (once a month or more) are between the ages of 18 and 34 years.

TABLE 8.2

Income Distribution, Three-Mile Radius,
Main and Kennedy Streets
(Anywhere in the United States)

Income Categories ($)	Number of Households (%)
Less than 9,999	5
10,000–19,999	12
20,000–29,999	30
30,000–39,999	7
40,000–49,999	25
50,000–59,999	20
60,000–74,999	1
75,000 and over	0
Total	100
Average Household Income	$33,540
Median Household Income	$31,980

Source: Census of Population, 1990.

Next, the income data of the most frequent visitors reveal the following:

Income	Percent
$20,000–$29,000	33
$30,000–$39,000	47
Total	80

Therefore, 80% of the most frequent visitors have incomes between $20,000 and $39,000. When reviewing the demographics within the trade area of a new location, the first items to look at are the age and income structure of the residents.

OTHER DEMOGRAPHIC SOURCES

Several other sources can be helpful, either to provide primary population and household data or to check the data provided by the demographic computer firms. In small towns, the local sources are often much more accurate than updated census data from outside sources.

Local Planning Agencies

City, county, and regional planning agencies usually prepare population projections, often using a census tract basis. Furthermore, the planners can explain the method used to arrive at the figures, and they frequently record the data on maps that more easily reflect the anticipated changes. Comparing these projections with the computer-generated forecasts will provide a solid check and balance against error.

Hospital Planning Councils

Large cities usually have hospital planning councils that are responsible for determining hospital bed requirements; they often make their own population projections.

Utility Companies

Most gas, electric, and telephone companies make projections, not only of population and households, but also of where they expect growth to occur. This information is important for them, since they must plan their service extensions and capital requirements.

University or College Forecasts

Universities and colleges may make population forecasts as part of a class project, a faculty study, a corporate-funded study, or a grant-funded population analysis. Unfortunately, the forecasts are most often not at a census tract level.

Local Post Office

When all else fails, the local postmaster's annual report can often be a source of population and household change information. Where considerable new construction is underway, the post office is an excellent source to determine population and household trends.

Each post office has delivery routes identified on a wall map that hangs in the back of the facility. If you discuss the data with the postmaster, he will usually allow you to make a copy of the map. It will not match census tracts but will give you a fairly clear picture of where the households are located. If you have further questions, talk to the mail carriers of specific routes.

Other Sources

Depending on the local situation, other sources may include the assessor's office, the title company, local school boards, and the water and sewer departments. Aerial photographs can provide a final source of assistance, because you can use them to count houses in areas of single-family homes and thus determine fairly accurately the number of households.

Before demographic computer firms were around, and the census was six to ten years old, hand-held counters were a surefire way to develop solid data. Available at most stationery stores, they fit in the palm of the hand. To use one, get in your car with the counter and a good up-to-date streetmap, and drive through the area, counting the dwelling units. In apartment areas, it is necessary to get out of the car and check the mail boxes. It takes time; however, the information will be current. Then, by determining the number of persons per household from the latest census, you can calculate the population within a specific trade area.

SUMMARY

Accurate demography forms the base for sound analysis and decision making. If your data are inaccurate, you may make a wrong decision. Unfortunately, most people find this out after making the mistake. At that point, they take the time to determine the characteristics of the population. Would it not be simpler and less costly in the long run to make the effort before coming to a decision?

Nine

Accessibility

A ccessibility usually occurs on three levels: community accessibility, trade areas accessibility, and site accessibility. Each is discussed on the following pages.

COMMUNITY ACCESSIBILITY

Community or city accessibility relates to the multidirectional accessibility of the metropolitan area. This has special significance for high-volume restaurants and some "special occasion" dinner houses that must draw from very wide areas because of a low frequency of visit. The following sections discuss the salient considerations in determining community accessibility.

Road Network

The road network comprises the major and minor traffic arteries and expressways that serve a community. We all know from experience that some roads are more important than others. It is important to identify which expressways and arteries are the most significant and why. Maps of metropolitan areas make it evident that cities are neither round, square, rectangular, nor circular. Instead, they are affected by the road network, topography, barriers, land availability, and other factors. Understanding the road network—where the significant traffic arteries extend, why some are much more important than others, what interchanges carry the most traffic, what changes are likely to take place in the future—will provide considerable insight into where the action is, and why.

Expressways

Expressways have changed the face of North America. Prior to the development of the U.S. interstate system, people often had to travel circuitous routes to reach destinations that presented topographic barriers. This access problem was especially true in cities that have hills or mountains precluding direct travel to one area from another, such as Pittsburgh, Atlanta, and Birmingham. In Atlanta, the interstate system now provides a loop expressway around the metropolitan area that allows drivers to travel from one sector of the community to another without going all the way back into the city and coming out on another radial artery.

Expressways are also important relative to their interchanges. In many sections of California, food operations have developed an interstate strategy designed to intercept traffic exiting and entering the interstate system (most often exiting). Such a plan can often be implemented without adversely affecting another strategy that might include locations in proximity to major commercial areas. Thus, expressway interchanges enable people to drive quickly from one area to another.

We are a time-oriented society. Expressways occasionally provide (although, not always) the ability to drive from one sector of a metropolitan area to another with a high rate of speed. Thus, some interchanges become more significant, since they are carrying a higher level of traffic. In most communities, the traffic counts on the expressway system are higher than the traffic counts on the other major traffic arteries.

In considering the activities within a metropolitan area and, more importantly, the expressway system, it is necessary to differentiate between "through" traffic and local traffic. These data can usually be secured from the state's Department of Transportation, (usually the Planning Division), which keeps records regarding the types of traffic utilizing the expressway system.

Traffic Counts and Traffic Flow

Perhaps the single greatest cause of misunderstandings in the study of accessibility is the meaning of an average daily traffic count.

Traffic counts are figures indicating the average daily number of cars passing a particular location within either a 12- or 24-hour period. In the past, it was common for traffic engineers to station people with handcounters on a particular traffic artery to count the cars, trucks, and other vehicles for either 15-, 30-, or 60-minute intervals. The objective was to determine the number and type of vehicles utilizing a particular street. Some communities conducted the counts for only 12 hours, while others conducted 24-hour counts. Inclement weather required an alternative counting method, and so the automated traffic counter was born. Generally, it is a black rubber hose approximately one inch in diameter, extending across the traffic artery from a counter chained to a tree or post. The counter has a time clock and records the traffic crossing the hose, usually by time intervals. Some recent models can count the vehicles without using a hose. In any case, the data can then be averaged over a period of time to determine the 24-hour averages. Figure 9.1 depicts an intersection with the counters deployed, identified alphabetically. Each letter represents a station that tallies vehicles passing over the counter strip in a specific direction. Thus counter station A counts cars entering the intersection from the north in a southbound direction, station B counts cars exiting the intersection in a northbound direction, and so on.

Contrary to popular opinion, the average 12- or 24-hour traffic count number is *not* the true measure of automobile activity. Unfortunately, most people looking for locations in the food business simply look at that average. I often will hear, "I won't take a location unless it has a traffic count of at least 15,000 cars." Or, perhaps, the number is 25,000 cars during a 24-hour period. Regardless of the number, *when the traffic occurs is the most important factor.* Therefore, traffic count data on an *hourly* basis, are crucial for evaluating the type of traffic, when it actually occurs, and how the hours of high-volume traffic will affect the peak sales hours in your particular food operation.

During the fast food craze of the early 1960s, food people on the East Coast and in the Midwest looked at the growth figures in California and, to put it mildly, got rather excited. Unfortunately, many site selection people rushed to California, saw the unusually high traffic counts (40,000 to 70,000 cars on a major traffic artery), and were eager to buy sites. As might be expected, the local California real estate community saw them coming and had a very profitable time. What the site selectors failed to recognize is that most of California is heavily automobile oriented; therefore, looking at hourly

FIGURE 9.1

Traffic Counters at an Intersection

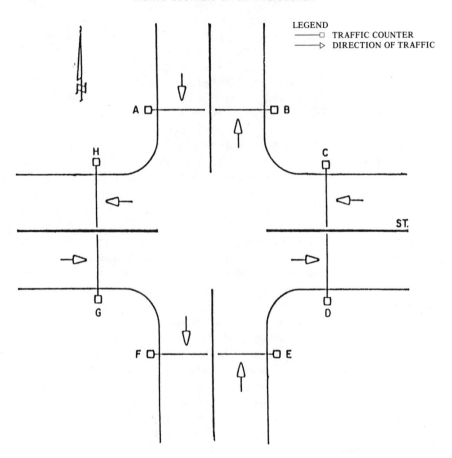

LEGEND
☐ TRAFFIC COUNTER
▷ DIRECTION OF TRAFFIC

traffic counts in that state is an absolute must. Had they evaluated the hourly counts at many of the intersections where they purchased sites, they would have discovered that the vast majority of the traffic occurred in the morning (going to work) and in the evening (going home). Thus, the traffic that they thought they were buying as a consistent pattern throughout the day and the evening did not exist. The mortality rate of food operations in California during the 1970s and early 1980s partially reflects this ignorance.

Traffic flow maps depict the flow of traffic within the community. Figure 9.2 shows that the widest lines are streets carrying the greatest amount of traffic, while the narrowest streets carry the least. The map simply reflects traffic counts visually. To determine the significance of traffic flow, record on the map the locations of the major shopping centers, industrial concentrations, office concentrations, medical concentrations, high schools, airports, downtown, and other significant traffic generators. The reasons for the areas of high-volume traffic versus the areas of low-volume traffic will then become readily apparent. A food operator needs to understand the traffic flow—the types of traffic, its origins, and its destinations.

FIGURE 9.2

Traffic Flow Map

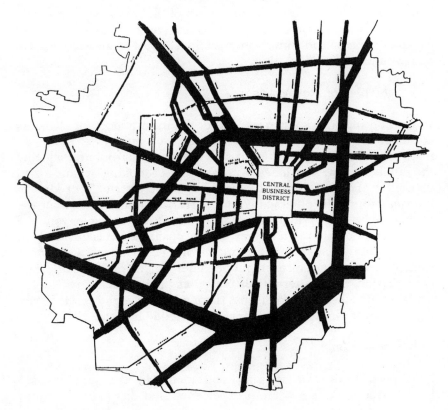

Community access to a region also indicates whether the community is importing dollars or exporting retail and food sales. Certainly, proximity to larger markets influences this situation.

TRADE AREA ACCESSIBILITY

Trade area accessibility represents access from the area that a restaurant or fast food facility will serve. It refers to the ability of residents to move throughout the area and to travel to and from a specific location. An analysis of accessibility must be done when considering trade area size and shape. The following sections describe the factors that must be evaluated.

Major Traffic Arteries

Major traffic arteries usually carry most of the traffic within a market area. These traffic concentrations are governed by the number of lanes, the speed limit, intersections, traffic signals, traffic counts, and traffic flow.

Number of Moving Lanes

In considering traffic arteries, one of the most important elements is the number of "moving lanes," not the total number of lanes. On many traffic arteries, parking is allowed on the curb lane, reducing the number of moving lanes. Another way of looking at lanes is to determine the capacity of the artery to move traffic. That kind of information can be obtained from the traffic engineer at either the state, county, or city highway department. If, for example, you find that the particular traffic artery under consideration is currently at capacity, then you need to determine from the local traffic engineer what alternative measures might be under consideration to alleviate the situation. Some alternatives may alter the volume of traffic. Examine them carefully and discuss them with the engineer. However, do not expect him to be an expert in the food business.

Speed Limit

The speed limit can be a critical factor in the success of a food business. We know from experience that distinct age groups usually react differently to higher or lower speed limits. For example, frequent customers of cafeterias, buffets, or smorgasbords tend to be elderly. Therefore, they are very sensitive to high speeds. Locations on fast tracks that do not have traffic lights usually do not meet sales expectations. Older people will not put up with the problems of getting in and out of a particular site. However, traffic lights that allow ease of ingress and egress can remedy that situation.

Younger customers are not as influenced by fast tracks, and therefore the speed limit is not as significant. In some instances, the speed limit can be too low: congested areas that have speed limits of 20 and 25 miles per hour are often avoided by younger people. This can be an important consideration in evaluating a location in a downtown area or business district that has a very low speed limit and must cater to a younger crowd. Naturally, it is only a major consideration if the majority of customers come by car.

In examining speed limits, you should conduct measured driving times through the area. Driving times indicate the distances that a person can achieve within, say, 5 minutes or 10 minutes, and the obstacles that the driver may encounter. Also, by conducting driving times, you will often find that the traffic is not moving at the posted speed limits. It may be moving faster or slower (usually faster). While the speed limit might be 40 miles per hour, you may find for example, that the traffic is basically moving at 50 miles per hour. Thus, the posted speed limit would appear to be acceptable, whereas 50 miles per hour is a fast track. Although a speed limit of 50 miles per hour can pose a problem for older customers, it may be acceptable if adequate breaks occur in oncoming traffic, permitting ease of ingress and egress.

Intersections

In reviewing an area for accessibility, it is important to recognize the streets, major arteries, and expressways that intersect with the primary traffic arteries throughout the area. Do the intersections have left-hand turning lanes and signals? Are the traffic lights signalized? How many seconds are permitted for a left-hand turn? How significant is the traffic backup in proximity to the interchanges? What is the time period of the green light? What is the time period of the red light? Are there any traffic impediments? Is any construction planned that will shut down or narrow the traffic arteries over a one-, two-, or three-year period? All of these are important considerations.

Traffic Signals

Traffic signals are designed to control traffic. Sometimes, because of poor signalization, they actually become impediments. Thus, the existence of a traffic light does not necessarily bode well for the food business; however, more often than not, it does. In considering traffic signals, you must recognize the time cycle, or the number of seconds or minutes required for a complete traffic signal rotation. Usually, concentrations of commercial facilities exist on major traffic arteries at traffic lights. In evaluating trade area accessibility, you can analyze the type of commercial development that has occurred at the intersections of the traffic artery.

Traffic Counts

Traffic counts indicate the number of vehicles passing a specific point on a roadway. Studying the traffic counts helps to determine the traffic concentrations versus lighter traffic areas. Again, it is important to review hourly traffic counts. Figure 9.3 is a traffic count map that indicates the counts at specific locations for an average 24-hour period.

Figure 9.4 depicts the type of peaks and valleys that some restaurant and fast food people who are open for lunch and dinner should worry about. Notice that once the peaks are over, the valley is so deep as to reflect little traffic at all on the artery. Nevertheless, the overall traffic count for this particular location exceeds 40,000 cars. Unfortunately, those cars are concentrated, both going to work and coming home from work. Thus, there is very little other activity during the balance of the day and evening. This type of location has been a "killer" to the food industry.

Traffic Flow

As previously indicated, traffic flow reflects the amount of traffic passing through an area on specific traffic arteries. The wider the artery appears, the more traffic it carries (see Figure 9.2). Studying traffic flow and the generative facilities that create that traffic is important in understanding the travel patterns throughout a particular

FIGURE 9.3

Average Daily Traffic Volumes

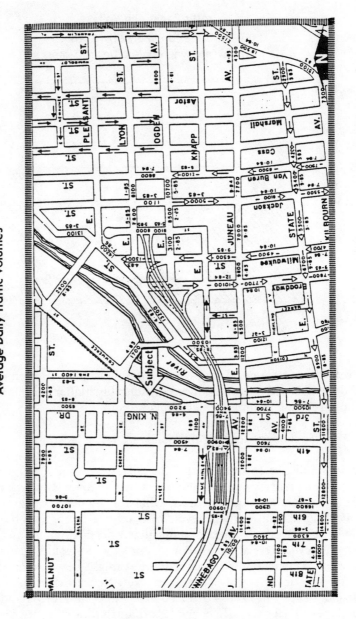

FIGURE 9.4

Traffic Peaks and Valleys

Main Street and Kennedy Avenue
Utopia (Anywhere in the United States)

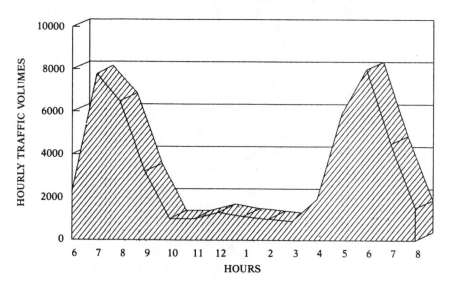

area. Placing potential units in an intercepting position to the traffic, if done correctly, can result in considerably higher sales, particularly those relating to impulse decisions.

Secondary Traffic Arteries

It is important to understand the difference between primary and secondary traffic arteries. Primary traffic arteries carry the majority of traffic through an area, whereas, secondary traffic arteries carry significantly lower levels of traffic. Varying community sizes make it difficult to create generalized definitions for primary and secondary traffic arteries. For example, what would be classified as a secondary artery in a major market might be thought of as a primary traffic artery in a small market. Nevertheless, most primary arteries carry in excess of 15,000 cars in a 24-hour period, and secondary arteries usually carry less than that number. In some larger markets, the primary traffic arteries may be carrying traffic in the range of 25,000 to 40,000 cars, while the secondary traffic arteries carry approximately 15,000 to 20,000 car range. Nevertheless, in studying the traffic patterns, you can quickly identify primary and secondary arteries simply by observing the volume of traffic throughout the day and evening. It is important to identify secondary traffic arteries and to establish their significance.

Identification

It is necessary to identify secondary traffic arteries because, in most instances, food operators do not belong on them. There are exceptions to this statement, depending on the restaurant's generative qualities. However, in most instances, secondary traffic arteries produce secondary results. They are also extremely vulnerable to additional competition. By identifying the secondary arteries, you immediately know which arteries to avoid and also on which primary streets or roads to concentrate.

Significance of the Secondary Arteries

Some secondary arteries are more significant than others, so being on a primary artery in proximity to a busy secondary artery can enhance success. To identify the significant secondary arteries, it is necessary to determine which streets are carrying more traffic and when it occurs, as well as the type of traffic they are carrying, and how it fits into the patterns of residents of the trade area. For example, it is important to learn if some of the secondary traffic arteries are a part of a "shortcut" pattern. All of us who drive daily develop shortcuts that we believe save time or at least allow us to continue driving rather than sitting in traffic. These shortcuts may contribute considerable traffic to a secondary artery. Recognizing their impact will help determine whether the artery should be a factor in choosing a location. While they can be important, usually the shortcuts do not carry enough traffic to warrant a restaurant or fast food facility.

Traffic Barriers

Physical and psychological barriers can adversely affect trade area accessibility. The following sections describe some of these barriers.

Railroad Crossings

Although the railroad industry has declined in many areas, railroad track crossing still exist on some major traffic arteries. The first thing to do is to look at the tracks and see if they have any rust on them. Second, ask some of the property occupants whether trains still run on the tracks. Is it on the main line, or a spur? You may find that the railroad runs a train or a locomotive through the area once a month in order to maintain their right-of-way. When does that occur? How long is the train? How long is the delay? Does that delay perhaps occur when you expect to be doing business?

Rivers

Rivers are physical barriers that often prevent people from traversing one side to another. Thus, they also proscribe trade areas. Bridges provide access across rivers but often still have an adverse psychological influence on the consumer. Therefore, although it is possible to drive across the river via a bridge, the river remains an overwhelming barrier with very little interchange from one side to another, except for working patterns. Another problem is that it may be necessary to raise the bridge periodically to allow water traffic to pass. The interruptions may cause people to find alternate travel routes. The only way to determine if these interruptions exist is by driving the arteries and by talking to people who use them.

Traffic Congestion

Traffic congestion can be both a physical and psychological barrier. People will avoid traffic arteries because congestion increases the time that it takes to get through an area. In the food business, there is such a thing as too much traffic and congestion. Ask the traffic engineer to identify the locations of serious traffic congestion.

High-Crime Areas

High-crime areas may not necessarily be physical barriers, but they certainly represent a psychological barrier. Most consumers, if they possibly can, will avoid high-crime areas because they feel unsafe and insecure. While they may, in some instances, drive through a high-crime area, they certainly will not stop in it. Also, if a major crime is perpetrated and emphasized in the media, drivers will almost immediately shift their travel patterns away from that particular area. The evening news can be an enemy to a restaurant pioneer who is on the edge of neighborhood change.

Other Barriers

Numerous other barriers affect traffic, such as heavy truck concentrations, which tend to scare women drivers and older people. The objective is to identify whether any barriers do, in fact, exist and, if so, to recognize them as impediments to traffic flow and accessibility.

SITE ACCESSIBILITY

It is absolutely essential that direct ingress and egress to the specific property under consideration be adequate for both present and future sales opportunities. Even if access to the community and the area is excellent, traffic to a specific location can be poor, and failure may result. The following factors affect site accessibility.

Positioning

Positioning refers to the placement of a food operation on a site that is adequate to serve the market area identified. Another element of positioning is having adequate parking facilities. (Guidelines for parking needs are discussed in Chapter 22.)

Type of Traffic Artery

As previously indicated, most high-volume food operations belong on a primary traffic artery "where the action is" rather than on a secondary road. Once again, certain unique restaurant and fast food operations may violate this axiom and be successful; however, they are rare.

Number of Moving Traffic Lanes

The number of lanes in front of a site is not as important as the number of *moving* traffic lanes. The better the traffic can move, make turns, and enter and exit specific sites, the better the opportunity for the food operator to do business.

Street or Road Changes

Nothing in our society remains static; things are constantly changing. This evolution is true for streets and roads as well. Therefore, it is important to discuss possible changes in the existing road network with traffic officials. Changes do not necessarily mean building a new street or highway but can be the addition of traffic lights, turning lanes, stop signs, medians, changing speed limits, parking probation, and highway upgradings. Food people are often surprised when some road change occurs that adversely affects them. They should not be surprised because, if they had done their homework, they would have known about the alteration long before it occurred.

Temporary, but significant, interruptions to the food business can result from street widening or resurfacing. Again, this information is available long before the work begins. Many food people have completed the construction of their facility and opened their doors to an excellent turnout, only to discover a month or two after opening that the Highway Department has commenced a street-widening program. Then, over one, two, or three years, the sales in the unit drop appreciably, and a struggle to survive commences. The scheduling of the road construction was an item that could easily have been determined prior to building the restaurant. Then, perhaps, the development of the restaurant might have been postponed because of an awareness of the construction and its impact on potential sales.

Median Strips

Median strips are by far the most significant locational killer of restaurant and fast food access. Median strips prevent the consumer from making a left-hand turn into a specific site and thus eliminate a considerable amount of potential business. When the food operator pays for being on a particular traffic artery and perhaps, more specifically, for the traffic on that artery, he or she should expect to have the possibility of intercepting or attracting all the motorists. The existence of a median strip precludes that from happening. If, for example, a particular traffic artery has a traffic count of 40,000 cars equally distributed on each side, or 20,000 cars in each direction, a median strip reduces the potential motorist–customer count to about 20,000. There are very few cities in the United States or Canada where people are conveniently oriented for comfortable U-turns. Therefore, the medians eliminate potential business.

Earlier in this book, I mentioned that it is often as enlightening to look at failed locations as it is to look at successful ones. Several years ago, I toured the country looking at closed-down restaurants. If there was a single characteristic that the majority shared, it was the existence of a median strip on their primary traffic artery. Avoid medians!

There are a number of different types of median. The strips to avoid are the ones that prohibit a convenient left-hand turn. They are the medians that—when you attempt to drive over them—take off your muffler, or at least the underside of your vehicle. You may also get killed making the attempted turn. Another type are known as "rumblers." These medians are perhaps two or three inches high so that the motorist can conveniently drive over them, but they make a rather loud noise as the tires pass over the rumblers. Making a left-hand turn across rumblers is usually not illegal, so they represent an acceptable median. Nevertheless, any median is deleterious if it precludes a *convenient* left-hand turn.

Traffic Counts

As previously indicated, the hourly traffic counts are more important than the overall traffic total. Given the traffic activity on an hourly basis, is it possible to conveniently make a left-hand turn into the site under consideration? How many seconds are allotted for a left-hand turn in the average traffic break?

Traffic Control

A traffic light on a major artery can represent excellent assistance to a location's ingress and egress. Customers should be able to enter and exit the property with relative ease from either the primary or secondary traffic artery. The size of the site usually will play a role. If the site is narrow or short, there may be some difficulty making a left-hand turn out of the property from the secondary traffic artery because of traffic backup. Usually, the larger the site, the easier it is for people to get in and get out of either the primary or secondary traffic artery. Where a median exists on one of the arteries, it can prevent convenient ingress and egress even though the site is on a corner.

As a general rule, locations on major arteries at stop signs are acceptable because the signs provide traffic control and make entering and exiting the site very easy. Obviously, in every situation, there are some exceptions. For example, where median strips or heavy traffic congestion exists, corner locations are not always as desirable as those somewhat removed from the corner. Each situation needs an individual review. Where there is traffic backup or congestion at a signalized intersection, an acceptable site would be away from the corner, at a point where the traffic interval is adequate for a left-hand turn. Remember, you can be in the right area, but in the wrong location, and fail. Once you have determined the side of the street at a signalized intersection, the far corner is generally the best location because it allows more time for decision making and is usually not affected by traffic backup. Successful locations are a combination of good access to the community, the trade area, and a specific location.

Traffic Backup

Traffic backup can change what appears to be a good location into an absolute disaster. For example, traffic backup in front of a site precludes people from getting into and out of the location. Traffic backup is especially harmful if it occurs during the hours of the day when you, as a restaurant or fast food operator, expect to do much of your business. Do not buy such a problem—there can simply be too much traffic. Where that situation exists, people may avoid the area, or potential customers may have difficulty getting in or out of properties that abut the roadway. It is easy to identify these detrimental factors by consulting with the state, county, or city traffic engineer prior to signing an agreement to buy or lease a location. Also observe the site during the hours that you would expect to be doing business and especially on the weekends, for additional insight into the situation.

Curb Cuts

Most states, as well as some counties and even cities, are becoming stingy about granting curb cuts on their respective roads. For success, however, a location needs an adequate curb cut or cuts. Adequate is enough to handle the anticipated customers on an hourly basis. A discussion with the jurisdictional officer (most likely the state, county, or city traffic engineer) should be held to determine the probability of obtaining the necessary curb cuts. Also, any deals certainly should be contingent on the receipt of curb cut permits.

Accident—Congestion Locations

Most food operators should avoid heavily congested locations, particularly if significant accidents occur there. The consumer may also avoid such locations, thus adversely affecting business potential. One way of making that determination is simply to ask a police officer on patrol to tell you the five most accident-oriented locations in his or her area. You can be assured that if some solution has yet to be found, the traffic engineers will be working hard to find it. While the answer may solve the traffic and congestion problem, it may also eliminate the business that you either have, or are about to pay to acquire. A little bit of effort and investigation goes a long way.

Left-Hand Turns

Left-hand turn ingress is extremely important to the food industry. More and more cities are recognizing the impact of left-hand turns that back up traffic on major arteries. Thus, it is becoming more commonplace to have left-hand turn lanes primarily at intersections and at major commercial concentrations. Some cities provide a center turn lane for access to locations along a major traffic artery. However, because the uncontrolled left turns cause frequent accidents, many cities are eliminating the center lane.

To facilitate traffic movement, some communities are limiting left-hand turns at intersections between the hours of 3:00 P.M. and 6:00 or 7:00 P.M. or, in some cases, early in the morning. Depending on your type of food business, you should determine how such prohibitions affect you. In any case, since left-hand turns are critical to the food business, try to evaluate the current ease or difficulty of such turns and the likelihood of future changes.

Shopping Center Locations

In evaluating shopping center restaurant locations, you need to consider the placement of curb cuts, the primary ingress and egress points, and the availability of traffic lights. Regardless of whether the restaurant is freestanding or situated in an "in-line" location within a shopping center, access to the subject property is paramount.

TRAFFIC DATA AVAILABILITY

A methodology for gathering the necessary data for market evaluation can be found in Chapter 7. That material includes answers to the hows, whys, and wheres of traffic data. Traffic information can also be secured from state, county, and city highway and traffic officials. They can tell you what is planned, what is likely to be funded, and what will be the probable time schedule for commencing and completing the projects. They are not always right, but at least they provide insight into what can happen, even if it does not happen quite as rapidly as they may have anticipated.

Ten

Attitudes, Trends, Habits, and Patterns

Consumer attitudes are the subject of many books, speeches, and articles. Most of us are aware of the aging of the population, increasing conservatism, orientation toward health, and concern for physical well-being. In contrast, habits and patterns are subjects that most restaurateurs and fast food operators find vaguely familiar and yet rarely consider. We all establish habits as a result of where we live, work, play, shop, travel, socialize, bank, and seek medical care. Habits establish patterns that affect our daily lives because they satisfy our comfort level, need, speed, or necessity, or simply represent the shortest distance between two points. This chapter will explore four important areas: attitudes, trends, habits, and patterns.

ATTITUDES AND TRENDS

Just as the youth revolution of the 1960s affected habits and patterns, so has the rising "adult era" of the 1990s. In the 1960s and early 1970s, the predominant age group was between 18 and 25

years, but mostly younger. They bred informality, so-called open-
ness, and truth; they brought blue jeans and work clothes into vogue,
as well as mustaches and beards, long hair, and beads; and they
taught us to "do our own thing." Hard rock pounded our ears—
profanity became the lyric, and the guitar the instrument of the mu-
sical revolution. Men who wanted to jump on the bandwagon bought
leisure suits; women outfitted themselves in hot pants and
miniskirts; haircuts became hair styling and hair spray a way of life.

Vietnam was the issue; marches and demonstrations, the action;
and civil disobedience, the solution. Youth was in vogue; love was
universal (or, at least, we were told); and peace was the sign.
Through it all, many traditional values were affected. Many mar-
riages were replaced by "live-in" arrangements; divorce predomi-
nated at all adult ages; sex became the new religion and social
change became the need; jogging became the social exercise, love
became "you're pad or mine," money (and profit) was truly the root
of all evil; and energy conservation, wildlife conservation, and other
social issues were key causes.

The 1980s added their own trends. Health was a high priority, and
dieting became the new cult. Health clubs became the norm, sweat
was in, and exercise suits were acceptable social attire. Herpes provided an initial scare, quickly followed by AIDS, which descended as
a plague. Casual sex was out, and condoms became a necessity. Divorce declined since the grass was not always greener on the other
side. Profit became acceptable; social change became business
school; the "soaps" provided the new evangelism; transportation
was by BMW; babies (at least trying to have them) returned; daycare
became a focal topic; moose was no longer an animal; laptops were
status; beef was out; and fish and chicken were in; oat bran was the
hot seller; and being vegetarian was "cool."

So things have changed and keep changing. Vietnam, thank God, is
long over for most of us, victory was ours in Kuwait, hair is shorter,
skirts are longer, and leisure suits are either collecting dust in the
closet or are hanging in some Salvation Army resale shop. The rabble-
rousers of the 1960s are today's young, or perhaps not so-young, professionals. The "yuppie" generation has been responsible for not only
social but also physical improvement. Gentrification of blighted
neighborhoods has created the era of the new urban pioneers.

The early 1990s will be best known, other than for the Persian Gulf
war, as the "age of frugality," recession (or possibly depression depending on the industry), and unsatisfied expectations. Our excesses

have resulted in too much debt and too many restaurants, stores, shopping centers, office buildings, hotels, resorts, cars, and houses. Following the recession of 1990–1991, however, the 1990s are likely to see considerable growth in consumer expenditures. Frugality of the 1980s and early 1990s will gradually shift to consumption, with a dramatic impact on the food service industry in the middle, and perhaps, later years of the decade. Also, while drugs are the inherited scourge of the 1990s, oil remains ever on our minds. The health craze will continue; thin remains "in"; materialism is the continuing religion; smoking is a killer; ownership is a must; notebooks take precedence over laptops; and hand-held cellular phones are an absolute. Alcohol is harmful; gray hair, acceptable; and social security, a worry; the "couch potato" has become a reality; and with population aging retirement is a now recognized possibility.

The number of working women will continue to rise, adding more spending power to more households. The current mild baby boom will have profound effects on education, as older mothers demand higher levels of accountability. Shopping will become an even greater chore as time demands on women reduce available hours. "Fashion with flexibility" will be the norm, with women continuing the shift away from dresses to coordinates and suits to meet the demand for daily individuality. Clothing brand name awareness will continue, benefiting some department stores and chain boutiques to the detriment of others. The aging of the population will see a decline in the demand for jogging shoes, jogging attire, and jeans. More and more meals will be eaten away from home, thus benefiting the food service industry. Moreover, these changes will lead to more informality, fewer bars, more value, lighter foods, lower alcohol content drinks, more fast service, more delivery (especially of fine dining meals), and the large kitchen going the way of the living room.

What does it all mean? It simply shows that we are an ever-changing society, and this fact will continue to have a significant impact on the food service business. Understanding the past attitudes and trends—and their causes—and anticipating future changes are essential to continuing success in the food business.

HABITS AND PATTERNS

A habit is a ritual. We establish habits without fully realizing that we have done so. I often suggest to audiences that they try for a full seven days to vary their habits. Try it! You will find that the attempt is disconcerting and difficult, because we do not like deviations. Try driving to work a different way each day. First, most people will say that they cannot, because of the expressway. Others will try for a day or two and then simply fall into the previous route. Our habits influence our patterns, as does where we work, live, play, shop, worship, and so on.

Often our patterns are dictated by others over whom we have little or no control. Regardless, it is important, especially in the fast food industry, to recognize these patterns and take advantage of them. A simple secret is to recognize the patterns of people whom you would like to have for customers and place your units within their patterns. You will simply do more business. If you attempt to force or encourage people to deviate from their patterns, you will often meet with failure.

Habits and patterns, in many respects, are interchangeable. The habits are what we do, and the patterns are what we follow in practicing our habits. Many habits are the result or indication of income, age, family size, number of children, type of employment, suburban versus urban locations, and other considerations. Patterns reflect the actions of different functions, for example, the employment pattern (home to work to home), the shopping pattern, the school pattern, the recreation pattern, and others that will be discussed in this chapter. The importance of these considerations is obvious. Habits affect what we do and the patterns reflect how we do them. Although we may vary established patterns somewhat, studying these patterns would reveal how habit-oriented we really are. In fact, it is very easy to evaluate people over a period of time and specifically identify their patterns.

The habits and patterns of people are extremely important to the food industry, particularly for fast food operations and restaurants that are oriented toward middle-income America. This concept is perhaps less true with respect to fine dinner houses, since consumers tend to violate their normal habits and patterns, particularly with respect to a special occasion or an unusually expensive function.

Work

Work patterns and their ramifications for the food industry have altered drastically during the past 15 to 20 years. Increasing numbers of working women, the decentralization of jobs to suburbia, the end of the industrial revolution, and the commencement of the service revolution have all had a significant market impact on the market.

Work patterns differ greatly throughout the United States. In the Northeast and portions of the Midwest, public transportation patterns to and from work still have considerable importance. In recent years, decentralized facilities in suburbia have caused these transportation patterns to decline in favor of a strong automobile orientation. Today, the automobile is the primary mode of transportation to and from work. Thus, work-oriented automobile patterns play an important role in both direct and indirect eating-out decision making. In the western part of the United States, the automobile has been "king" since its invention. Thus, most commercial facilities in that part of the country were developed with the car in mind.

Think for a moment of the last time you decided where you were going to eat lunch. The work pattern experience plays an extremely important role in that decision. Carry the thought a little bit further, and consider the last time you made a decision regarding where to eat dinner. Did the work pattern play a role? It may not have been obvious. For example, the place you selected maybe one that you rarely visit but that happens to be in the general directional pattern that you follow to and from work. We tend to establish overall directional patterns and follow them in deciding where to eat out. If it was not in the work pattern, are there any other patterns that may have influenced your decision? Perhaps a shopping pattern?

The variation in this selection experience occurs as the amount of money to be spent at the restaurant increases. For example, the selection of a fine French restaurant where the bill of fare might be $50 to $100 per person, may override many normal patterns. Conversely, however, the decision to take the family out for dinner to, say, a "funky" restaurant or, for that matter, to eat at McDonald's or the Olive Garden, is dramatically influenced by preestablished patterns.

Today, there is often a twofold work pattern because both the husband and wife are employed and they may use different routes to and from work. Thus, each party is exposed to different roads, restaurants, and fast food facilities. They may not be consciously aware of this exposure, but our research indicates that it does, in fact, affect the decision-making process. Think about it. Where do you eat out most often? In what travel pattern is it?

Public transportation commuter patterns also affect the decision-making process. For example, in Manhattan, the position of the subways, train stations and transfer points plays a role in the market for eating-out facilities, which are found in a greater concentration closer to work–commuter concentrations. In the West, and especially in California, food facilities are concentrated near the interchanges of major expressways leading to and from primary concentrations of employment. This is no coincidence; it is an attempt to maximize a particular pattern.

Shopping Patterns

Shopping patterns have been changing for the past 25 years and will continue to change. Initially, the shopping pattern shifted from the downtown area or older business districts to commercial highways and then expanded to major regional shopping centers and malls. In fact, in suburbia, major regional shopping centers provide the largest concentration of activities.

Shopping patterns are influenced by at least two factors: convenience goods and shoppers' goods. Convenience goods include food, drugs, hardware, liquor, and other consumable items generally purchased on a highly frequent basis. Thus, the convenience goods shopping pattern represents a high-frequency visit. Because the newest major convenience goods facilities are large and generative, they are greatly influencing shopping patterns. Supermarkets may range between 50,000 and 200,000 square feet and capture sales varying from $300,000 to $3,000,000 per week.

Shoppers' goods are durable goods that are purchased less frequently, including apparel, accessories, appliances, furniture, television sets, stereos, and other more expensive items. Some of these facilities, which are generally found in large concentrations, are quality oriented, while others are price–value directed. Still others take a combined approach.

A shopping pattern is a critical pattern. It is more female oriented than male oriented, although the pattern is shifting to a more equal representation in many areas of the country with a high concentration of singles and divorcees. Also, with the time pressure on working women, a larger percentage of business will be done at night and on weekends. Also, men will be taking on a greater shopping role in the future as more chores become shared. The shopping pattern is important because of the shopper's exposure to various types of food facilities while traveling to the convenience goods or shoppers' goods facilities, as well as those that he or she encounters on the return trip. As previously indicated, we are creatures of habit, and whereas the days on which shopping occurs may vary somewhat, the road patterns followed are generally the same.

There is less variation in convenience goods shopping than shoppers' goods patterns. Mothers tend to visit supermarkets on similar days throughout the week, often dictated by the schedules of their children. Because of the increasing incidence of working women, however, shopping days are more often being dictated by the availability of time. In evaluating the shopping pattern, you must identify when shopping occurs. Furthermore, it is no accident that many food facilities are located in proximity to regional shopping centers and, in more recent years, within the shopping centers themselves. Today, more and more shopping is being done evenings and weekends, especially in areas where a majority of families are composed of two full-time workers. In older or more affluent neighborhoods, housewives are still at home and thus can shop when they choose. It is important to know what the situation is in any area under consideration.

Eating-out decisions are seldom made to and from convenience goods shopping. This is especially true for the consumer coming from a supermarket with frozen goods in the car. A drive-thru decision is then more likely. Also, the consumer is more money-sensitive because of the cost of food. Conversely, a trip for shoppers' goods will often stimulate an eating-out decision. Actually, we have found that the dinner decisions are not made directly on the shopping trip. Rather, the exposure to the dining facilities influences the decision at home later on in the day.

School Pattern

The school pattern is also twofold. The first part is established by people driving children to and from school. The second part is the eating-out pattern that develops in proximity to an elementary school, high school, college, or university. Probably the most obvious example of this pattern is the ubiquitous McDonald's located near high schools throughout the United States. A further amplification of this pattern is the concentration of food facilities in proximity to major universities. Our studies indicate a decline in the number of students eating meals in dormitory facilities, whereas there has been a considerable increase in the number of students eating meals in fast food facilities located on or adjacent to campuses. The driving pattern that is developed in traveling to and from school, to a varying degree, influences the decision-making process for eating-out facilities.

Travel Patterns

The United States is a country on the move, particularly for the younger and older generations. Middle-aged Americans generally have fewer disposable funds and, therefore, are less travel oriented. Old patterns influence numerous eating decisions. The airline travel pattern influences eating decisions at airports or nearby hotels in the destination city. Railroads (principally commuter service) affect eating-out patterns both at embarkation and disembarkation, as well as in the cities that people visit. This is also true of bus transportation and the patterns of the people who ride buses in traveling around the United States. The interstate highway system has a continuing impact on eating-out habits and patterns, creating some markets while destroying others.

Studying the patterns for each mode of transportation can provide useful information. For example, Las Vegas, with its unique gambling facilities and big name shows, is influenced by the airline travel pattern, the bus pattern, and certainly the interstate highway system pattern. Atlantic City has some similar attractions, but reflects different patterns, because more people in the surrounding megalopolis visit the city more often, usually by automobile or bus, but for fewer days. A broader influence is felt in Hawaii, where the economic base fluctuates with airline travel patterns. Convention facilities have created numerous food opportunities oriented toward conventioneers and visitors to the host cities. All of these cities are influenced by various travel patterns.

Recreational Patterns

The country continues on a "body beautiful" jag. Almost every closet holds a jogging suit, running shoes, and sweat bands. Health and diet are frequent topics of conversation. Even if a person does not practice the art of diet and exercise, it may seem necessary to look the part. As a result of all of this activity, recreational patterns play an increasing role in decision making. That role is not as major as you may be led to believe, but it should be considered, particularly in major cities where recreation alternates with lunch, afternoon snacks, and after work "hoisting a few" activities.

Social Patterns

Existing social patterns within the community can play an influential role in the success of a fine dining restaurant. In many southeastern and southwestern states, buying a drink across the bar was prohibited for years. Thus, cocktails were consumed in the home prior to dining out. Whereas the law has changed in most states, people's habits have changed more slowly. Thus, alcohol consumption in restaurants is generally lower. In considering a restaurant opportunity, it is important to understand the social patterns that exist within the community. North Carolina, for example, is a state where restaurants have experienced below average liquor sales.

Another social pattern is the availability and desirability of entertainment in the restaurant facility. This is especially important at the cocktail hour or later in the evening. There are, of course, many variations to the entertainment theme. The promotion of cocktail hours has been banned in many states in an attempt to reduce drinking-related-driving accidents, and more states are expected to pass similar legislation. The day of the advertised happy hour is apparently over.

Entertainment Patterns

Age and income, and, to some extent, ethnic characteristics significantly influence entertainment patterns. Uniqueness of a particular type of restaurant operation can also play a critical role in the entertainment pattern. For example, a restaurant that features classical music and operatic singing will attract a specific segment of the population oriented toward that type of music. Likewise, an ethnic restaurant, featuring both appropriate cooking and entertainment, creates another type of attraction. The dinner house theater also combines dining with a specific kind of entertainment. Along with concerts and the legitimate theater, movies also play a big role in this category—especially with younger people.

Special Patterns

Special patterns include the impact of special uses, such as medical complexes that encompass a cluster of hospitals and attract people both locally and throughout the region. Whereas food facilities are provided within the complex, often market opportunities develop for adjunctive facilities, for those people who find the hospitals' food too institutionalized.

Special patterns also include those established with respect to anniversaries, birthdays, weddings, and funerals. Special occasion restaurant facilities oriented to these special patterns must identify the appropriate patterns and locate so as to capitalize on them.

The religious pattern is most prevalent on Sunday and certainly influences eating-out decisions. This pattern has a significant impact on the Sunday breakfast or brunch. Religion is going to play a growing role in our society, coming back from decades of decline. This will have a more important impact on the food service industry.

Eating-Out Patterns

The most critical patterns for a restaurateur or fast food operator who is considering a new opportunity are the existing eating-out (and/or eating-out and drinking) patterns. It is essential to determine where competitive facilities are located and why people patronize them, including elements such as income, age, number of children, number of working women, and ethnic characteristics. For example, areas with a strong European background will evidence more orientation toward cocktails or drinks with meals, while predominantly Jewish concentrations will reflect a much higher incidence toward food and a much lower orientation toward alcohol, other than wine.

Most fast food operators and restaurateurs pay considerable attention to the existing eating and drinking patterns and competition within a community. However, they often ignore the other patterns that have contributed to the overall picture of what people do, why they do it, when, and with what frequency.

SUMMARY

We are all creatures of habit, and we do follow specific patterns. Market analysis will identify those patterns and capitalize on them. The more patterns that can be capitalized on, the greater the opportunity for maximizing sales and minimizing the competitive hazard.

Eleven

Competition

Competitive evaluation is perhaps the easiest to undertake and yet it is often, especially for restaurants, the most difficult to define. It is easy simply because most food people think they can identify their competitors. They sample a meal, look at the decor, get a feeling for the turnover, and arrive at a judgment. It is complicated because many restaurateurs as well as some fast food operators are often wrong about their competition. The measurement of competition is most difficult because, in determining its effectiveness, there are so few rules to go by. Furthermore, how often have these questions been asked: "How much is too much? What is saturation? How will I be affected by saturation?" Unfortunately, in many markets, we are seeing the answers now.

The first step in assessing competition is to define it properly. Competition may be categorized into two types: direct and indirect. *Direct* competition represents those food service facilities that are competing directly with a specific menu. For example, a steak and lobster restaurant operation is directly competitive with other steak and lobster operations, and a fast food hamburger facility is directly competitive with other fast food hamburger operations. *Indirect* competition represents competition that is less direct such as a steak restaurant compared with a fish restaurant, or a fast food chicken operation compared with a pizzeria. In reality, they are each somewhat competitive with the other, although it may be at different times and in different situations. The important consideration is which ones are competitive with your individual or chain operation, and at what daypart.

My experience has been that very few food operators truly evaluate competition, especially in relation to the sales being captured by the competitors. How can you understand the competition if you do not know what the competitor's sales are and when the business is occurring?

If you have asked your customers questions about the competition, they have probably identified your competitors. If you are starting a new business or concept, it is necessary to look at similar facilities. Either interview their customers or spend at least a week observing the customers and analyzing each daypart. Observation usually is not good enough; because of limited resources, however, it may be the only way. Certainly it is useful if it is done correctly. The following sections describe some important elements of analyzing competition.

IDENTIFYING COMPETITORS

As previously indicated, existing food operators should determine their customer profile and their specific competitors, so that there is no guessing. Others, who do not have an existing restaurant, should talk to as many people as possible in the area under consideration. This discussion will help to identify where the area residents and workers eat out and will suggest the potential competitors. Talking to suppliers about "the who, where, why, and how much" of competition and sales can also provide information.

COMPETITIVE INVENTORY

Figure 11.1 depicts an inventory form used in quantifying restaurant competition, while Figure 11.2 is for fast food competitors. They are not gospel, but rather examples of what an inventory form might look like. Actually, each form should be tailored to fit the specific situation. The important thing is to inventory the competition in a uniform manner, so that you can compare the data realistically.

Usually the inventory of restaurants is more extensive than that of fast food operations because restaurants normally have more individual considerations in comparing competition. This does not mean that the inventory for a fast food operation is any less important. On

FIGURE 11.1

Restaurant Competitive Inventory

Map key _____   Date _____
City _____   Location _____

Name _____   Side of the Street _____
Chain or independent _____
Type: Direct _____   Seating:
        Indirect _____   Dining Room _____
Size (sq. ft.) _____   Bar _____
                              Seating efficiency _____
Hours: Weekdays _____
        Saturday _____   Primary daypart _____
        Sunday _____
                              Seating turnover _____
Sales (annual) _____
Source _____   Seating setup:
Take-out _____   Fours _____
Check Average _____   Twos _____
Source _____   Larger tables _____
Parking spaces _____
Valet _____   Saturday night wait _____
Curb cuts _____
Primary menu items _____   Prices _____

Primary traffic artery _____   Traffic counts _____

Ease of entry _____   Date of counts _____

Secondary traffic artery _____   Hourly counts _____

Ease of entry _____
Number of lanes—primary road   Speed limit _____

                              Traffic speed _____

FIGURE 11.1 *(Continued)*

Distance to traffic light _____	Ingress _____
Light timing sequence _____	Egress _____
Visibility	
Directional _____	Describe customers _____
Distance _____	_____
_____	Age _____
_____	Income _____
Other characteristics and observations _____	

Sketch location on the attached sheet, including adjacent uses, competitors, curb cuts, traffic lights or signs, number of lanes, median strips, topographical changes, one-way streets, and other items. Include photos of front and both directional views.

the contrary, a mistake in competitive analysis can quickly spell the demise of a new unit.

Notice that both forms require a fair degree of detail. Most of us do not want to get that involved. However, many food people have stopped me in airports, at conferences, or in restaurants to tell me that they wished that they had seriously followed what I had said regarding competition. Unfortunately, the omission proved to be their downfall, often resulting in the complete loss of all business and personal assets. A number of items in the inventory forms are common to both restaurants and fast food operations, including type of location, size, number of seats, customer counts, type of traffic artery, parking, visibility, turnover of seating by daypart, peak periods, menu, menu variations, menu specials, prices, ingress and egress, condition of the facility, and presentation. Items specific to the fast food industry might include drive-thru windows, drive-thru timing, pickup, delivery, product packaging, advertising, promotions, giveaways, activity areas, generative concentrations, traffic counts, resident population, and driving times. To the inventory for the fine dining industry, you might add unique menu, price, atmosphere, valet parking, proximity to hotels and convention centers, personality of the owners, community involvement, and business people attraction.

FIGURE 11.2

Fast Food Competitive Inventory

Map key _____	Date _____
City _____	Location _____
	_____
Name _____	Side of the street _____
Chain or independent _____	_____
Type: Direct _____	Seating _____
Indirect _____	Drive-thru _____
	Number of lanes _____
Size (sq. ft.) _____	Primary daypart _____
	Saturday _____
Hours: Weekdays _____	Seating turnover _____
	Peak days _____
Sunday _____	_____
	Seating setup:
Sales (annual) _____	Fours _____
Source _____	Twos _____
Take-out _____	Cleanliness _____
Check Average _____	Signs _____
Source _____	_____
Parking spaces _____	
Curb cuts _____	Prices _____
Primary menu items _____	_____
	_____
_____	Specials _____
_____	_____
_____	
	Traffic counts _____
Primary traffic artery _____	
_____	Date of counts _____
Ease of entry _____	_____
	Hourly counts _____
Secondary traffic artery _____	_____
_____	_____
_____	_____
Ease of entry _____	
	Speed limit _____
Number of lanes—primary road	
_____	Traffic speed _____
_____	_____
	Ingress _____

FIGURE 11.2 *(Continued)*

Distance to traffic light _____	
	Egress _____
Traffic light timing sequence	
	Describe customers _____
Visibility:	Age _____
Directions _____	Income _____
Distance _____	Chain market share _____
Seconds _____	
Other characteristics and observations _____	

Sketch location on the attached sheet, including adjacent uses, competitors, curb cuts, traffic lights or signs, number of lanes, median strips, topographical changes, one-way streets, and other items. Include photos of front and both directional views.

It is especially important to inventory the "uniqueness" of a particular facility. Failure to recognize this factor has had serious repercussions, especially for chain restaurants going into a market that appeared to be understored. The strength of a few good restaurants can often handle what appears to be the opportunity for many. Do not let your ego get in the way of a critical decision; it is the customer, not you, who will decide whether you have used good judgment.

Figure 11.3 depicts a competitive evaluation form that was designed for a specific situation in downtown Chicago. We used it to evaluate the food facilities competitive with food operations located in the Sears Tower. Based on the competitive evaluation of all types of food operations within the building's trade area (determined by interviewing), we made recommendations regarding the types of facilities for which there was a market.

VISIT, DINE, AND EVALUATE THE COMPETITIVE FACILITIES

Try to eat at the competitive facilities as both a restaurateur and a customer. Especially try to be objective in your reactions. Remember,

FIGURE 11.3

Restaurant Evaluation Form

Date _____   Ref. No. _____ _____
                                                      01   02

Restaurant Name _____ (03)
Address _____ (04)

Type of Facility   **Type of Location**

Dining room   _____ (05)   Store front   _____ (10)
Pub   _____ (06)   Inside office building   _____ (11)
Coffee shop   _____ (07)   Basement   _____ (12)
Cafeteria   _____ (08)   Two levels   _____ (13)
Fast food   _____ (09)   Other (specify)   _____ (14)

Overall Site Characteristics

Visibility: Poor   _____ (15)   Appearance: Poor   _____ (16)
             Good   _____   Good   _____
             Excellent _____   Excellent   _____

Restaurant Characteristics

Specialty: Type _____ (17)
Appearance: Poor _____ Good _____ Excellent _____ (18)
Unique features: _____ (19)

Carry out service: _____   _____ (20)
                           Yes   No
Cocktails: Table   _____   _____ (21)
                           Yes   No
           Bar   _____   _____
                           Yes   No
           Both   _____   _____
                           Yes   No
Price change at dinner _____   _____ (22)
                           Yes   No
Specials of the day   _____   _____ (23)
                           Yes   No
Accept credit cards   _____   _____ (24)
                           Yes   No
Accept reservations   _____   _____ (25)
                           Yes   No

FIGURE 11.3 *(Continued)*

With reservations, how long a wait? _____ (26)
                                                    Minutes
Other: _____ (27)

Hours of Service (by time and day of week)

Breakfast _____ (28)
Lunch _____ (29)
Dinner _____ (30)
Cocktail hour _____ (31)

Seating and Size

Dining area: Seats _____ Tables _____ Stand-up counters _____ (32)
Lounge: Bar _____ Seats _____ Tables _____ (33)
Square footage: _____ (34)
Time arrived: _____ (35) Time left _____ (36)
Meal ordered
   (full description): _____ (37)

   _____

Cost: _____ Tip: _____ (38)
Waiting time:
   To be Seated _____ (39) Served _____ (40)
Customer counts:
   Time in: _____ Number _____   (41)
   Time out: _____ Number _____   (42)
Number of table turns

	Observation	Waitress	Manager	
Breakfast	_____	_____	_____	(43)
Lunch	_____	_____	_____	(44)
Dinner	_____	_____	_____	(45)

Rating System

	Score								Total
Quality of food	1	2	3	4	5	6	7	8	
Quality of service	1	2	4	4	5	6	7		
Ambience and atmosphere	1	2	3	4	5	6			
Overall value/price	1	2	3	4	5				
Food presentation	1	2	3	4					
Cleanliness	1	2	3						(46)

General experience _____ (47)

FIGURE 11.3 *(Continued)*

Estimated Sales

Weekly _____ (48)

Monthly _____

Yearly _____

Estimated average check _____ (49)

Length of time at present location _____ Years   (50)

Obtained Menu   *Reviewer's Initials*

Yes _____   _____

No _____

Menu Description

Appetizers   _____   _____

               Yes   No

Number _____

Type _____

_____

_____

Average cost $_____

Salads   _____   _____

               Yes   No

Number _____

Type _____

_____

_____

Average cost $_____

Sandwiches   _____   _____

               Yes   No

Number _____

Type _____

_____

_____

Average cost $_____

Entrees   _____   _____

               Yes   No

Number _____

Type _____

_____

_____

Average cost $_____

the customer does not look at food cost, labor cost, controllables, and uncontrollables. Instead, the customer looks and reacts to taste, quantity, service, price, value, perceived quality, comfort level, perhaps atmosphere, maybe speed, and sometimes entertainment. Taking this attitude can be very difficult, since food people often are more critical than the customers. Visit the competitive facilities during both peak and quiet times. Ask your server or counter person which items are purchased most often and then order those selections. Try to gain some insight into check averages by daypart. Talk to the host or hostess, servers, bartenders, and the manager regarding sales and activity.

For fast-fooders, talking to the manager or assistant manager during quiet times can get you the information that you need. They are often more receptive to conversation at those times and will either brag or moan about sales and customer counts. Sometimes it is best not to let them know that you are in the food business, while other times it is better to be in the food business and to sympathize with them. You must decide your approach by listening to how the individual reacts. If you start on a neutral note, not indicating that you are in the food business, you can become a knowledgeable food operator or simply a good and interested customer, depending on the response. Also, you might ask questions about new menu items that might be in the offing. Since health is "in," most food people have been adjusting their menu to accommodate this consumer demand. Using this subject for an opening question or statement can get the ball rolling.

TALK TO OTHER COMPETITORS

Over the years, I have found that asking each competitor about the others helps to get operators talking and comparing. Usually before long you are both comparing the facility you are in to the others, on very specific terms. *You may actually get to see both sets of books!* Following this procedure with all the competitors develops a network of information, often including the sales of the various competitors, their prime hours of business, and food and labor costs. In fact, I have been astounded at how much information can be gathered with some perseverance and cleverness. Do not be bashful; go for it!

COUNT THE CUSTOMERS

When securing the necessary information is extremely difficult, count the customers by daypart, for several days. Next, attempt to determine the average check and multiply this times the customer counts to determine the probable level of weekly sales. This figure can be extended to an annual sales figure. Some adjustment is almost always required because of seasonal variations, nontypical weeks, promotions, conventions, and other factors.

STOCK OFFERING PROSPECTUS

A number of food companies have been selling stock in the public arena. For each, there is a prospectus outlining the number of units, sales, operating data, plans, financing, areas of expansion, and other important data. This information can be useful in assessing competitors. Also, public companies must submit 10-K reports annually and 10Q reports quarterly to the Securities and Exchange Commission, regarding changes in the company's ownership and other data. Often, these data can be helpful.

FORMER EMPLOYEES

Finding former employees can at times be both easy and difficult. Nevertheless, the search can be worthwhile if the result is greater insight into a competitor's operating data, as well as his or her strengths and weaknesses.

ASK! ASK! ASK!

I am constantly surprised by the number of people in the food business who, when asked about their sales, respond with pride or concern. You might, on the other hand, be upset at how willingly your employees pass around your operating data and perhaps your shortcomings. (We all have some, so do not feel persecuted.) The risk of asking is hearing "No." Better to have asked and been refused, than not to ask at all. What have you lost?

SUPPLIERS

Talk to the meat man, the bread man, or some of the other suppliers; they know the volume of their deliveries and can provide insight into other competitors. Beware, however, that some responses can be misleading. That is why it pays to talk to competitors, customers, and suppliers, to get a more complete picture.

SUMMARY

Acquiring insight into your competitors' sales, profitability, and breakeven points will help you determine how much impact they can take and yet survive. When you have finished, you can add up the sales of the competitors and truly evaluate the extent of the market, as well as their individual market shares. This is a critical juncture! Often the analysis indicates that the situation is marginal for your planned facility. Again, do not let ego get in the way. If no market exists, do not go ahead. Conversely, if there is a market, you will recognize it, based on facts.

Competition usually exists or is planned. It can destroy before there is an opportunity to succeed. I know of many examples. However, the one that flashes to mind is the restaurateur who risked more than $3,000,000 in a new restaurant venture that lasted only six weeks. Naturally, he lost his entire investment including his home. It pays to take the time to truly analyze existing and proposed competition.

Twelve

Visibility and Exposure

V isibility represents the ability of consumers to see a facility from one, two, or more directions. More specifically, visibility relates to the amount of time that someone, either driving, or walking can see either a sign or a building. This factor is critical to impulse decision making, namely, the decision to stop and turn into the facility.

Exposure refers to the possibility of being seen by consumers over a long period of time. Exposure is especially important to most fast food operations and to many family restaurant facilities since the ultimate decision of where to eat is influenced by what the consumer sees on a regular basis. Because frequency of customer visit is vital to success, the continuing exposure helps to keep a fairly high level of awareness. Although the persons receiving the exposure will not necessarily become customers, that factor, along with advertising and promotion, increases the likelihood.

THE MAIN ASPECTS OF VISIBILITY

Adequate visibility is an arguable item; while there are numerous examples of successful units with limited visibility, the road is paved with hundreds of failures. Visibility is a crucial element in

site selection, especially in the fast food business. If potential customers cannot see the facility, then you greatly reduce your chances
of encouraging their impulse visits and, moreover, their general decision making.

Is visibility in one direction acceptable? In many instances, it is. A
positive evaluation of one-directional visibility depends, first of all,
on whether the characteristics of the people residing within the potential trade area are highly compatible with the most frequent visitor profile. Second, the competitive aspect of the marketplace also
dictates making a review of adequate visibility and exposure with
the realization that a competitive facility will be developed somewhere nearby. The position of existing competitors relative to a proposed location and consumer driving patterns is critical. When
competitors are between you and possible customers, a difficult
problem may exist. Third, a thorough study of directional traffic
counts by hour is essential. This study will provide insight into the
number of potential customers who will have visibility versus those
who will not be able to see the unit. Finally, a study of people's
habits and patterns regarding the particular traffic artery is necessary. Whereas the proposed unit will have no visibility for some people, it may be visible to others on their return trip. Selecting the
proper side of the street is critical. Therefore, understanding where
traffic originates and where it is going is extremely important in
determining directional visibility.

You have probably noticed that I have not mentioned the acceptability of units with no visibility. That is because I generally do not
like units that have no visibility, especially in a suburban location.
Without question, some unique restaurants can compensate for the
lack of visibility, but that is not true in the fast food business. I can
count on one hand the fast food units that I have known to be successful without decent visibility. Restaurants that might be able to
overcome the lack of visibility would include a high-price bistro
with ambience and atmosphere, a restaurant developed on a lake
away from a main artery, serving good food in a delightful atmosphere, or a restaurant on top of an office tower. What we are primarily concerned with, however, are restaurants and fast food
facilities that are *not* unique (because most establishments fall into
that category) and few of them can succeed without some degree of
visibility.

What is adequate? The determining factors are the driving speeds,
distance covered, and seconds available for visibility. Table 12.1

TABLE 12.1

Distance Traveled per Second
at Varying Driving Speeds

Speed	Feet per Second
20	29
25	37
30	44
35	51
40	59
45	66
50	73
55	81
60	88
65	95

depicts various speeds and the corresponding distance traveled in feet per second. It shows that a person driving 35 miles per hour covers 51 feet per second. Thus, a food operator who wants a maximum of 300 feet of visibility in essence is saying that, given a speed limit of 35 miles an hour, consumers will have 5.8 seconds to make a decision regarding the food operation. Given the same 300 feet for decision-making purposes, a motorist traveling at 45 miles per hour will have 4.5 seconds to make that decision, since the vehicle will be traveling at 66 feet per second. At 55 miles per hour, the consumer will have 3.7 seconds, since 81 feet will be covered per second. Adequacy for a fast food operation and a chain coffee shop unit, which must allow time for the prospective customer, is a minimum of 3 seconds; 5 seconds is desirable. For a dinner house, which depends less on impulse, minimums are often acceptable.

To maximize visibility, food operations are usually located as close to the street as possible, in contrast to retail locations, which are often set back so that the consumers can park in front. Furthermore, other buildings may obscure visibility; thus, most food operators have prominent signs, varying in size, color, and illumination, to overcome the lack of visibility or to maximize as much visibility as is practically possible. Unfortunately, everybody has the same goal. Therefore, in food facility concentrations, particularly of fast food units, signs can become so numerous that they obliterate visibility. Some food executives have attempted to develop the building into a symbol so that, when viewing it from most directions, the consumer automatically associates the building with the product. Design has been effective for some and not so effective for others. Ineffectiveness is more often related to the product than to the building.

Property owners do not have control over what somebody else may do on an adjacent piece of land. Nevertheless, a restaurant operator can attempt to maximize as much visibility as possible while recognizing that someone can build on nearby vacant property and affect that visibility. This recognition certainly should be considered in placing the building on the site.

The seasons of the year can affect visibility. When picking a location in the wintertime, visibility may look spectacular. However, trees do grow, and the impressive winter visibility may become totally obliterated in the summertime when the trees come into full foliage.

A location on a curve or hill limits visibility. Furthermore, these locations often have access problems, particularly for customers exiting the parking lot, given a reasonably heavy traffic load. It is difficult for consumers to see approaching traffic.

Many food operators, to avoid the fast food row or restaurant concentrations, have opted for locations away from food competition. My experience has been that this strategy works if the restaurant has a degree of uniqueness or the operator is prepared to take several years developing a customer base. For the fast food operator, all of the needed market and locational elements must be appropriate.

THE INFLUENCE OF EXPOSURE

Exposure, as previously indicated, is being seen for a long period of time. Exposure is extremely important to fast food operations, moderately priced dinner houses, family restaurants, and certain other types of restaurant. Exposure even matters to high quality, higher priced dinner houses with considerable competition. It is less significant for superior French cuisine in an atmosphere-oriented environment with an expensive menu. It may also be less significant for the special purpose restaurant where a unique environment is coupled with good food and an exciting atmosphere.

Why is exposure important? Because so much of our decision making is influenced by our patterns and those facilities that we see on a regular basis. The more often a restaurant is seen, the greater its possibility of being selected, when the decision is made. The less it is seen, the less it is thought of, and often it is forgotten. The lack of exposure requires that the restaurant be generative and usually admits little or no possibility of an impulse decision. Advertising and, perhaps, yellow pages placement can somewhat offset this disadvantage, but in a highly competitive environment, advertising is usually insufficient to overcome the lack of exposure and, more specifically, the lack of visibility. Since the "average deal" is for 15 to 20 years and competition certainly does not remain static, it pays to pick the best location available with both visibility and exposure.

Advertising is exposure of another dimension. Advertising and promotion, if done properly, create an awareness of a restaurant or fast food facility; however, if the product is not good or excellent, the consumer will not repeat the visit. Repetition is the root of the restaurant success tree.

Thirteen

Market Employment

Employment is important for a number of reasons. First, it reflects the vitality of a community. Second, the extent of employment in an area can indicate the potential for capturing breakfast, lunch, or perhaps, cocktail hour and dinner business. Finally, indirectly, the type of employment suggests income availability, which in turn determines discretionary buying power. This chapter presents the various aspects of employment that relate to locational choices for restaurant facilities. Also, several methods for determining employment in an area will be explored to assist operators in making such estimates.

Nearby employment is the mainstay of many restaurant and fast food facilities. Employment concentrations, passing motorists, and nearby or adjacent employees can ensure the success of a restaurant that might otherwise fail. Employment within an area is often confused with activity within a market segment. For example, numerous restaurateurs and fast food operators flock to positions near major regional malls under the assumption that the facilities, along with employment in the area, will sustain at least a luncheon and dinner business. Unfortunately, they often find that the mall attracts a high preponderance of women. The small number of men, along with limited initial employment in the area, results in insufficient sales. Usually, this situation corrects itself in several years. They can, however, be very costly years.

OVERALL EMPLOYMENT WITHIN AN AREA

The overall employment types and trends within a community or an area mirror the dynamics of the community. As the United States has shifted from an industrial society to an service-oriented economy, the impact of major employment change has been felt throughout the country. Manufacturing jobs have been exported to Asian countries because of our high standard of living and our inability to compete with cheaper wage rates. This change continues to affect almost all parts of the United States. I am sure that you have seen this in your own community. Plants close; jobs are lost and are not replaced because there are no new manufacturing plants. In some communities, total employment will look static, but further inspection indicates that considerable changes have occurred in various categories of employment. For example, many communities have shown a significant decline in the number of manufacturing jobs, while a major increase has occurred in service-oriented jobs. Thus, the total number of people employed may be approximately the same, but the types of employment will have been drastically altered.

Labor Force

Although the unemployment rate has drawn much attention, a major recycling of the labor force has also been occurring. Namely, numerous manufacturing jobs, paying more than $12 an hour, have been replaced by service jobs, paying between $6 and $7 an hour. Thus, while total employment may have remained relatively stagnant within a community, the overall purchasing power has declined. This problem has often been overlooked in evaluating the changes in fast food demand and flat restaurant customer counts. Also, these changes are partially responsible for the rise in home entertainment and the proliferation of video rental shops.

In studying the labor force relative to the food industry, the focus has often been on unemployment, whereas the critical factor is the change in the total number of jobs. It is even more crucial to know where, geographically within the community, employment has grown versus where employment has declined. Even in metropolitan areas that are showing negative growth or atrophy, some sectors may reflect vitality because of job growth created by shifting patterns within the community.

Major Employers

Typically, major employers have a significant impact on a community. The first step in determining the extent of that impact is to obtain a list of major employers from the Chamber of Commerce. As indicated earlier in this book, the Chamber of Commerce almost always maintains a list of major employers, along with the number of persons employed. In some instances, this information is also made available with a map depicting specific locations within the geographic area. Understanding the type of employment, where it is concentrated, and the number of people employed by location helps to establish some of the community's patterns. Also, any seasonal variations in employment can be noted and evaluated.

Geographic Location of Employment

The location of the employment or its concentrations is as important as the number of total employees. Furthermore, it is useful to be aware of changes or trends in employment growth by geographic area (or trade area). This information can help in identifying the work patterns that are likely to have been created. For example, major new office concentrations have created a significant demand for restaurant and fast food facilities in the Schaumburg community of suburban Chicago. The same kind of concentration also exists along the LBJ Expressway in Dallas. Incidentally, the identification of the growth in employment should be coupled with an analysis of the growth of competition, since other restaurants are drawn to these areas for the same reasons.

Types of Employment

Historically, employment opportunities have generally been categorized as white-collar or blue-collar jobs. White-collar represents people who principally work in offices, while blue-collar designates those persons working in factories, construction, maintenance, warehouse, and distribution functions. Moreover, blue-collar was often segmented into three additional categories: skilled, semi-skilled, and unskilled. In recent years, these designations have been modified, particularly with the significant increase in service industries. The continuing decline of manufacturing jobs has resulted in considerable change in our society, and the rising number of women in the workplace has added other considerations in classifying types of employment. Today, white-collar reigns number one in overall employment. Second place however, has been taken over by people in service jobs, which are often referred to as "tan-collar" jobs. The blue-collar category remains approximately the same.

The overall definitions—white-collar, tan-collar, and blue-collar—are further subdivided into these specific industries: manufacturing, construction, transportation, communications, wholesale trade, retail trade, finance/insurance and real estate (F.I.R.E), service industries, and public administration. Furthermore, individual occupation categories include the following:

- Executive
- Administrative and managerial
- Professional specialty
- Technicians and related support
- Sales workers and administrative support
- Service workers
- Agriculture
- Precision production
- Machine operators, assemblers and inspectors
- Transportation and material moving
- Handlers, equipment, cleaners, and laborers

While some of the preceding information may have little meaning to a restaurateur, these factors indicate income levels and, to some degree, employment growth and stability. Furthermore, if manufacturing jobs are declining in an area under consideration for a food service unit and the area is heavily industrialized, then it is necessary to explore in greater detail the longevity of employment in that market segment. You want to ascertain that the market will remain at least stable, and not decline, thereby jeopardizing your investment. On the other hand, an area with growing office development, particularly with a large number of branch or regional offices of major corporations, usually signals an opportunity for extensive food service growth. Data are available regarding the hourly wage rates and salary levels for the different types of employees within the community.

Daytime Working Population

The restaurateur or fast food operator is normally interested in the *daytime working population* because it represents a significant level of business. For most food operations—depending on the type of location and food service—the primary market is the resident population, while the daytime working population represents a strong secondary market. Identifying the daytime working population within an area helps in assessing the potential dollars available for a new food facility. The fact that the daytime working population exists does not mean that it represents potential business. The buildings or industries that generate the daytime working population may provide their own dining facilities or commissaries, which would limit the number of people who leave the premises for lunch. Furthermore, the amount of time available for lunch, particularly in industrial areas, often precludes the employees leaving the premises during the luncheon period.

The Chamber of Commerce usually can furnish data regarding industrial employment concentrations, and the number of persons employed in the various industries in the geographic area under consideration. Office employment is sometimes more difficult to determine. However, if the buildings have been built in the past five years, you can usually assume that there are approximately 200 to 250 square feet of space for each employed person, if the building is fully occupied. Thus, by obtaining an office inventory (by individual building square footage) for the area, less vacancy and dividing by 200 or 250 square feet, you can determine the approximate number of people working in each building. While this is not completely accurate, it serves as a fairly general guideline. The ratio of 200 square feet per employee is more universal than 250 square feet. Headquarters or major regional offices often have more space per employee because of conference rooms, commissaries, large reception areas, and other nonoffice space. Thus, it is necessary to allot the higher figure. When in doubt, use 200 square feet per employee.

If there are major retail facilities in the area, you can assume that they provide approximately 300 square feet per employee. This figure, again, assists in determining the number of workers in the area. Remember that estimates of daytime employment using office or retail space are guidelines; there will be variations, depending on the kinds of office buildings and retail facilities. Nevertheless, "on average," they are fairly reliable.

Should the area have a military base or complex, it is usually necessary to call the base commandant regarding the number of military and civilian employees. Given the world situation and the U.S. budget deficit, there will probably be a continuing decline in the number of military bases throughout the United States, and many that remain open will see their military and civilian complement considerably reduced. Therefore, in evaluating a location in proximity to a military base, it is necessary to tread with caution regarding its future, particularly if the planned facility will be wholly or partially dependent on the military base for its survival.

Shifting Employment Patterns

Nothing is static; everything changes; the difference is the degree. Since most restaurant and fast food facilities need a survival time of at least 5 years and, more realistically, 10 years, the changing employment patterns within a geographic area can affect success. For example, are plants closing and moving to other areas, or is the location in an area where new plants are relocating? Furthermore, are new office buildings being developed, and are smaller companies being created in the area or relocating to the area? Simply stated, determine whether this is a *recipient of employment or an exporting area.*

In recent years, the southeastern, southwestern, western, and northwestern parts of the United States have been the primary recipients of new industries and businesses. This shift has resulted in new jobs, major construction, large residential developments, and numerous new restaurants and fast food facilities in those areas. Even so, during these periods, segments of cities such as Buffalo, New York, Philadelphia, Pittsburgh, Minneapolis, and Chicago, while exporting jobs, experienced a shift of employment from the central city to certain suburban sectors. These changes, regardless of the area where they occurred, have generated opportunities for food service development. It is, therefore, necessary to evaluate the shifting patterns to fully capitalize on them. Often people, both in or out of the restaurant business, either do not consider the changing patterns or misread the results when planning a new food facility.

Cyclical changes must also be considered relative to shifting employment patterns. For example, food facilities in resort areas must capture 60% to 90% of their sales during "the season." Unfortunately, in many of these areas, there are simply too many restaurant and fast food facilities for the mediocre to survive. In some cases, even unique fine dinner houses have difficulty because the market is simply too small to accommodate all the local food facilities. Developing areas, such as Florida, provide examples of too many people chasing too few eating-out dollars.

Another consideration in employment patterns relates to "work shifts." Shift work is usually predominant in manufacturing or industrially oriented locales, where it can have a considerable impact on the restaurant and fast food business. The main consideration here is to recognize the significance of the shift as a business generator. For example, the normal dayparts (breakfast, lunch, and dinner) are often totally confused. People working the all-night shift may want a steak and beer in the morning instead of breakfast. Moreover, lunch can be dinner; and dinner can be lunch. It is also necessary to evaluate the strength of the industry, the likelihood of shift work continuing, and the downside risk, if shift work were to be eliminated. Evaluating areas with a preponderance of employment shifts also requires understanding the starting and quitting times of the shifts, the types of employees, their wage and salary rates, their habits and patterns, and their discretionary buying power. Fully understood, opportunities abound for successful restaurant and fast food facilities.

Employment and Household Trends

The labor force has changed dramatically in the past 10 to 20 years. We have gone from the single wage earner or salaried person to multiple employed persons in individual households. In the early 1970s, married women were predominately homemakers. When they went to work, often it was to provide discretionary income for a second home, a boat, special vacations, and the like. With the decline of the family unit, at least two major periods of inflation, and a major shift from manufacturing employment to a service economy, the U.S. household has found itself in a negative position. For the most part, mothers now work outside the house, not simply to provide the "extras" but, more importantly, to maintain the standard of living enjoyed by the 1970 and 1980's household.

To achieve material goals today, in the face of the high price of housing, the cost of raising children, and the expectations developed through childhood, usually both husband and wife must hold full-time jobs. Furthermore, a large number of women today want a career that provides something to fall back on should marriage fail or not materialize. Currently, women have opted for independence, career opportunities, compatible income, and more control over their future destiny. The housewife who does not hold a paying job often finds herself defending her position against those women who have opted for careers. Moreover, household sizes have declined; fewer babies are being born and when children do arrive (other than minorities), they are cared for by someone other than their parents. Regardless of the pros and cons, all of these changes have had a major impact on the number of meals eaten away from home.

In the latter 1990s and the early part of the next century, the most important labor group sought by both industry and commerce, will comprise persons older than 60 years of age. Age and the wisdom of experience will be recognized again. The decline of the teenage labor market (already underway) will necessitate looking to the largest population group, the over-65 category. Their stability, their need for income (which certainly will occur), and lower turnover will become significant factors in our society. These individuals with their longer life cycle, their boredom with retirement, and the decline in sufficient pension funds will fill the labor market. The young generation coming out of school will not meet this demand, simply because there will be too few of them to accommodate the overall need for service employment.

TRADE AREA EMPLOYMENT AND DAYPARTS

The importance of trade area employment depends on the type of restaurant or fast food operation. Fine dining restaurant facilities have a different orientation to trade employment than do fast food operations. Moreover, restaurants that are open only for dinner may have no orientation to trade area employment. Breakfast-oriented operations have varying degrees of employment orientation. Some are dependent on businesspeople who meet to discuss sundry topics before heading to the office; others cater more to salespeople and route delivery workers who stop prior to getting into the business day. Restaurant facilities that have lounges or after-work meeting and socializing amenities, must also be concerned with the type and location of employment.

Dayparts, which represent the time spans when significant amounts of business occur, generally include breakfast, lunch, dinner, and for many, the evening entertainment hours. For some others, it also includes the late night daypart, from midnight to 6:00 A.M.. The breakfast daypart usually necessitates being on a major commercial traffic artery in the employment pattern, that is, an artery used by a large number of people traveling to work. This situation also requires being on the "going to work" side of the street. That numerous people travel a particular road en route to work does not ensure breakfast business. In fact, probably the most difficult group to stop within the employment pattern are people heading to work. Since the average person ordinarily allows only sufficient time to get to work, the concept of stopping is contrary to the objective. The majority of breakfast patrons are senior citizens, employed persons who have a flexible business schedule in the morning, or other workers who need morning nourishment before going to their jobs. Older people or retirees who are under no time pressure constitute one of the most significant breakfast customer segments. They usually are very price oriented.

The most significant employee daypart is luncheon. Potential customers can plan where to eat lunch and usually have sufficient time for the meal, if the service is fast. Also, for many, the luncheon hour is staggered. The restaurateur or fast food operator should identify the extent of the employment in the area, luncheon eating-out patterns, timing, and locational opportunities that maximize luncheon employment potential. It is also essential to know how much time employees in the area have for lunch. In industrial areas, it is not unusual for the lunch period to be limited to 45 minutes, while in still other areas, commissaries or lunchrooms are provided to discourage the employees from leaving the premises. Once you have identified the principal employers of an area, a simple series of telephone calls can determine the extent of the luncheon hour and whether there are on-site facilities.

The dinner daypart includes the cocktail hour. In recent years, considerable pressure has been brought to bear on the restaurant industry to eliminate the "after work" cocktail hour and, more specifically, the promotions related thereto. Nonetheless, the early evening business can represent a significant portion of a restaurant's sales, whether it is a bar–grill facility serving a blue-collar neighborhood or an elegant restaurant with a strong professional following.

For many restaurant facilities, the cocktail hour is a prelude to their dinner business, and helps to ensure sufficient potential to achieve the necessary dinner volume. Nonetheless, the restaurant industry must adjust, since enforcement of "drinking and driving" laws is having a major impact upon the country. This shift in attitude is another reason it is so important to determine the employment activity, as well as employment trends within an area, prior to making a locational decision.

The after-dinner or late evening daypart usually is not directly employment related, but instead is more recreational or entertainment oriented. Nevertheless, in some areas, particularly where shift work exists, this daypart can also be influenced by employment. The late night daypart (midnight to 6:00 A.M.) usually consists of late night revelers or employed persons. For example, cross-country truck drivers will identify restaurants that have good food, are convenient to an interchange, and have adequate parking. Truckers as well as other travelers represent this daypart. For highway locations and within major cities, particularly where high density population exists, it is not unusual to find all-night restaurants that cater to both the area residents and employees. In still other cases, the site may be in proximity to hotels that provide some business.

SOURCES OF EMPLOYMENT DATA

The United States Census

A census of population and housing is conducted every 10 years for each state and metropolitan area with more than 10,000 persons. The data, which includes information about employment, industries, and other elements related to employment travel patterns, can serve as a base for measuring employment change.

United States Department of Labor—Bureau of Labor Statistics

The U.S. Department of Labor compiles data regarding labor statistics and employment changes. Furthermore, the department carries out expenditure studies to provide insight into the costs of maintaining a family of two or four. The Bureau of Labor statistics for small geographic areas are generally of limited value.

Chamber of Commerce

The Chamber of Commerce in most communities is an excellent source for a list of significant employers within the community, along with the number of employees. While all the information may not be in published form, the individual responsible for tracking employment can usually either verbalize the information, record it on a map for you, or can get it for you.

Information about office employment is less precise. Some chambers keep such records, while others do not. Nevertheless, they usually can tell you where you can obtain an inventory of office buildings by location and size. The inventory will not indicate the number of people employed in the various buildings; however, by applying the rule of thumb that allots 200 to 250 square feet per employee of occupied space (as explained earlier in this chapter), you can quickly determine the approximate number of employees per building. The Chamber of Commerce will also probably not have an inventory of retail facilities, but they usually will be able to direct you to someone who does. Normally, this information is available at the local newspaper. As mentioned earlier, retail facilities normally have about 300 square feet per employee. Therefore, by dividing the total retail space by 300 square feet per employee, you can arrive at the number of employees in concentrated retail facilities in a given area.

Industrial Commissions

More often, industrial commissions are state related. Larger cities, however, tend to have industrial development commissions. These groups assemble information regarding employment within the state, as well as the names of the primary employers and the number of employees. Furthermore, they usually have access to other sources of data that can aid the employment analysis.

Local Planning Agencies

Almost all cities have a planning commission or a planning department. Larger communities often have regional planning commissions or agencies. The first step is to identify which is the strongest and which is the most active. Many keep running inventories of employment by subsector within the metropolitan area. Often, their data are more comprehensive and detailed than that provided by the Chamber of Commerce because planning requires evaluating individual neighborhoods and determining needs.

State Employment Services

The states are empowered to deal with employment, unemployment, and job search assistance. In this capacity most states operate employment offices in every county. In most of the offices the data are not as formalized as at the Chamber of Commerce or the planning agency. Nevertheless, the head of the local office is acutely aware of the community's employment situation and is required to file employment reports with the primary state agency and the federal government on a regular basis. Discussions with the head of the office or a designated assistant can often clarify employment by specific geographic areas.

Utility Companies

Major utility companies continuously plan for the needs of their services throughout their franchise area. Moreover, they often maintain definitive records and employ talented personnel to evaluate the changes that are likely to take place within their service area. Thus, they often have employment data for small geographic areas.

Major Real Estate Firms

In medium to larger cities, major real estate firms that deal specifically in either office development or industrial buildings maintain inventories of existing facilities. If you are reviewing the types of industry and number of employees within a trade area, such inventories can be most helpful in identifying the locations of industrial and office facilities.

Unions

In areas where unions are strong, they keep track of the number of employees for each industrial firm. Although the food industry may not be partial to unions, they can represent a good source of data, particularly if the prospective location happens to fall in an area with a high preponderance of industrial facilities.

Computer Demographic Service Companies

The computer demographic service companies, such as Urban Decision Systems, Equifax/National Decision Systems, CACI, National Data Planning Corp., Urban Decision Systems, and R. R. Donnelley currently provide preliminary 1990 employment data. Additional data from the census will be incorporated as the information becomes available. These services also estimate daytime working population. All the data can be purchased. (See Chapter 8 for 800 phone numbers.)

SUMMARY

For the individual restaurateur or fast food operator, it is not necessary to reinvent the wheel when it comes to evaluating employment. It is in your best interest, however, to understand the types and sizes of employment within the potential market area, as well as any positive or negative job trends that are taking place. A careful review before committing yourself to a specific area or location not only can avoid a misconception but also can clarify areas of greatest opportunity, thereby increasing the potential for higher sales and greater profitability.

Fourteen

Income and Expenditure Dynamics

Consumer income is the most critical variable in the determination of expenditures for food services. The amount of income, fixed-expenditure commitments, discretionary dollars, household size, age of family members, type of employment, and other factors play a role in how income is spent. This chapter explores the importance of income, the elements that affect its distribution, and methods for determining expenditures of food service dollars within a trade area. To obtain some idea of how much potential exists within a market area, it is necessary to identify income, evaluate its components, and estimate the food expenditure portion from which your share can be captured.

During the 1980s, the United States experienced a significant shift in household income. While it did not directly affect all households, it certainly had an indirect effect on most of them. The switch from an industrial to a service economy has markedly influenced discretionary buying power, which, in turn, has had a dramatic impact (both positive and negative) on food service. These changes are expected to continue in the early 1990s.

As a result of the shift to service economies, numerous wage earners have seen their earnings decline. Average household income may not reflect that decline, however, because the reduction in salary or wages to one individual employed in the household has usually been offset by the salary or wages contributed by a working spouse (or roommate). Nevertheless, hourly manufacturing wages at $13 to $15 an hour have been replaced with service-type wages at about $6 to $8 an hour. *The decline has had a notable impact on the demand for food service facilities in many markets throughout the United States.*

VARIATIONS IN INCOME

Income has undergone volatile gyrations during the 1970s and 1980s, as witnessed by the tremendous inflation of 1972–1973; the "depression" of 1974–1975; the continued inflation of 1976–1978; the recession of 1979 to 1981; the slow recovery of the early 1980s; and the recession/depression of the early 1990s. While most of the 1980s did not experience the wild fluctuations of the 1970s, for many families, income did not keep pace with expenditures. In fact, the incomes of more and more Americans are not meeting their expectations, nor will they in the near future. More specifically, many low- and middle-income families, and even upper-middle and high-income families, are having difficulty maintaining their standards of living. Union wage and fringe benefit concessions also have often resulted in lower disposable income. These changes in income are partially responsible for the "couch potato." While the couch potato is frequently considered to be a phenomenon of our casual and lazy society, people sometimes sit at home watching television for more cogent reasons, such as pressure on discretionary buying power, the lack of babysitters, the aging of the population, and fatigue in households where both spouses are wage earners.

The squeeze on income varies geographically, and the federal government's forecasts of changes in personal income often do not accurately reflect what is happening in area households. Important income variations occur in normal everyday life in every neighborhood. If, in the search for a location, you were looking for a group of households with incomes above $50,000, you might be satisfied to know that there are, say, 10,000 households with incomes above that figure. However, this information can be very misleading. Here are five households with incomes of $50,000.

Household 1

This household is composed of two young professionals who recently completed college and who have a combined income of $50,000. They currently rent an apartment, have two cars and two car payments, eat almost all their breakfast and lunch meals away from home, and eat dinner out two to three times a week. In addition, they take two vacations a year, utilizing one week for skiing and one in the Caribbean. They live on "plastic" and most often have significant credit card balances. They are a restaurateur's ideal.

Household 2

This household is composed of two working adults and two small children. The husband is a truck driver, and the wife works as a salesperson in a department store. Household 2 has owned a house for three years and has a mortgage payment of more than $1,000 a month. In addition, this household has a woman who comes in and watches their children daily while the parents are at work. Both members "brown bag" lunches, and eat only an occasional dinner meal away from home because of the high operating expenses of the household, including babysitters.

Household 3

In this household there are also two wage earners making a total of $50,000. Their two children are in college. The mortgage on the home is about $600 a month. The family has one car, which is paid off. The children attend a state university, nevertheless, tuition, room, board, and expenses are running about $12,000 a year. Student loans supplement the expenditure to the extent of $7,000, leaving $5,000 as a direct cash outlay from the household budget. The parents eat most breakfast and lunch meals away from home, and most dinner meals at home. Only occasionally do they go out for dinner, normally on Saturday night.

Household 4

There are five household members—the husband (who is the sole wage earner), his wife, and three children. Two of the children are in high school, while one is elementary school. The family owns a home and two cars. The mortgage payment is approximately $1,000 a month, and the loan installments on the two cars amount to about $800 a month. The household is trying to save some money for college expenses; however, they are not achieving much success. The majority of this household's meals are consumed at home, while the principal wage earner brown bags his lunch. Occasionally, the parents go out for dinner, but more often, they eat at friends' homes as part of a dining club that rotates through the member households.

Household 5

This household consists of a single professional person who eats most workdays meals near work. Dinner is occasionally consumed at home. This individual's primary expenses are rent and car payments. Most weekends are spent eating out or going to parties. Outside social life is extremely important to this individual.

Comparison of the Households

Each of the above households has the same income. However, their expenses and commitments vary considerably. *A specific income figure does not adequately reveal anything other than the income level of people.* It does not indicate their potential disposable eating-out dollars. Experience indicates that if adequate numbers of people earn a given income, there is probably sufficient potential for certain kinds of restaurant facility. Nonetheless, spending patterns can vary widely. It is also necessary, then, to look to the structure of the households and families in the area to better estimate the discretionary buying power.

SOURCES OF INCOME DATA

The primary source of most income data for forecasting purposes is the decennial Census of Population and Housing of the United States. Income data is compiled by states, counties, cities, census tracts, and other civil subdivisions (see Chapter 8), so it is possible to review income structure by relatively small areas. Also, the demographic computer services can provide estimates of income for almost any part of the country. However, as the 1990 census becomes more removed in time, the potential increases for errors in forecasting income.

Today, very few people evaluate income by means of census data. The problem is simply that income data by census tracts usually is not available for at least three years after the census. Thus, income data from the 1990 census will probably not be available until 1993, when the information will be essentially outdated. Instead, individuals either make their own forecasts or utilize forecasts from other sources, primarily the computer demographic services that estimate current household and family income and make forecasts for three, four, or five years.

Income data have proven very difficult to forecast accurately, particularly during the past 20 years. Personal income has both enjoyed the roller coaster ride and suffered on it. The periods of high inflation often eliminated any real income change, while at other times, deflation actually allowed the consumer to get slightly ahead. Overall, given the changes in our society, the average consumer is worse off today than he or she was in the 1960s. Fortunately, the food industry largely escaped the impact from these changes because of the significant rise in the number of working women and the growth of white-collar employment. Recent changes in food service sales and customer count growth have awakened the industry to the importance of income, household structure, and the age of the population.

It is necessary to review *household* income, rather than *family* income because of societal changes, such as people living together, single parents raising children, and other unorthodox living arrangements. Households include all the people residing in a particular dwelling unit. In contrast, family income relates only to those blood members of the family residing in a dwelling unit.

Another way to assess income change is on a "per capita basis," which is simply the income per person. To utilize per capita income and compare it with other markets or other locations, it is necessary to review household size, since larger households will bring down the per capita income and smaller households will raise it. Per capita income is an excellent way of evaluating possible future income, as well as the changes that have taken place in income and household sizes. It takes into consideration household size, which household income does not. Sources of household income information include the following:

- *U.S. Department of Commerce, Bureau of the Census*
  1990 Census of Population CP-2: Social and Economic Characteristics
  Special Census Data for individual cities (usually not available)
  Series P-25 (see Chapter 8)
  Series P-26 (see Chapter 8)
  Series P-60 (see Chapter 8)
- *Demographic Computer Services.* Most provide per capita, household, and family income, as well as forecasts of income for three or five years. They are described in detail in Chapter 8.
  Urban Decision Systems
  Equifax-National Decision Systems
  CACI, Inc.
  CLARITAS/NPDC
  Donnelley Marketing Information Services
  Compusearch (Canada)
- *Sales and Marketing Management Survey of Buying Power (Annual).* Detailed Income and Five-Year Forecast by metropolitan areas, cities, and counties; often available in local libraries; provides data in greater detail for a fee.
- *Editors and Publishers Market Guide (Annual).* Current income estimate by metropolitan areas, cities, and counties; usually available in local libraries.
- *Restaurant Business Magazine (Annual).* Current income estimate by metropolitan areas; generated from *Sales Marketing Management* data and modified for the food service industry.
- *Others*
  Occasional Internal Revenue Service studies of income by metropolitan areas
  Income data generated by newspaper consumer research
  Detailed consumer research studies conducted in specific metropolitan areas

Income forecasting is both simple and difficult. Some forecasters use the simple "straight line method" (the same growth percentage over a given number of years), reflecting the trend of income within a metropolitan area, a neighborhood, or a trade area. Others carry out a more definite evaluation of income, recognizing the impact of changing age, types of employment, household size, local wage rates, and other factors necessary for definitive income forecasting.

In recent years, the computer demographic data services have made it easy for the average layperson by providing income estimates and forecasts. Variations in income forecasts exist among the individual data services. If you evaluate the key elements of household size, look at the income structure by income range, including the number of households in each income range, consider the age of the children, and gain some insight into the size of the mortgages, any of the major computer demographic data services will be acceptable.

You may also encounter income forecasts by local planning agencies in both *constant* and *real* dollars. A *constant income forecast* simply holds the value of the dollar constant for a specific year (excluding any inflation) in forecasting income for the future. While this is not realistic in relation to what will actually happen, it removes the inflationary element, which in itself is often difficult to forecast. *Real income forecasts* represent the actual dollars that people are expected to have (including inflation) at some future date. Most income forecasts, particularly the computer demographic data services, provide for both real and inflationary change, especially when the forecast is for a five-year period. Since restaurant and fast-food people are working in the "real world," actual forecasts of income for the next five years, including both real and inflationary dollars, are important to assess probable sales five years into the future.

EXPENDITURE DYNAMICS

The term *expenditure dynamics* refers to the dollars for which restaurant and fast food operations are competing. The primary source of data is the Census of Business—Retail Trade, updated every five years. The reports are available from the United States Department of Commerce, Bureau of the Census, Census of Business. The reports include a category known as Eating and Drinking Place sales, or further stratification of the sales category includes: eating places, drinking places, restaurants, cafeterias, lunchrooms, and fast-food. Figure 14.1 depicts two pages from the United States Department of Commerce, Bureau of the Census, Census of Retail Trade, Geographic Area Series for the State of Illinois, 1987. The

FIGURE 14.1

Sample Report from the U.S. Department of Commerce

Table 8. Summary Statistics for Metropolitan Statistical Areas: 1987—Con.

[Includes only establishments with payroll. For meaning of abbreviations and symbols, see introductory text. For explanation of terms and comparability of 1982 and 1987 censuses, including revised methodology for presenting establishment counts, see appendix A. For definitions of CMSA's, MSA's, and PMSA's, see appendix D]

1987 SIC code	Geographic area and kind of business	Estab- lishments (number)	Sales ($1,000)	Annual payroll ($1,000)	First quarter payroll ($1,000)	Paid employees for pay period including March 12 (number)	Unincorporated businesses	
							Individual proprie- torships (number)	Partner- ships (number)
	CHICAGO-GARY-LAKE COUNTY, IL-IN-WI CMSA—Con.							
	Chicago, IL PMSA							
	Retail trade	**31 656**	**38 752 961**	**4 764 648**	**1 129 572**	**457 320**	**5 500**	**1 252**
52	**Building materials and garden supplies stores**	**1 178**	**1 530 367**	**204 830**	**46 685**	**15 286**	**191**	**47**
521, 3	Building materials and supply stores	585	1 039 925	125 724	28 873	8 646	56	12
521	Lumber and other building materials dealers	359	893 897	105 235	24 087	7 025	27	8
523	Paint, glass, and wallpaper stores	226	146 028	20 489	4 786	1 621	29	4
525	Hardware stores	423	329 938	54 736	12 783	4 725	96	25
526	Retail nurseries, lawn and garden supply stores	154	149 880	22 513	4 610	1 823	38	9
527	Mobile home dealers	16	10 624	1 857	419	92	1	1
53	**General merchandise stores**	**491**	**4 345 739**	**471 277**	**110 066**	**46 237**	**67**	**11**
531	Department stores (incl. leased depts.)	176	4 006 232	(NA)	(NA)	(NA)	—	—
531	Department stores (excl. leased depts.)	176	3 759 178	417 856	96 672	40 158	—	—
531 pt.	Conventional	32	1 234 371	141 073	33 700	11 008	—	—
531 pt.	Discount or mass merchandising	105	1 224 155	124 000	27 884	14 422	—	—
531 pt.	National chain	39	1 300 652	152 783	35 088	14 728	—	—
533	Variety stores	123	102 854	16 248	3 945	2 011	20	4
539	Miscellaneous general merchandise stores	192	483 707	37 173	9 449	4 068	47	7

54	**Food stores**	**3 638**	**6 692 081**	**694 781**	**178 001**	**69 117**	**798**	**168**
541	Grocery stores	2 130	6 138 780	599 056	155 533	56 996	439	66
542	Meat and fish (seafood) markets	275	161 828	18 386	4 436	1 605	83	19
546	Retail bakeries	620	194 414	51 517	12 194	6 686	145	39
546 pt.	Retail bakeries—baking and selling	560	173 884	47 340	11 145	6 116	138	38
546 pt.	Retail bakeries—selling only	60	20 530	4 177	1 049	570	7	1
543, 4, 5, 9	Other food stores	613	197 059	25 822	5 838	3 830	131	44
543	Fruit and vegetable markets	92	67 592	6 000	1 315	870	27	10
544	Candy, nut, and confectionery stores	263	60 354	10 353	2 443	1 495	29	19
545	Dairy products stores	96	17 204	2 274	438	505	49	2
549	Miscellaneous food stores	162	51 909	7 195	1 642	960	26	13
55 ex 554	**Automotive dealers**	**1 419**	**7 757 989**	**666 159**	**150 389**	**27 222**	**117**	**32**
551	New and used car dealers	460	7 013 845	561 231	125 927	20 447	19	9
552	Used car dealers	170	145 397	13 757	3 240	798	33	6
553	Auto and home supply stores	670	436 049	74 858	17 749	5 011	54	14
553 pt.	Tire, battery, and accessory dealers	635	409 408	72 793	17 271	4 757	43	13
553 pt.	Other auto and home supply stores	35	26 641	2 065	478	254	11	1
555, 6, 7, 9	Miscellaneous automotive dealers	119	162 698	16 313	3 473	966	11	3
555	Boat dealers	40	40 042	3 853	812	256	3	—
556	Recreational vehicle dealers	21	45 350	4 375	1 062	226	3	1
557	Motorcycle dealers	51	62 522	7 244	1 393	446	4	1
559	Automotive dealers, n.e.c.	7	14 784	841	206	38	1	1
554	**Gasoline service stations**	**1 875**	**2 128 561**	**126 571**	**30 366**	**12 403**	**635**	**91**
56	**Apparel and accessory stores**	**3 844**	**2 883 820**	**364 295**	**86 849**	**39 296**	**410**	**100**
561	Men's and boys' clothing stores	477	337 007	53 039	13 703	3 924	71	13
562, 3	Women's clothing and speciality stores	1 549	1 126 586	142 962	34 347	16 774	177	44
562	Women's clothing stores	1 302	970 120	121 348	28 667	15 126	141	33
563	Women's accessory and speciality stores	247	156 466	21 614	5 680	1 648	36	11
565	Family clothing stores	380	762 277	81 292	18 657	9 591	41	15
566	Shoe stores	1 105	504 143	68 265	15 671	6 642	57	14
566 pt.	Men's shoe stores	149	72 956	10 263	2 306	757	8	2
566 pt.	Women's shoe stores	335	166 260	25 259	5 787	2 168	6	3
566 pt.	Children's and juveniles' shoe stores	41	11 326	1 895	437	218	1	—
564 pt.	Family shoe stores	580	253 601	30 848	7 141	3 499	42	9
564, 9	Other apparel and accessory stores	333	153 807	18 737	4 471	2 365	64	14

FIGURE 14.1 *(Continued)*

1987 SIC code	Geographic area and kind of business	Establishments (number)	Sales ($1,000)	Annual payroll ($1,000)	First quarter payroll ($1,000)	Paid employees for pay period including March 12 (number)	Unincorporated businesses Individual proprietorships (number)	Partnerships (number)
564	Children's and infants' wear stores	142	93 662	9 532	2 264	1 433	25	7
569	Miscellaneous apparel and accessory stores	191	60 145	9 205	2 207	932	39	7
57	**Furniture and homefurnishings stores**	**2 374**	**2 262 463**	**292 740**	**67 815**	**19 426**	**291**	**34**
5712	Furniture stores	619	743 851	108 622	25 100	6 209	69	9
5713, 4, 9	Homefurnishings stores	811	565 211	80 594	18 131	5 872	110	9
5713	Floor covering stores	292	296 941	40 505	9 154	1 991	42	3
5714	Drapery and upholstery stores	122	45 900	7 707	1 816	656	21	2
5719	Miscellaneous homefurnishings stores	397	222 370	32 382	7 161	3 225	47	4
572	Household appliance stores	127	182 529	18 514	4 346	1 117	29	3
573	Radio, television, computer, and music stores	817	770 872	85 010	20 238	6 228	83	13
5731	Radio, television, and electronics stores	424	497 053	52 154	12 500	3 511	50	8
5734	Computer and software stores	97	75 129	9 605	2 146	561	6	—
5735	Record and precorded tape stores	187	128 159	12 178	2 840	1 496	11	5
5736	Musical instrument stores	109	70 531	11 073	2 752	660	16	—
58	**Eating and drinking places**	**9 605**	**4 217 873**	**1 079 801**	**251 123**	**159 251**	**1 762**	**500**
5812	Eating places	8 092	3 946 163	1 021 689	237 365	151 304	1 424	461
5812 pt.	Restaurants and lunchrooms	3 720	2 028 715	555 845	131 453	76 859	630	208
5812 pt.	Cafeterias	86	43 892	11 285	2 526	1 633	19	3
5812 pt.	Refreshment places	3 310	1 406 254	322 702	73 236	56 035	640	219
5812 pt.	Other eating places	976	467 302	131 857	30 150	16 777	135	31
5813	Drinking places	1 513	271 710	58 112	13 758	7 947	338	39
591	**Drug and proprietary stores**	**1 397**	**2 034 900**	**222 707**	**54 191**	**19 987**	**111**	**30**
591 pt.	Drug stores	1 331	2 001 838	218 821	53 076	19 536	105	29
591 pt.	Proprietary stores	66	33 062	3 886	1 115	451	6	1
59 ex 591	**Miscellaneous retail stores**	**5 835**	**4 899 168**	**641 487**	**154 087**	**49 095**	**1 118**	**239**

table presents retail sales data for the Chicago Primary Metropolitan Statistical Area (PMSA). Note especially the sales information under the Eating and Drinking Places category. Provided are subcategories for various types of eating and drinking establishments. The Census of Business is completed every five years and is published approximately two to three years later. The next census will be conducted in 1992 and will be available in 1994 and 1995. The following individual publications are available for each state:

- Census of Retail Trade—State.
- Census of Wholesale Trade—State.
- Census of Service Industries.

The report that will interest you most is the Census of Retail Trade, which contains data for counties, cities, and towns, as well as detailed sales data for downtown areas, cities, and metropolitan areas. These documents also include sales comparisons with previous censuses. The Census of Business provides a historical base, indicating the number of dollars that have been spent by consumers in the Eating and Drinking category, along with the number of establishments.

An annual evaluation of expenditures in the food industry is provided in the September issue of *Restaurant Business* magazine. The magazine's Restaurant Growth Index has been published for more than 20 years. This compendium of market data provides major market segment trends, sales, units, growth rates, five-year forecasts, for regional sections, metropolitan areas, and ADI (area of dominant influence), and market rankings. Moreover, sales forecasts are provided for eating and drinking places, eating places, fast food operations, and restaurants. The basic data are derived from *Sales Marketing Management, Market Statistics*, and the annual forecasts are adjusted every five or six years through the use of the Census of Business results.

Additional sources of expenditures include the computer demographic data services that utilize the 1987 Census of Business to compute dollars generated in expenditure categories including Eating and Drinking Places. Thus, they can provide expenditure estimates for any trade area for the Eating and Drinking Places category. Some provide more detail than others. *The data from the computer demographic data services represent an estimate of the potential within the trading area.*

Some of us like to evaluate retail sales trends and convert them into a more usable form as a basis for forecasting future potential. This procedure is a good check and balance against the estimates furnished by other sources. To do this, it is necessary to analyze the changes that have taken place in the Eating and Drinking Places category for at least the past five years and, perhaps, for a full 10-year period. This is especially important in evaluating a particular city or town. In going through the fieldwork process and developing a clear understanding of the components of change within an area, it helps significantly to evaluate the changes that have taken place in eating and drinking sales. The first step is to determine which segment of those sales pertains to your type of operation.

The 1987 Census of Business provides sales in the Eating and Drinking Places category, as well as a number of subcategories (see Figure 14.1). Eating Places, under Eating and Drinking Places, includes restaurants and lunchrooms, cafeterias, refreshment places, and other eating establishments. For example, if you have a full-service restaurant providing cocktails, the dollars for which you are competing are generally the total Eating and Drinking Places category. You might wish to define a specific potential more clearly by referring to the forecasts in *Restaurant Business*. If you are in the cafeteria business, you might want to take the data from an overall cafeteria sales basis and try to relate it to a smaller market size by adjusting the relationship of the cafeteria sales to the total sales in a particular area. Regardless, you are probably not going to be competing for the total Eating and Drinking Places dollars.

Another way to evaluate changes in eating and drinking, or fast food sales is to analyze the changes that have taken place on a per capita basis. To arrive at that data, take the census data (the most current now being distributed is 1987) and divide it by the population for the same defined area (city, county, town, and the like). You might use the *1988 Statistical Abstract of the United States*, available in most local libraries. It may also be purchased from the U.S. Department of Commerce.

An additional method for determining sales potential within an area is to consider the relationship of household income to eating and drinking sales. Historically, local residents have spent between 3% and 6% of their household income on meals away from home, but this percentage has been rising. By reviewing a community's retail sales data (1987 Census of Retail Trade), you can divide the sales by the total number of households and determine the per capita household eating and drinking sales. Next, by dividing that figure by average household income, you can determine the general percentage of sales that are derived from household income. It should be between 3% and 6%. This will provide local parameters of income that can be a check and balance against the computer demographic services.

In some markets, you may find that the amount of dollars being spent is below normal levels. This may be because a majority of the residents work in another community and thus spend the dollars elsewhere, or it might represent an untapped market. A comparison of the potential sales with what has actually been spent may indicate an opportunity. A word of caution! There are very few markets in the United States that, on a *quantitative* basis, reflect an unmet need; and conversely, there are numerous markets throughout the United States that, on a *qualitative* analysis, reflect an opportunity. Qualitative implies various levels of quality, value, and service. It is important to study not only the income and household expenditures but also those market segments that are successfully capitalizing on that potential. Whereas the dollars are being spent somewhere, the restaurants and fast food operations are not necessarily meeting the market need effectively. Obviously, that is why different restaurant and fast food operations can enter markets that appear to be overstored and compete very successfully. Nonetheless, you must understand the potential dollar availability, compared with the strength of the existing competitive facilities within a market segment, to truly understand the potential that may or may not exist.

The eating and drinking expenditures generated from the Census of Business—Retail Trade, and modified to today, usually represent the lowest estimate of eating and drinking potential, unless the community generates considerable tourists or convention business. That is primarily because it includes the entire metropolitan area (all incomes) and is generated from actual retail sales. Since it shows all socioeconomic groups and areas, it tends to pull down the actual figures generated. Finally, it measures actual, not potential, sales.

The personal income approach involves taking the average income of the households and applying expenditure ratios. For example, if the household income were $43,500, and we applied a 5% expenditure ratio, the household would spend approximately $2,175 annually for food and drink consumed outside the home. Next, if we divide the $2,175 spent annually by the household by the number of persons per household (2.3), we would arrive at an estimate of per capita potential for the household of $946. We can then compare this figure with the forecast of per capita expenditures in the September issue of *Restaurant Business*. We can also buy a report from a computer service with their expenditure estimates of eating and drinking potential.

If you are looking at a specific site and have purchased a demographic report from a service, you can make your own computations. Take the median household income and multiply it by both 4% and 5% (4% for fast food and 5% for restaurants). Next, divide it by the persons per household provided in the report to arrive at the per capita eating and drinking expenditures. If you apply this figure to the population within your trade area, you will have computed the total eating and drinking potential for which your unit may be competing.

SUMMARY

All the methods for estimating income and expenditures can provide a check and balance system to review the information that you use. Once you are satisfied with the per capita figure comparison, you will know which set of data appears to be the most reliable. Income is a critical factor in the determination of sales potential. If you understand the data sources, their meaning, and the methods to evaluate them, you will find that it is a fairly simple task to determine your food operation's potential.

Fifteen

Generative Areas

Generative areas are concentrations that attract "people and automobile" activity. The majority of restaurant and fast food facilities require generative activity to succeed. That is why so many operators locate their establishments near generators. Some equate generative activities with traffic, while others recognize patterns and the need for interception. Regardless of the reason, the objective is *action for opportunity.*

Of the numerous types of generative areas, perhaps the first in our cities were the downtown areas. They were the concentrations of commerce, and gateways for new arrivals. Inns, stables, railroad stations, harbors, boarding houses, financial markets, shopping with adjacent housing, and numerous other activity-generating facilities were located downtown. As a result, hotel and food facilities developed within these areas, until the growth of cities and the advent of the automobile brought about a dramatic change in our society. Following World War II, the automobile increased consumer mobility significantly, thus creating new concentrations of activity, while changing others. Today, there are numerous generative areas, both in the central city and suburbia.

Generative areas are vital to the average fast food operation and to many restaurants because they establish patterns and attract large numbers of people, generally on a highly frequent basis. Generative areas are not necessarily important to the higher priced, ambience-oriented dinner houses. Nevertheless, generative areas should be taken into consideration when thinking about a location for any facility, simply because good locations can protect against competitive erosion.

As indicated in Chapter 10, people are, in fact, creatures of habit. Thus, awareness of generative areas and the extent of their activity generation is important in identifying the types of locations that each individual fast food or restaurant facility must have for success. The significance of generative areas is determined primarily by two major activities: *work* and *shopping*. Of course, there are other activities, such as visiting the health club; however, they usually occur with less frequency. From an operator's viewpoint, generative areas might include hotel or motel concentrations, airports, major medical centers, marinas, universities, recreational facilities, and industrial parks. Extremes in activity generation include such places as Disney complexes, Las Vegas, and Atlantic City.

Let us examine the different types of concentrations and their impacts on varying types of food operations. *Exceptions have occurred in the past and will occur in the future. Once again, however, they are few and far between.* If you want to make the most of your location in relation to customer characteristics and profile and, at the same time, to protect the facility from competitive hazard, it is wise to fully understand the activity ingredients that will maximize the opportunity and minimize the risk.

WORK-ORIENTED CONCENTRATIONS

Since people usually work five to six days a week, employment concentrations are significant to food operators. Initially, employment was concentrated in or near the downtown area. The advent of the automobile expanded consumer mobility, and the decentralization of employment shifted the concentration of employment away from downtown. Moreover, new opportunities were created for additional restaurants to serve the expanding employment and residential development. Ultimately, the massive development of suburbia occurred and, along with it, the proliferation of restaurant and fast food facilities.

More recently, the shift from an industrial economy to a service economy has further resulted in major changes in our society. These shifting patterns not only have affected the past but will have a profound effect on the future of individual market opportunities. In many areas, the proliferation of employment is in offices; while in other areas, it is concentrated in industrial parks. In still others, it might be a combination of the two. In a few cities, one or more major employers may dominate the market, such as NCR in Dayton, Ohio, Boeing in Seattle, Washington, or insurance companies in Hartford, Connecticut. Regardless, employment concentrations are major activity generators. In determining how significant they are and what possibilities they individually offer for food development opportunities, the first step is to know whether this factor is significant to your business. For example, a food operation doing a strong breakfast and luncheon business is generally highly oriented toward employment activities. Conversely, a restaurant that relies heavily on dinner trade usually does not depend on employment activities. The difference depends on the clientele and the hours that the facility does business.

Office Complexes

The original office complexes in almost all cities occurred downtown, with subsequent decentralization to suburban sectors. That the offices exist by themselves is not the primary consideration. What matters is the employment factor itself. Downtown employment and ways to collect employment information and its impact or opportunities are discussed in Chapter 24.

It is also important to review the kinds of office users and the numbers of visitors that are generally attracted to an office concentration. A word of caution: *Daytime activity does not mean nighttime activity;* an office complex may be "dead city" at night. If your facility requires a strong dinner business, you may want to avoid such areas.

Governmental office complexes often contain substantial numbers of employees. However, our studies have found that this category has a higher than normal incidence of "brown baggers," and that these complexes usually generate lower than normal restaurant potential and sometimes limited fast food opportunities. Also, governmental complexes do not usually generate dinner business. An exception may be a location in proximity to the state capitol, which may be a gathering place for legislators and lobbyists.

Another influential factor is that the majority of employees traveling to and from work are like cattle on a stampede; they are difficult to stop. The old adage: "Be on the 'going-home' side of the street" does have validity in some areas but is not an absolute rule.

Age, family size, marital status, and other factors play a role in the likelihood of intercepting office or home-bound workers. Older, married workers are likely to have fixed habits, and thus are difficult to intercept. Young people who are single, or married without children, are much easier to intercept, since they usually do not want to bother with fixing a meal at the end of the workday. Middle-aged individuals with children are the hardest to intercept, because they often have less discretionary buying power and eat more meals at home.

Industrial Concentrations

Opportunities usually exist for various types of food service facilities in industrial concentrations, particularly if considerable shift work occurs throughout a 24-hour period. Bars and grills, fast food units, and roadhouses have been quite successful in many areas, especially, in the northeastern and midwestern states. The secret to capitalizing on locational opportunities in industrial concentrations is to understand the type of employment in the industrial concentration, hours, shift changes, amount of time for "lunch," the size of the employment market, the streets leading into and out of the area, the strength of competition, and the presence or absence of company food facilities for employees.

You should consider the future of the industrial area, especially where heavy industry is concerned. While it is difficult, if not impossible, to forecast the demise of a major industry, there are clues. For example, the steel industry has been hard hit by imports; because of labor costs, the printing industry has shifted to the South, as did the textile industry decades ago. On the positive side, the southeastern and southwestern states are the recipients of new industry of all types. It is important to recognize shifting trends and to consider their implications for the area under consideration.

Special Employment Concentrations

This category refers to employees who represent a market for a food facility while providing services to another group, who may also represent a potential market. An example of a special employment concentration would be an airport. The food orientation there usually is in two directions, toward the passengers or toward the employees. Most often, these are separate groups, and each food facility must be positioned to intercept the specific market for which it is oriented.

There is a more detailed explanation of airport facilities later in this chapter.

Military Installations

Military bases have long been generators of varying activities, including fast food units, restaurants, bars, and other entertainment facilities. The most important consideration, initially, is the installation's stability. Changes in military appropriations apparently will reduce the size of some bases and close many more. To determine what the current and likely future situation might be, talk to the base commandant or the public relations officer. Also, talk to your local congressman or senator regarding their thoughts on the subject.

SHOPPING COMPLEXES

The second largest generative concentration (sometimes the first) usually includes shopping centers, malls, or large commercial areas. While often the second in overall concentration, malls are usually first in activity for restaurant and fast food facilities. The primary reason is that the activity occurs throughout the day and evening and especially on weekends. Thus, it has consistency and generates customers at an additional daypart. Furthermore, trips to go shopping are usually more relaxed than work-oriented activities.

Neighborhood or Convenience Goods Shopping Centers and Districts

These centers are basically composed of supermarkets, drugstores, hardware stores, liquor stores, cleaners, laundromats, banks, savings and loan associations, currency exchanges, and other small retailers. Such retail clusters usually serve a narrow trade area and are probably the least desirable locations for most restaurants and fast food facilities. In the northeastern states, where population density is extreme, and land availability is often scarce, restaurants can sometimes do well in these areas.

Convenience goods shopping centers and smaller commercial districts, to be discussed more fully in Chapter 25, usually range in size from about 10,000 square feet to 100,000 square feet, depending on the size of the supermarkets. Because of economies of scale and other reasons, today's supermarkets range between 30,000 and 100,000 square feet, capturing *weekly* sales between $200,000 and $1,500,000 or $10,000,00 to $80,000,000 annually.

The point to keep in mind is that convenience goods shopping centers and districts usually serve narrow trade areas and a restaurateur planning to capitalize on the number of people generated to the area, must recognize that fact. Conversely, these shopping complexes usually enjoy a high frequency of customer visit. As a result, such a location often makes up for the lack of trade area size by the frequency with which the residents patronize the commercial facilities. These locations are usually desirable for pizzerias, bars and grills, deli's, Chinese restaurants, sandwich shops, and small family restaurants.

Community Shopping Centers and Districts

Normally larger in size than neighborhood and convenience goods shopping centers and districts, community shopping centers and districts usually contain a limited-line department store, a discount department store, or a major off-price store as its primary generator. In some cases, it might be a major catalog store (Service Merchandise), a promotional electronics store (Comp USA), a toy store (Toys R' Us), or an appliance store (Silo), which in the past few years has produced unusually high sales volume. Perhaps the stores most often associated with community shopping centers are K-Mart and Wal-Mart; similar facilities are usually located in community shopping centers throughout the United States. These complexes generally range in size from 100,000 to 250,000 square feet.

Many fast food operations and restaurant facilities have taken locations on discount department store pads or in proximity to community shopping center developments. Some have been successful; it appears, however, many restaurants have been less fortunate. The primary reason for the dichotomy is that some community shopping centers simply are not generative enough activity. Successful facilities, in addition to meeting a market demand, normally have a strong match of customer characteristics to the resident population characteristics, and traffic counts adequate for the type of facility at the times of day necessary for the particular restaurant operation. Community shopping centers, by themselves, seldom will generate enough activity to provide the market for most restaurant and some fast food operations. If the shopping center is situated on a street with adequate traffic, then the location may represent an excellent opportunity. Naturally, the characteristics of the resident population and the driving public must be compatible.

Power Centers

Large numbers of power centers are being developed throughout the United States. Power centers are a collection of highly promotional retailers (generally known as "category killers" because of their advertising and pricing), who generate very high sales per square foot. The power center normally has a large warehouse-type supermarket of more than 50,000 square feet, along with major off-price stores, such as T. J. Maxx, Mervyn's, Marshall's, and Phar-Mor Superstores. They also normally have a limited number of small stores. It is common for power centers to generate between $400 and $1,200 per square foot. Power centers generally range from 200,000 to 400,000 square feet, although some are much larger.

Older Major Business Districts

The northeast, midwestern, and some southern cities have older business districts with concentrations of commercial facilities that usually exceed 1,000,000 square feet. Most often, one or more department stores are part of the older business district complex. Parking is usually provided in parking decks or on the street, and there is very little coordination between retailers. These areas can represent opportunities for restaurants and fast food operations, particularly on the major arteries leading to and from the business districts. In come cases, public transportation is an important factor, particularly at the points where passengers transfer from one route to another. As usual, it is necessary to have appropriate ingress and egress.

Regional Shopping Centers and Malls

Other than the downtown areas, the greatest single generative complex within our metropolitan areas normally is the major regional shopping center or mall. Most complexes contain anywhere from two to six department stores and occupy more than 1,000,000 square feet. Highly successful shopping centers and malls generate sales in excess of $200,000,000 per annually. In medium-size communities, and in some older urban areas, shopping centers generally range between 400,000 and 800,000 square feet; whereas in smaller communities, they may range between 200,000 and 400,000 square feet. Nevertheless, they are the focal point of all major shoppers' goods shopping activity within significant trade areas. As a result of this high focus of attention, consumers visit such centers on a highly frequent basis making them an integral part of their shopping habits and patterns. This is one reason so many restaurants and fast food facilities are in proximity to regional shopping centers and malls.

Perhaps a clearer way to examine the impact of a regional shopping center is to consider its trip generations, that is, the number of trips that are created to and from a major mall on an average day. A shopping center capturing sales of $200,000,000 with the usual compliment of secondary centers and stores might expect to generate between 25,000 and 40,000 car trips per day (one trip each way). Conversely, a community shopping center that captures sales of approximately $30,000,000 annually might expect to generate approximately 7,000 to 10,000 car trips per day. Notice the significant difference between the two facilities. Thus, as discussed in other chapters, the significant factor in evaluating activity generators is not necessarily their size, but the number of people that they attract to specific areas. Therefore, *sales per square foot* for a regional shopping center or mall or, for that matter, any commercial complex, are far more important than the number of square feet in the complex.

HOTEL CONCENTRATIONS

There are numerous places throughout North America where a concentration of hotels or motels has generated markets for restaurant facilities. Hotels in proximity to the international airports in Chicago and Los Angeles represent examples of such a concentration. Such clusters of hotels and motels create markets for food facilities although, over the years, hotel restaurants have improved. Historically, they were avoided by travelers since the hotel's dining facilities were secondary to the primary purpose of providing rooms. Food, in that context was a "necessary evil."

To evaluate opportunities, you should identify the hotel or motel's total number of rooms, occupancy levels, room rates, dining facilities, and level of amenities (budget versus luxury). Additionally, you must determine the in-house restaurants' degree of success, their utilization, quality of food, excitement, and special qualities. Also, you must look at the competitive restaurant and fast food facilities that have been developed in proximity to the hotel or motel and their relative success.

RESORT AREAS—FAMILY AND ADULT PLAYGROUNDS

This category can be divided into several subcategories. For example, there are gambling resorts, family resorts, resorts oriented principally toward adults, and resorts that focus on seasonal activities. Regardless of the resort's orientation, you must identify the types of visitors, the extent of their stay, the places where they consume most of their meals, the structure of the party (adults versus families), and the size, type, and price structure of hotel facilities. Another serious consideration is the extent of the visitors' orientation to eating facilities outside the hotel or resort, as well as the primary activity that attracts consumers to a particular area, and the mode of transportation usually employed to travel there. This data will indicate the who, what, where, when, and why of consumer movement, which can be vital to decision making.

AIRPORTS

Major airports generate restaurant and fast food opportunities for servicing the passengers in the terminal and also the employees concentrated in and around the airport. Sometimes the facilities can meet both markets, particularly, in small communities. However, in medium and larger cities, the food facilities are often segmented.

In the past, airport food facilities have been selected on the basis of food service contracts, that give a single company control over the entire development of dining, fast food, and bar facilities. Most cities and airports today are fighting the revenue battle. As a result, more and more of them are looking for additional income. A new trend is likely to emerge shortly, encouraging the location of major food operations in airports because they have a high degree of acceptance and the potential to generate considerably more sales dollars. Furthermore, passengers are beginning to voice their objections to the sameness and mediocrity of most airport food. Thus, the major food contracts will probably have exceptions, allowing for the placement of exciting concepts and highly acceptable and well-known food operations in airports. The consumer will benefit, and the food industry will be allowed to flex its innovative muscle.

Food facilities that serve employment at an airport are not necessarily on the airport grounds. Rather, they are often on the major road network entry and exit points to and from the facility.

DOWNTOWN AREAS

The original generative concentrations in most cities were the downtown areas. Chapter 24 contains a discussion of downtown areas and how to determine their generative appeal, the extent of their daytime working population, and the shifting patterns that are taking place in these areas throughout the United States. The changing nature and functions of downtown areas have had a major effect on opportunities for food facilities located there.

MAJOR CONVENTION FACILITIES

Many cities throughout the United States have recently developed or are attempting to develop major convention facilities to attract business to their respective communities and also to service the business that either exists or is planned in the future. Because the extent of the convention activity will determine the market for food operations, those facilities that attract large concentrations of visitors will generate opportunities for dining establishments. Normally, the market for food facilities is either in the complex, near the hotels, or in restaurant row. Most often, the least successful is in the complex. This is especially true if the convention center is located on municipally-owned property. Nevertheless, the activity it generates creates the opportunity for the development of restaurants, bars, and fast food facilities to serve the visitors.

MAJOR UNIVERSITIES AND COLLEGES

Because of concern about the possibility of declining enrollment in the face of significant competition, major universities and colleges are not as much in the forefront as they were approximately 10 years ago. Enrollments, however, have held fairly steady and, in some cases, have actually increased. Universities and colleges are basically of two types: resident schools and commuter institutions. The two are very different in their generative aspects. Resident universities usually have a fairly large student body living on or near campus. Furthermore, they have their own commercial orientation to a specific area or street. The students' habits and patterns—and the placement of the facilities in relation to the primary university buildings—are very important. A commuter school has less potential because the students are far more scattered, as are their expenditures. Nonetheless, there usually is a street that is the acknowledged location for school-related businesses. This concentration can represent an opportunity for student-oriented food and drinking facilities.

A number of fast food operations have also secured locations within student unions of universities and colleges across the United States. This experience has had mixed success. While sales have been excellent, profits have been difficult to maintain because of the unusually high labor turnover. Furthermore, students are perhaps one of the most unpredictable consumer groups because they shift from one favorite place to another, often for quite whimsical reasons. Nonetheless, they are generative and do represent a market opportunity.

With the new emphasis on adult education and erosion in the number of young people, the nature of the student body in many colleges and universities has been changing. In the past, the age structure was between 17 and 25 years. Today, however, the age span can range from 17 to possibly 70 years.

MAJOR MEDICAL COMPLEXES

Some large medical complexes with teaching facilities do provide opportunities for restaurant and fast food facilities, which most often are not in the medical complex itself. Rather, they are often in the general vicinity to serve the employees and those people who are either visiting the medical complex or staying in the area to be near hospitalized relatives and friends. Examples of generative complexes are Mayo Clinic in Rochester, Minnesota; Duke University Medical Complex in Durham, North Carolina; and Northwestern Memorial Hospital Complex in Chicago. Naturally, the extent and the quality of the food facilities within the hospital complex must be evaluated, along with the nearby hotel food facilities, to determine the likely market.

MAJOR RECREATIONAL COMPLEXES

There are three types of major recreational complexes. The first represents pro-active recreational complexes, where individuals participate, either individually or as a team, in a particular sport or recreational activity. The second type is the passive complex, where people participate as spectators of a major event at a stadium, auditorium, or amphitheater. The third type are major amusement parks, such as Disney World, Disneyland, Busch Gardens, and Six Flags.

Recreation for "the body beautiful" has been popular for the past 10 years. Much of this orientation is because the largest population segment in the United States is between 25 and 35 years of age and is very ego oriented. Thus, the number of health clubs and spas of all sizes and varieties has grown significantly as has the number of people participating in their facilities. This strong focus on nutrition and recreation has created new markets in the food field, both in and out of the actual complexes. In fact, recreational complexes in general have become a significant growth activity in our society. Passive recreational facilities, because of their infrequent utilization and, in some cases, because of the changing nature of sports, represent a highly selective food opportunity that requires careful study.

ENTERTAINMENT CONCENTRATIONS

Live theater usually generates dinner business. When theaters in major cities are active, nearby restaurants can expect increased business. Nonetheless, a theater alone will rarely generate sufficient business to ensure a restaurant's success, unless it is part of the theater complex. In that case, the restaurant is packaged with the theater at a single price. When the shows are good, the restaurant usually prospers; however, each case must be examined individually to determine if the location is adequate and accessible.

Movie theaters, miniature golf, baseball batting cages, golf driving ranges, water slides, and go-carts can represent generative opportunities, depending on the extent of the customer attraction, their level of success, longevity, and customer characteristics. For example, a multiplex theater complex may generate afternoon traffic, early evening, after dinner, and "after the movie" traffic. Regardless, the food service operator must determine if the market is compatible with his or her planned customer characteristics. The theater seldom can provide enough customers for success. The food units that benefit usually offer quick service, a desert-oriented menu, and reasonable prices. In addition, they have other customers who have been generated to the location.

Each of the other activities mentioned generate specific age groups, usually in the evenings and on weekends. The food service operator must examine the attraction and its customers to determine the desirability of being in proximity to them.

OTHER GENERATIVE AREAS

Other areas that generate activity and sometimes represent opportunities for various types of restaurants, bars, and fast food facilities include the following:

- Marinas
- Major residential complexes
- Major redevelopment projects in downtown areas
- Highway interchanges
- Restaurant concentrations
- Unique geographical areas
- Railroad depots
- Bus depots
- Others

SUMMARY

"Is my concept or restaurant unique?" Repeat that five times, answer in the affirmative, and you will be typical of the average restaurateur. As a result, you may believe that many of the factors described herein are not applicable or do not matter. Truly unique operations are the exception, and as I have previously indicated, there are some exceptions. They are, however, a minority and even so often are failures. Generative areas are important because they establish habits and patterns. It is much easier to intercept business than to generate it totally on your own. Finally, rental rates and land costs may be higher in generative areas; however, if competition is not excessive, if you are located in the right demographic market, and if you have acceptable access, such areas almost always deliver higher sales.

Sixteen

Market Penetration

Market share and market penetration may seem to be interchangeable terms, but as used herein, they have different meanings. This chapter explores the definitions with regard to restaurant and fast food site selection.

MARKET SHARE

Market share represents the percentage of business captured by a food operation (single or multiple units) in an entire market. The market share approach is normally a "macro" approach, which considers large segments or whole markets in determining market shares. Thus, this chapter will address market share on a macro basis and will consider the relevancy and realism of this approach. We will also discuss a property approach to the micro analysis of the market share.

MARKET PENETRATION

Market penetration is the share of market captured by an individual unit within its own trade area. Therefore, it represents the "batting average" of an individual unit. Market penetration, in my definition, is a "micro" approach. Mainly, it deals with small areas (trade areas and their subparts) and, more specifically, with those areas from which the most frequent visitors originate. Another definition might be the primary trade area. Again, the following pages address the micro approach and my methods of computing market penetration levels.

UNDERSTANDING THE MACRO AND MICRO APPROACHES

The terms *macro* and *micro* are simply technical terms to express a restaurant or fast food unit's batting average for the trade area in which it is competing, or the city or community in which the unit is located.

Consider the following *market share* (macro approach) example: A restaurateur has three units in a city, generating total sales of $4,000,000, and the units are competing for "total eating and drinking expenditures" generated within the market of $80,000,000. Therefore, the market share amounts to 5% ($4,000,000 divided by $80,000,000) of the total market eating and drinking expenditures.

Market penetration (micro approach) approaches the percentage of capture differently. Instead of including the overall city, market penetration addresses the performance of each unit within its own trade area. Table 16.1 depicts the market penetration for each of the trade areas. Notice the difference between the two approaches. The macro, or market share, approach takes the total potential for the entire market ($80,000,000), even though some segments of the market are obviously not served by the three restaurants. In contrast, the micro, or market penetration, approach recognizes that the true measure of potential ($67,000,000) is against the dollars for which the operation is actually competing, and thus, only the trade areas within the market of the units are actually influenced by existing

TABLE 16.1

Market Penetration for Three Restaurants

Unit	Annual Sales	Trade Area Eating and Drinking Potential	Market Penetration(%)
1	$1,600,000	$25,000,000	6.4
2	1,400,000	20,000,000	7.0
3	1,000,000	22,000,000	4.5
Total	$4,000,000	$67,000,000	6.0

restaurants. On that basis, market share reflects an overall share of the market of 5%. In contrast, market penetration reflects that the individual restaurants are competing for a total of $67,000,000 against a total capture of $4,000,000. Thus, the overall market penetration amounts to 6%. Moreover, unit 2 has a market penetration of 7%; unit 1 has a market penetration of 6.4%; and unit 3 has the lowest market penetration, at 4.5%.

Market penetration (particularly if combined with performance in relation to the most frequent customers) can be a highly effective measure of a restaurant's performance on an overall basis, as well as on an individual basis, within a city or metropolitan area. Furthermore, it is an excellent measure against the individual trade area, whether you operate one unit or 1,000 units.

What is the value of understanding the micro application? There are many benefits, including the following:

1. It will provide a better measurement of true performance in the marketplace.
2. If combined with the characteristics of your most frequent customers and the market potential, you can quickly determine the market penetration of your trade area.
3. It provides parameters for analyzing potential new locations. For multi-unit operators, it can provide an effective comparative data bank, which can be utilized in reviewing potential new locations.
4. It can be used to establish specific criteria for identifying potential high volume sites.

USING THE MACRO AND MICRO APPROACHES TO GAUGE SUCCESS

While sales and profits are financial measures of performance, market penetration helps to explain why a particular unit is successful or why it is, perhaps, an underperformer.

The Macro (Market Share) Approach

As previously indicated, the simple method to the market share approach is either to compute or to gather, from a secondary source, the eating and drinking (or just eating-out food) expenditures and compare them with the total sales of the unit or units. This, however, may not be the best method. A better way may be to determine, first of all, a restaurant or fast food unit's detailed customer characteristics. The process identifies who your customers really are. Eliminating noncustomers from the market share computation allows a clear picture of the realistic market share.

Consider the Louisville Metropolitan Area. Assume that a food operation has 10 units in the area, averaging $600,000 per unit, each located in a sector with an average household income of more than $30,000. Moreover, the company determines that they have very few customers with incomes below $20,000. It is realistic to eliminate anyone with less than $20,000 income from the market share computation. Considering the incidence of households with incomes below $20,000 in the Louisville area, such a decision would probably reduce the overall market population by 20%. Thus, the potential for which the 10 restaurants are actually competing would be significantly less than if the potential for the entire Louisville Metropolitan Area were utilized. Eliminating those households who are not potential customers and then comparing the total sales of the restaurants to the potential generated by households with similar characteristics results in a much higher and more realistic market share. The market share computation must consider the differences in socioeconomic characteristics, in relation to the customer profile. Without removing those persons who are not customers, an inaccurate market share percentage will be calculated.

An even more accurate method is to identify your most frequent visitors by their socioeconomic characteristics (these are often referred to as analogs by those who work in this business). Next, identify the people within the metropolitan area who have similar characteristics. By utilizing these data and the eating and drinking (or eating-out food expenditures), you can determine even more accurately the potential or market share possibilities, based on the most significant customer. This information will help in identifying acceptable unit development areas. There are two primary approaches:

- Application of *customer characteristics*, such as age and income, to the resident population's characteristics within the metropolitan area, to identify possible locations.
- Application of *characteristics of the most frequent diners* to the resident population, thereby identifying more specifically,

those geographic areas within the metropolitan area that best match the profile.

A word of caution! In a metropolitan area, the population is often scattered. Whereas many suburban areas share similar socioeconomic characteristics, older areas often do not. Therefore, the metropolitanwide stratification for your customers and, more particularly, your most frequent visitors, may appear to offer a market opportunity for additional stores that does not exist. This discrepancy occurs because the people with matching characteristics are spread over a wide area and thus are not concentrated enough to justify an additional unit. This is one of the failures of the macro approach.

Look at the Louisville Metropolitan Area example again. The area has approximately 1,000,000 people and 361,300 households. Eliminating all the households (and population) with incomes under $20,000 leaves a total of about 880,000 persons in 289,056 households. Next, applying the $733 per capita eating and drinking expenditures for persons with incomes in excess of $20,000 annually gives a total potential of $645,040,000. Since this restaurateur operates 10 units in the Louisville market, capturing a total of $6,000,000, the market share amounts to about 0.9%. Further stratification of the market based on the socioeconomic characteristics of the most frequent visitor revealed that this customer is between 25 and 35 years of age and has an annual income of $25,000 to $40,000. Next, the application of these characteristics to the total population of the Louisville Metropolitan Area indicates that approximately 235,000 people fall into the same categories as the most frequent visitors. Applying the per capita eating and drinking expenditure figure ($733) to this stratified population results in a potential of $172,255,000 for which the units are competing.

Application, then, of the current $6,000,000 in sales must be modified by the percentage generated by the most frequent visitors, which is 65%. Therefore, 65% of the sales equals $3,900,000. The potential generated by people with the same characteristics as the most frequent visitors amounts to $172,255,000. Thus, the market penetration of the existing restaurants, in contrast to the potential, amounts to 2.3%. It is essential to look for concentrations of persons with the characteristics of the most frequent visitor, for their absence could result in the selection of a location with inadequate *true* resources.

The Micro (Market Penetration) Approach

The market penetration approach utilizes a similar evaluation but relates to specific units and their *individual* trade areas. This approach was designed to develop market penetration or market shares for single food units within their trade areas subparts, as well as for the trade area as a whole. Researchers and statisticians refer to the resultant data as analogues. To the less sophisticated, the conclusions represent parameters of market penetrations. The micro approach is an excellent measure of a unit's effectiveness, since it compares the relationship of the sales of an individual unit (and its trade area parts) with the total market for which the unit is competing within its trade area (as seen in subsequent examples). Sales and returns on investment are certainly critical measures of the success of a single or multi-unit operation. Nevertheless, an additional ingredient is the level of market penetration, which often varies considerably.

The market penetration approach can be accomplished in one of two ways, as follows.

The Customer Distribution Method

The customer distribution generated from the interview program can be used in computing market penetration. Earlier in the book, I described how to plot the customers on maps, thus depicting the trade area of the restaurant. The customer distribution reflects where the customers originated their trip to the restaurant and their frequency of visit. Trade area demographics could then be compiled by the actual trade area, mile radii, some type of a grid system, an amoeba (lines reflecting the actual trading area), or some other designation. The potential for which the restaurant is competing could then be determined by small segments or subparts of the trade area. Therefore, at this point, you would have the customer distribution reflected by smaller parts of the trade area and the potential that also exists within those subparts.

Table 16.2 depicts a sales analysis and customer distribution designed to verify the number of customers required for a successful unit. The frequency distribution and check average are used to determine the sales per customer and the total sales per frequency of visit category. Finally, it presents cumulative sales by frequency category. For example, 60% of the customers visit the unit at least once

TABLE 16.2

Sales Analysis of Required Customers

Fast food unit sales: $1,200,000
Type of location: Intersection of two major commercial arteries
Check average: $4.00
All competitors are present: Average management

Customer Distribution (%)	Number of Visits	Number of Customers	Number of Annual Visits	Sales per Customer	Sales	Cumulative Sales
5	3 × a wk. + (156)	96	15,000	$625	$ 60,000	$ 60,000
4	2 × a wk. (208)	58	12,000	828	48,000	108,000
11	Once a wk. (52)	635	33,000	208	132,000	240,000
12	Every 2 wks. (26)	1,385	36,000	104	144,000	384,000
8	Every 3 wks. (17.3)	1,387	24,000	69	95,980	479,980
20	Once a mo. (12)	5,000	60,000	48	240,000	719,980
7	Every 2 mos. (6)	3,500	21,000	24	84,000	803,980
5	Every 3 mos. (4)	3,750	15,000	16	60,000	863,980
3	Every 4 mos. (3)	3,000	9,000	12	36,000	899,980
2	Every 5 mos. (2.4)	2,500	6,000	9	22,500	922,480
5	Every 6 mos. (2)	7,500	15,000	8	60,000	982,000
3	Every 9 mos. (1.3)	6,900	9,000	5	34,500	1,018,000
7	Once a year (1)	21,000	21,000	4	86,000	1,104,000
8	First visitors	24,000	24,000	4	96,000	1,200,000
100	Total	80,744	300,000		$1,200,000	

a month. They represent approximately $719,980 in annual sales. Also, the table reflects the sales per customers. Obviously, the more frequent customers represent higher sales per customer. This kind of information can help in estimating sales for new sites and selecting areas for new locations. It can also be inputted into a sales estimation model and to help define what you need in the way of population resources.

The area containing the most frequent visitors is the primary trade area, whereas the less frequent visitors originate from the secondary trade area. Combining the two obviously provides the total trade area. Within those same segments, the total potential for which the restaurant is competing could also be computed. On an overall basis then, by simply dividing the sales of the restaurant by the total potential, you would have the overall market penetration. Repeating the procedure for the primary trade area would determine its level of market penetration. Table 16.3 depicts the trade area segments (primary and secondary), population, income, eating and drinking expenditures, sales derived from each segment (primary and secondary), and the market penetration.

The example is admittedly simplistic, and furthermore makes the following important assumption: *The customer distribution equals the sales distribution.* I am the first to admit that is not totally true. Nevertheless, in more than 30 years of evaluating all types of retail and food operations, I have found this method to be effective for measuring market penetration within a specific area.

TABLE 16.3

Trade Area Fine Dining

	Primary Trade Area	Secondary Trade Area	Total Trade Area*
Population	27,565	89,512	117,077
Household income	$43,560	$39,889	$42,046
Per capita expenditures	$815	$763	$781
Eating and drinking dollars	$22,465,475	$68,297,656	$90,763,131
Customer distribution	30%	55%	85%
Actual sales*	$1,038,589	$1,904,080	$2,904,420
Market penetration	4.6%	2.8%	3.2%

*Approximately 15% of the customers and the sales are from beyond the trade area.

Most Frequent Customers Method

A more sophisticated method for determining market penetration is to recognize the importance of frequent customers. Using the frequency distribution of customer check averages by date, permits allocation of the sales by trade area segment. For example, if 60% of the customers were coming to the unit once a month or more, it could normally be assumed that the 60% of customers equaled 60% of sales. However, given frequency of customer visits, the computations could be made on the basis of check averages versus visits, to more adequately place the sales dollars in their respective segments.

Usually frequency of customer visit allocations will result in a higher level of sales being captured within the primary segment versus the secondary segment. It is also a truer picture of the situation. Therefore, if there is a bias in the axiom that a customer distribution equals a sales distribution, that bias favors the secondary portion of trade area over the primary portion. Without question, utilizing frequency of customer visits and allocating sales by market segment to compute market penetration is a much more accurate methodology. Unfortunately, many people do not have the resources nor the understanding to accomplish this procedure. Nonetheless, it is an effective model for measuring market penetration performance.

Information about market penetration performance can be used in a number of ways. First, it reflects the overall performance of an individual unit or units, and these results can be further subdivided to clarify variations in market penetration levels by type of location. Second, the penetration levels can be computed by segments or subparts of the trade area to further evaluate the variations that may exist in access and competition, as well as in the socioeconomic characteristics of the resident population. Market penetration computations help to explain why, among units with similar demographics, one unit captures a higher level of penetration than another. Often the existence of significant competition will be clearly apparent. Finally, it can be a way to measure performance changes, size of acceptable markets, and competitive impacts.

Table 16.4 depicts nine different units of an existing restaurant operation. It shows population within a three-mile and a five-mile radius, total eating and drinking expenditures, restaurant sales distribution (based on all customers), and the percentage of business being generated from beyond five miles. Finally, it reflects the

TABLE 16.4

Penetration Analysis of Nine Selected Restaurants

Unit	3 Miles	3–5 Miles	Total	Sales	Total Eating Out Food Expenditures	3 Miles	3–5 Miles	5-Mile Market Penetration	Beyond 5 Miles
A	90,979	209,452	300,431	$770,000	$33,048,000	3.71	0.83	1.70	26.7
B	32,013	48,113	57,272	450,000	9,996,000	2.79	1.31	2.10	53.2
C	78,587	362,514	441,101	600,000	47,638,000	2.80	0.60	1.10	17.5
D	89,383	38,931	128,314	500,000	13,851,000	2.42	2.28	2.38	34.0
E	106,721	161,113	267,834	500,000	32,568,000	1.73	0.41	0.94	38.5
F	307,892	308,450	616,342	600,000	71,404,000	1.00	0.29	0.65	22.8
G	54,496	42,385	96,881	450,000	9,882,000	4.10	2.57	3.43	24.6
H	148,220	117,552	265,772	800,000	32,329,000	2.40	1.10	1.82	26.1
I	64,602	132,357	196,959	300,000	19,186,000	0.76	0.76	0.76	51.3

market penetration levels for three miles, three to five miles and the total five-mile radius.

Units A through I in Table 16.4 represent several different types of locations. Units B and I are highway locations as reflected by the high percentage of business being generated from beyond a five-mile radius. Units A, C, D, and H are located in commercial areas that have a strong population base, along with an excellent mix of demographics related to the customer characteristics of the unit. Thus, it is not a surprise that those units have strong levels of market penetration. Unit G has the highest level of penetration; however, its sales are one of the lowest. Unit G is in a small town, and the statistics indicate that this small town, even with a high incidence of compatibility with the age and income statistics, is *inadequate* to support the necessary sales. No matter how well the manager is motivated, insufficient resources make it impossible to generate sales of the required level. This finding is very helpful because it also helps to establish minimum criteria. From Table 16.4, we can conclude that even though age and income structure may be highly compatible with the customer characteristics, no unit should be placed in markets with less than 50,000 population.

The primary advantage of calculating market penetration by individual units is to establish parameters of market share for the best units, average units, and poor units. This process reflects more adequately, not only the parameters of market penetration for a respective restaurant or fast food operator, but also the requirements for future market and site selection. Each fast food operator or restaurateur should want to duplicate high sales and strong market penetration units by studying their characteristics (or others). Both locationally and demographically, it is possible to determine minimum penetration requirements for maximum sales. If done correctly, the process can assist in establishing the fundamentals for computer modeling by providing the weights for sensitive market elements. Thus, a quick "go/no go" screening process can eliminate certain areas and simplify others.

Perhaps one of the most significant factors regarding this exercise is that it will begin to reflect the minimum number of people, income levels, and age structure required. Also provided are minimums for the development of a new restaurant or fast food operation. It certainly clarifies many of the axioms constantly heard regarding food site selection, such as "I need 50,000 persons within three miles to justify a new unit." This statement is unrealistic without a full analysis of customer and market needs and a determination of the actual requirements. For most operators, it should be a statement such as "What I need is approximately 25,000 people between the ages of 20 and 35 years with incomes between $25,000 and $30,000." Often those 25,000 people in the proper age and income categories make or break the unit. In other situations, it might require 75,000 to 100,000 people to identify adequate resources within the required age and income structures.

Table 16.5 shows an example of five full-service, casual restaurants, each with a popular bar (units A through E). Units A, C, and E are located in dense-urban locations. The unit with the highest annual sales ($6,400,000), unit C, is also competing for the largest five-mile potential ($295,000,000). Thus, unit C has a market penetration within five miles of 0.98%. Also, notice that 54.8% of its sales originate beyond five miles. Nonetheless, unit C also has the highest percentage of customers who reside within five miles.

Unit D has sales of $4,500,000, competing for potential sales of $66,850,000, and a market penetration of 2.6%. The unit captures only 38.7% of its business within five miles. As you might have guessed, these units are located near major malls. Unit B has the lowest sales, but the highest market penetration. Table 16.6 provides some of the answers to this situation, by providing the ages of the most frequent customers. Notice that the age category ranges from 25 to 44 years. This age group contains the highest customer frequency rate. In fact, they represent more than 80% of the customers.

TABLE 16.5

Annual Sales and Market Penetration
Casual Restaurant and Popular Bar

Unit	Sales	5-Mile Sales Potential	Market Penetration (%)	Sales Within 5 Miles (%)	Market Share (%)
A	$2,000,000	$102,850,000	1.95	35.5	0.69
B	2,600,000	34,066,500	7.73	35.5	2.71
C	6,400,000	295,000,000	2.17	45.2	0.98
D	4,500,000	66,850,000	6.73	38.7	2.60
E	3,640,000	105,500,000	3.45	35.5	1.22

TABLE 16.6

Annual Sales and Market Penetration
Customers between the Ages of 25 and 44 Years

Unit	Sales	Persons 24–44 Years	5-Mile Expenditure Potential	5-Mile Market Penetration (%)
A	$2,000,000	76,300	$26,904,700	2.64
B	2,600,000	21,361	9,050,400	10.20
C	6,400,000	222,500	79,298,000	3.65
D	4,500,000	39,200	18,366,000	9.48
E	3,640,000	61,134	26,399,300	4.89

Their eating and drinking expenditures are provided as well. Unit B has the highest market penetration with 10.2%, followed by unit D at 9.48%. Unit B appears to have the highest penetration and yet has had the lowest sales. The market area is limited in its population resources, and therefore this type of area should be avoided, if the sales level is too low.

The restaurant's most frequent customers have incomes in the $35,000 to $49,999 category. Table 16.7 depicts the market penetration for this predominant income category. The table shows that unit B has the best match of income, indicating a 15.5% penetration in this income category. Again, there simply are not enough people within the five-mile radius to generate higher sales. Unit C has all

TABLE 16.7

Annual Sales and Market Penetration
Customers with Incomes between $35,000 and $49,999

Unit	Sales	Customers' with Incomes of $35,000–$49,999	5-Mile Expenditure Potential	5–Mile Market Penetration (%)
A	$2,000,000	12,540	$14,086,200	5.04
B	2,600,000	4,980	5,951,200	15.51
C	6,400,000	34,467	34,310,800	8.43
D	4,500,000	9,100	12,542,700	13.88
E	3,640,000	15,160	18,913,100	6.83

the proper ingredients: location, population, age and income characteristics, high sales, and a strong market penetration.

SUMMARY

An analysis of market penetration or an analysis of multiple units by types of locations and geographic locales will provide the parameters necessary for adequate market identification and site selection. Food operations that generate a significant amount of their business from the most frequent customers might do well to carry the computation through to the most frequent customer visitor level. Others will probably do just as well by simply accepting the axiom that "customer distribution equals sales distribution" and proceed to compute the levels of penetration. The most important factor that the penetration level analysis can provide is *performance parameters*. Market penetration defines the share that a food operator is capturing within a specific market segment. In looking at new locations, the absence of adequate resources will show up immediately. If a prospective trade area looks good on paper, but when the market penetration parameters are applied, produces inadequate sales, it is necessary to ask, "Is it possible for the new unit to *outperform* the existing units?" Furthermore, market penetration analyses help to determine the minimum requirements for success.

Seventeen

Estimating Sales

Estimating sales is at best a complicated process. It is especially difficult in the food service business, where entrepreneurial operated facilities, management personality, and uniqueness can result in unusual success. This is not quite as true for the fast food industry, since franchising, standardization, controls, and competition have reduced considerably the importance of the individual entrepreneur in influencing attraction.

I am reminded of the successful restaurant operator who had three restaurants, all of which were grossing more than $2,000,000 annually. In his words, "I'm making big money!" He briefly discussed with me the need to estimate sales for the planned fourth restaurant. When he discovered that I would go so far as to charge him for the service, he told me that he felt he had mastered the business and was not worried about the future. In fact, he said that he could not miss, because he had a reputation and could open units just about anywhere and bring in $2,000,000 annually. He then went out and selected an additional site. Well, the fourth unit bombed. Could it have been avoided? The answer is an unequivocal, Yes!

So many of the fourth site's locational attributes were negative that it should never have been selected. Had the operator simply applied the market penetration from the other units, he would have realized that the potential for the new location was insufficient. As he later told me, "It was a real good real estate deal." Unfortunately, the mistake proved much more costly than the expense of determining if the restaurant should have been built at all. He is not making big money anymore, and he continues to pay semibig money for the rent on the now defunct restaurant. "Ego-city" often gets us all.

In the food business, sales estimates have historically been computed on the back of an envelope, a napkin, through a car windshield, or on the back of the building plans. This normally consists of determining the cost of the land, building, and equipment. Based on these figures and several computations, the amount of sales necessary to justify the new facility is determined. Not very realistic!

Knowing your customer characteristics and profile is essential in establishing an effective sales estimation program (or model, if you prefer). Without adequate understanding, it is extremely difficult to estimate sales accurately. A number of methods are used in preparing a sales estimate for a food operation, including the following:

- "Guts" method (Dreamland!)
- Windshield method (Pray for a sunny day!)
- Market penetration method (see Chapter 16)
- Eating and drinking potential allocation method
    Macro method
    Micro method
- Comparative method (chain operator's approach)
- Correlative method (see Chapter 18)
- Market saturation method (advertising method)

There are other procedures, perhaps more narrow in their approach, for estimating sales; however, the preceding are usually tough enough, without further complicating the process.

"GUTS" METHOD

This method, which might also be called the "I got a great deal" method, is the most common method for choosing a location and estimating sales. Actually, sales are not really estimated; instead, to justify the rent or the purchase price, they are assumed. I must admit that it is the cheapest way of estimating sales; however, as the man said, "You can pay me now, or pay me later." While this method may be cheap initially, users often end up paying for it later. People who are truly good at using this method usually have been in the business for 15 or 20 years, and they mentally run through a checklist of a successful location's necessary components to arrive at a good decision. However, the average food operator cannot handle the "guts" method with any degree of accuracy because it requires a great deal of luck. Even after selecting locations for more than 30 years, I shy away from relying on instinct since without the proper market data, it is very easy to be wrong.

WINDSHIELD METHOD

This method utilizes some locational selection experience; however, the site is frequently chosen by looking at locations through the windshield of the real estate broker's car, in either heated or air conditioned comfort. While this approach may include some locational criteria, the benefits are minimal because it is impossible to see through a windshield everything that needs to be taken into account. On the basis of looking at one or several locations, the interested parties make a sales estimate on the back of an envelope or on the fender of the vehicle. The benefits of either are seldom worthwhile.

MARKET PENETRATION METHOD

This method, which was described in detail in Chapter 16, allows food people with at least one existing operation to apply their success to another potential location. For the multi-unit operator, it is an excellent procedure for measuring opportunity against existing performance. The market penetration method, a micro approach, depends on the analogs developed. For example, the data may indicate a strong pattern of penetration performance, say, within three miles or within three or four minutes' driving time. A market penetration figure might be applied to the eating and drinking potential within either of these areas to determine the likelihood of achieving an acceptable level.

To further refine the process, market penetration can be computed by age and income categories for subareas of a trade area. When market penetration analogues (or parameters) have been developed, the tools are available to apply to any new location. Once the necessary data are developed, the market penetration experience can then be applied to the market data of new locations. If the required sales levels are not forthcoming, then you must ask: "Is the new location going to do better than the existing location or locations?" If that appears unlikely, the new location's success is questionable.

After determining the profile of your most frequent customer, you may find that a new location's prospective trade area has a better mix of demographic resources than your existing location or locations. In that case, the new location may outperform the existing restaurant or restaurants. You cannot make that decision unless you have the base data for comparison. Also, if a new location is in a market with a strong overall market share (macro), assisted by strong advertising, the final sales estimate may need upward adjustment. This should only be done if the sales performance of the existing units in the market are actually experiencing higher sales per unit.

EATING AND DRINKING POTENTIAL ALLOCATION METHOD

Macro, in considering an area, means "large" or "wider." In contrast, *micro* means "small" or "narrow." Obviously, these two methods can be in conflict, or they can be combined to arrive at the best general area or city for restaurant development. The micro method can be used to determine the potential of a location, by studying the opportunity in minute detail. Thus, while both methods will result in a sales estimate, the micro method should, but unfortunately does not always, provide more accurate results. The macro approach often considers an overall market share target. The method most used by site researchers is commonly referred to as the "amoeba" system of estimating sales for retailers and shopping centers. The trade area is divided into two or three parts—the primary trade area, the secondary trade area, and the tertiary trade area—and the population, households, income, and potential expenditures are calculated for each part. A percentage of market share is then assigned to each area. The most frequent customers normally originate from the primary trade area. It usually receives the highest percentage of market share because of customer frequency and also because of its proximity to the location. Market share percentages are assigned to the secondary trade area. More often than not, a tertiary trade area is not designated. This system falls in the macro family because the trade area parts are usually fairly large, and only a few decisions regarding share–capture–percentages are used. Figure 17.1 shows an example of an amoeba trade area, and Table 17.1 lists the pertinent data. Totals have been rounded off.

The micro approach focuses on areas with acceptable characteristics and explores the data in detail by very small geographic areas. The objective is to assess each small component of the trade area, in order to make decisions about consumer actions, assuming a new restaurant facility is built. Analogues are then applied to determine how the location under consideration compares with other existing unit performances. (*Analog* is simply a technical term for isolated comparative data, i.e., market penetration percentages). This method usually involves delineating a trade area, which is subdivided into smaller parts. The investigator estimates the present and future population, determines the number of households for each part, estimates the household income, and calculates the eating and drinking (or eating only) expenditures. In addition, a full understanding of accessibility and competition is necessary. The objective is to allocate the eating and drinking business generated from each subarea. Next, the competitors are listed on a worksheet similar to the one presented in Table 17.2, and percentage shares of the potential eating and drinking (or eating only) are allocated to the proposed restaurant and also to competitors. There should be an "Other" column, since some business cannot be quantified, for example, people passing through the area for other cities or other market segments in major cities.

The process forces the user to truly think through allocation, since the totals, when completed, often add up to more than 100%. Naturally, this requires starting over and relocating the numbers. This process is repeated for each subarea. When completed, the numbers are totaled to determine the dollars that you expect your proposed restaurant to capture. First of all, do you believe? How did the competitors do? You may find the numbers outlandish, or you may find that they are much too low, given the market potential. Therefore, it may be necessary to go through the process once again. Repeat the steps, add up the competitors' allocations and compare them with their current sales. If the variation is large, then repeat the procedure again. Remember, however, that your restaurant may have an adverse impact on competitors' sales, and thus the allocation may correctly result in lower sales for them. If you go through

FIGURE 17.1

Trade Area Map

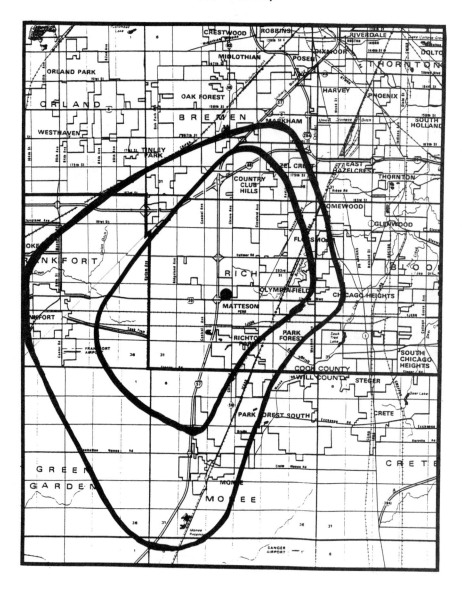

TABLE 17.1

Macro Trade Area

Trade Area Segment	Population	Households	Household Income	Per Capita Eating and Drinking Expenses	Potential Eating and Drinking Expenses	Market Penetration (%)	Estimated Sales
Primary	22,546	6,754	$33,690	$693	$15,624,400	11.0	$1,718,700
Secondary	48,792	32,971	29,733	623	30,397,400	1.7	518,000
Total	71,338	39,725	$30,234	$645	$46,021,800	4.9	$2,236,700

this process, you will see that it can be maddening. However, you will have a much better understanding of where the business (or your estimate) is going and why.

In growing areas with generative concentrations, and in areas where the ages of the residents are oriented toward eating out, the impact of new restaurants is usually not as great, unless the competitors are *direct competitors*. Impacts of new restaurants vary considerably, depending on the location of the new competitor, the menu, pricing, promotion, operation, and certainly, the extent to

TABLE 17.2

Sales Allocation Proposed New Restaurant

	Subareas					
	Primary (%)			Secondary (%)		
	1	2	3	4	5	6
Proposed restaurant	5	10	8	1	3	4
Johnny's	9	15	4	3	1	1
The Barn	12	8	2	12	1	2
Rose Cafe	15	7	3	15	2	8
Barnaby's	8	11	12	5	1	2
Junior's	3	7	15	9	2	9
Red Lobster	12	9	3	4	18	8
Other—in area	21	22	27	28	28	33
Other—outside	15	11	26	23	44	33
Total	100	100	100	100	100	100

which the competitor provides *good food*. The allocation of percentage shares is subjective. Nevertheless, if you follow the process outlined in this book—namely, the customer profile; the demographic analysis; accessibility study; competitive inventory; and assessment of habits and patterns, viability, income dynamics, and eating and drinking expenditures—then the subjective allocation is less subjective and much more informed.

The more data that you obtain and analyze logically, the better your opportunity to arrive at a reasonable estimate of potential sales. You may find that the analysis indicates that the potential for your proposed restaurant is too low to proceed. *Do not* fudge the numbers to produce pleasing answers. The investment is risky enough without adding an additional element of chance. I cannot over emphasize the importance of experience in carrying out this exercise. Unfortunately, there is no substitute for the wisdom gained from years of going through this process. Without experience, it is difficult to know if the number arrived at is realistic. Nevertheless, if you go through the process, the analysis required will help you to understand the variables and their importance.

COMPARATIVE METHOD

This method can be used alone or in conjunction with another method, and often is. To use it, you need to have more than 5 units, and preferably 10 or more units. The more units, the better the method works. The first step is to get similar data on each existing unit, so that you have something to compare. This includes population and household data for similar trade areas, average household income, roadnet description, traffic data, competition and the history of competitive change, sales performance (by year for three to five years), type of location, and age structure. Next, the data are compared with locations under consideration to see how they match. Are the prospective locales better or worse, than the existing ones? Make the comparison with your better performing units. Is there a good match? If so, why? Often, either a "plus or minus" system or a numerical rating system is used in comparing locations.

Either a numerical rating system or a plus or minus system might compare the existing locations to a prospective one by allocating 5 or 10 points either positively or negatively for each important market and locational element. When completed, the total numbers are added up to see how they compare. A negative number reduces the sales forecast of the proposed unit. Conversely, a positive number should probably raise the sales forecast. Regardless of the system, what is important is that individual existing locations are compared with a prospective location by sales, income, visibility, accessibility, competition, traffic counts, population characteristics, generative activity, daytime employment, and daypart activity. Many companies follow this approach on either a formal or informal basis to determine if a location is acceptable. Also, sales are estimated based on the sales of comparable existing units.

MARKET SATURATION METHOD

The market saturation approach is based on the premise that a certain number of units are needed in the marketplace to develop high sales levels and sufficient advertising impact. Therefore it is important to get as many units into place as quickly as possible, and sales will then rise to an acceptable figure. In actuality, sometimes yes, more often, no! Although a certain level of gross advertising rating points may elevate sales of secondary locations belonging to major chains with good consumer acceptance, it certainly does not have that effect on newly developing companies. Advertising, marketing, good food, and efficient management go hand and hand with good location selection. Each is important to the success of a restaurant or fast food facility.

SUMMARY

Whatever method you may use, it is important to evaluate the market and estimate sales. If you gather accurate information and study it carefully, you will learn to understand the market and reach error free conclusions. We send our children to college, so that they will have a better opportunity in life. Is it not logical to conclude that the more we know about both the operation and the locational issues, the better we will be at selecting locations?

Eighteen

Computers and Site Selection

The restaurant industry, like other industries, has moved toward electronics for control and cost reduction measures by formalizing more and more elements. An outgrowth of this has been more sophisticated computerized cash registers designed not only to keep cash records but also to track inventories, maintain sales of individual menu items, and help plan labor costs. Additionally, there has been an effort to develop computer-assisted site selection techniques or "models" to streamline and improve the accuracy of restaurant locational decisions and sales estimation techniques.

Computerized methods of site selection and sales estimation are not really new; they have been around since the early 1960s. While very few were operational at that time, they have been tried for more than 30 years. *Computers do not select sites.* Instead, they can compare and weigh data for a potential site, against a given set of criteria. If the program is adequate, computers can identify areas for the possible placement of restaurants or fast food facilities.

The appeal of computer use in this process is obvious. Once you have input data in a usable format and worked out the bugs, you can systematically and quickly analyze large amounts of data. Moreover, you can compare the data with existing units or known parameters to test how the new location might perform. Thus, the operator is not necessarily confined to a few key factors but rather can deal with the varying influence of a host of variables. Theoretically, once a workable method has been developed, three things can occur: (1) The time and expense needed to evaluate additional sites can be greatly reduced, (2) a systematic procedure can be established for gathering consistent and comparable data, and (3) an enormous amount of data regarding existing units can be quickly examined in relation to a potential location. As a result, it should be possible to reach timely, informed decisions when opportunities present themselves. Sounds terrific? Unfortunately, it does not always work that way.

Computer technology has expanded geometrically, especially the personal computer. Today a desktop computer can handle tasks that in the 1970s and 1980s were only available to those with mainframes. Both the large and small entrepreneur now have the computer power necessary to develop a data base regarding existing units and markets. Also, the services of specialized consultants who offer a range of methods for estimating the value of a particular site now proliferate the landscape.

With all these advantages, the real issue becomes how *reliable* are computerized methods? More than one restaurateur has been skeptical of a computer sales forecast, when the results far exceeded or fell below the expectation. The problem usually is not with the equipment, but rather with the software program, the data variables, their weightings, or the data itself. Like any analytical tool, programs tend to work best when applied in certain controlled conditions and tend to be less reliable under other less controlled conditions. By knowing how computerized methods work, the food operator can exercise judgment on whether such an approach is suitable and, if so, how much confidence can be placed in the results.

THE LOCATION MODEL

The basis for a computer-assisted site selection technique is a location model. It is possible to have a market and location model without a computer; however, to manipulate considerable data or to speed up the process, a computer is necessary. A model is an attempt to create an approximation of the real world. Although location models may differ with regard to the number, kind, and measurement of specific variables, they tend to utilize a common approach. Namely, they attempt to rate potential or to predict sales for a proposed restaurant site as a function of qualitatively and quantitatively measured site attributes. The latter includes such varied characteristics as trade area delineation, traffic in proximity to the site, resident population within the trade area, age structure of the population, a weighting of generative activity, existing potential customer patterns, income or discretionary buying power of potential customers, and frequency of customer visits. There are several types of models, including linear regression, multiple regression, gravity, and comparative models.

The first task in developing a computer-assisted location technique is to build a model that includes the minimal factors necessary for predicting potential site sales. These factors should be identified from past experience, customer and site profiles, or the advice of market and location experts. Moreover, the multiple-unit operator must undertake a thorough evaluation of the sensitive market, location, and sales factors of existing locations. Once all the possible factors affecting site sales have been listed, the next step is to examine statistically the relationship between each factor and potential sales. This is usually done using a sample of actual cases (restaurant or fast food operations), where total sales are already known, and the site and market characteristics of each restaurant have been quantified.

For example, a food service operator may believe that the potential restaurant sales of a site are directly related to the traffic volume in front of the site, and in some cases that is true. To construct and test the model, the operator would take a sample of existing restaurants and examine the statistical relationship between sales and traffic counts, perhaps hourly traffic counts. The use of *linear regression* can produce the following simple prediction equation:

$$Y = a + bX$$

where Y = Potential site sales, X = Automobile traffic count, a = Constant, and b = Linear regression coefficient.

Figure 18.1 provides a graphic illustration of this equation. In this example, the single line that best fits the relationship between sales and traffic counts for the sample restaurants is found to be $Y = 100 + 20k$. This represents the mathematical expression of the model, which will be used to predict potential sales at future sites. Consider the following example. There are four existing fast food units with the following sales and traffic counts:

Unit	Sales	Traffic Counts
1	$740,000	32,000
2	700,000	30,000
3	660,000	28,000
4	620,000	26,000

The graph in Figure 18.1 depicts the relationship between the dependent variable (Sales) on the vertical axis and the independent variable (Traffic Counts) on the horizontal axis. The diagonal line indicates the linear relationship between restaurant sales and traffic counts. Although the process appears simple, many have tried it only to discover that it does not accurately reflect the real world. Nevertheless, to apply the model in selecting future sites, you need only to include the traffic count for any site under consideration in the prediction equation.

If, for example, the traffic count for a site were 35,000 vehicles, then the resulting sales forecast for the site would be $800,000 (or $100,000 + (20 × 35,000)). Furthermore, by examining the standard

FIGURE 18.1

Relationship between Dependent Variable (Sales) and Independent Variable (Traffic Counts)

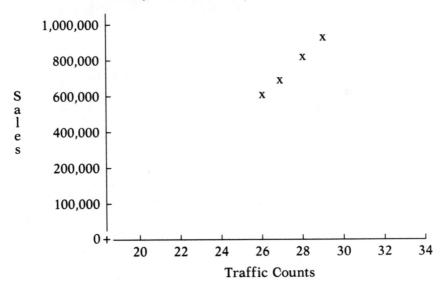

error of the estimate, the operator can determine the range within which the forecasted sales volume can be expected to vary on average. Theoretically, the model yields not only a potential sales forecast but an estimate of the site's most likely sales range.

Linear regression for the food business is too simplistic. There are usually multiple variables, and they certainly do not cluster as the example does. Instead, the formula most often used, at least at the beginning, is the *multiple regression* approach. In most applications, the location model incorporates a number of key factors in predicting site sales potential. With sufficient cases (existing restaurants or fast food operations) to build and test the model, it is possible to include a wide array of explanatory variables. The sales prediction equation is developed using multiple regression and takes this form:

$$Y = a + b_1X_1 + b_2X_2 + b_3X_3 + \ldots bnXn$$

where Y = Potential site sales, $X_1, X_2, X_3 \ldots$ = Market and location factors, $b_1, b_2, b_3 \ldots$ = Regression coefficients, and a = Constant.

This statistical technique yields a measure of predictive accuracy for the equation and the individual location factors. The overall accuracy of the equation is expressed as R^2, the coefficient of determination, which reflects the percentage of total variation explained by the locational factors included in the model. The actual range of estimated sales in absolute units (dollars), is further reflected in the standard error of estimate for the regression equation. Thus, the method provides the forecasted sales for a potential site, as well as the probability of error. The contribution of each locational factor to the overall accuracy of the prediction equation can also be determined by examining the respective partial regression coefficients, which can be subjected to the statistical significance test to establish their significance.

The statistical technique of multiple regression imposes a number of limitations on location model building. The technique assumes, for example, that the regression of Y on each X is linear. This assumption may be tested, and adjusted for, if need be, by transforming the measurement scale of the independent variable. The statistical technique also requires that the variable to be regressed be ratio or interval scale measures, although this assumption can often be relaxed without damaging predictive accuracy. Multiple regression is a variable dependent on several independent variables, which further demands that the independent variable not be highly intercorrelated. Where they are, the reliability of partial regression coefficients which are associated with each individual location factor is greatly reduced. In such an instance, one or more of the intercorrelated variables can be dropped or a new combined variable can be created to restore predictive accuracy. Another limitation imposed by the model's statistical basis is the need for sufficient cases to develop the prediction equation. The necessary sample size will depend partly on the number of independent variables. In no case can there be no independent variables in the equation than there are sample cases. It is also advisable to have a reasonable sample to reduce standard error.

I expect by now that, unless you are into this stuff, you have moved along to subsequent chapters or laid down the book in favor of a cold frosty. I cannot blame you. While it is boring stuff, it can be a very useful tool in identifying sensitive factors in site selection and sales estimation. When conducted by a skilled analyst with the correct market, locational, and customer factors, the multiple regression technique can produce a reliable sales prediction equation. The serious limitations of this management tool do not derive from the statistical method so much as from the need to apply valid measures to the several independent factors affecting site potential. The factors that are included and the method of measurement are crucial to the reliability of the explanatory model.

The identification of locational attributes on which to base sales potential assumes first a logical or conceptual understanding of how various factors influence restaurant sales. Frequently, the conceptual basis is vaguely taken for granted—*this is a critical mistake*. To proceed correctly with the application of the process and the collection of the appropriate data, the operator must clearly specify the underlying conceptual model at the outset. This is really the heart of the model-building process that eventually reveals its quantification in the multiple regression solution. If the identification of the sensitive market, customer, and locational factors, and the application of the statistical formulas are handled correctly, the model can yield impressive results.

The first step in building a conceptual model is to define the problem as concisely as possible. This means that the model should focus on predicting sales for a *particular type* of food service operation at a specific *type of location*, since there are differences in the effect of locational and market characteristics by type of location. Thus, it is likely that locational factors will similarly influence a defined operation and its type of location. For example, a freestanding fast food operation offering a standard menu in proximity to a commercial concentration will expectantly exhibit one pattern of dependence on such factors as trade area size, population, traffic volumes, and activity generators. In contrast, this same set of locational factors would influence a traffic-oriented restaurant operation differently. The predictive location model with the most accuracy would be the one that clearly relates the dependent variable—potential site sales—to a specific food service operation and type of location. Again, models often fail at the outset because the type of location is not adequately defined along with the type of food service operation.

To enhance the model's predictability, the criteria for definition should specify such additional characteristics as menu, pricing, population, age structure, income structure, hourly traffic counts, a visibility rating, a competitive weighting adjustment, and physical site characteristic requirements for the particular operation under study. Obviously, definitional uniformity is most easily accomplished when the model attempts to reflect the locational factors influencing a standardized operation, such as McDonald's or Subway. In this instance, the model is based on the current performance of units that are virtually identical, by type of location, to the proposed site. Where this strict uniformity is lacking, as in the case of small operators who must base a location model on a sample of similar, but not identical cases, the margin of predictive error is greater. The margin of error will also be greater if the fast food units are not evaluated against the specific type of location that is compatible with one under consideration.

Once the defining characteristics of the locational type have been established, the next step is to identify the independent factors that can be expected to account for sales variations. A broad range of factors may be initially considered for input into the regression equation. These locational characteristics include, but are not limited to, the following categories: customer base, expenditure level, major generative facilities, competition, and site characteristics.

Customer Base

The customer base of a food service operation refers to both distance and customer profile characteristics of a specific market or trade area. While the total number of area residents is important, what matters more is the actual number whose characteristics compare favorably with the most frequent visitors. In measuring the customer base, it is common to use a defined area unit corresponding to the potential trade area. One such approach, is to use a standard radius of a specific number of miles to the site. While this is perhaps convenient, it is also often inaccurate, since the characteristics of one direction may differ greatly from those of the opposite direction. Another method for determining the customer base is to use driving time to the site. Residents living within so many minutes of driving time are then compiled to make up the population base. The most accurate method usually is to create the actual trade area through the use of customer origin studies. Regardless of the method used, it is necessary to maintain consistency and to consider accuracy as it relates to your particular type of food service facility.

In evaluating the characteristics of the customer base, it may be that neither the *aggregate* income level nor the *average* age level of the resident trade area population adequately predicts the site's potential sales. Prior consumer surveys may have established, however, that the key factor is the total number of persons within a certain income bracket, or within a limited age grouping. Having discovered this from customer research, the operator can tailor the collection of relevant locational data to yield the most productive results.

Expenditure Level

The potential amount spent for food service by the trade area population represents a key factor to include in the location model. Depending on the type of food service operation, consider expenditures for food alone or food together with alcoholic beverages. Moreover, expenditures can further be defined by fast food, restaurants with or without alcohol, cafeterias or others. Various sources can be used to develop expenditure levels (see Chapter 14), including local retail sales reports, state sales tax receipt data, or various customer expenditure surveys. Expenditures may be referenced to the total population on a per capita basis or to households.

Major Generative Facilities

Usually of prime importance to the location model is an accurate accounting of major activity generators in the immediate area. Each type of activity generator creates a distinctive customer flow in terms of total number, time of day, type of trip, demographics, spending habits, and others. Office buildings, for example, usually stimulate breakfast and lunch business. Cinemas enhance evenings and weekend trade. Shopping malls generally build up business throughout the day, with evenings and weekends representing the most active periods.

As important as major generators are to sales, their individual contributions are not easily classified or measured. For example, accounting for the gross leasable area (in square feet) of a shopping center or commercial strip as a measure of activity level can be very misleading, since it does not consider performance. While in most cases, these data are readily available, they fail to measure the extraordinary shopping appeal of particular stores, or the position of the center relative to competing shopping areas. Conversely, store or retail complex sales volumes are a highly relevant measure of shopping activity. An even more relevant measure is sales per square foot performance, which combines sales and square footage to develop a productive measure. Unfortunately, sales data are the most difficult to obtain and, in inexperienced hands, they are difficult to estimate.

Similar measurement and data collection problems are encountered with other types of activity generators. Office buildings differ by the number of employees (with various orientations to eating out), as well as the number of visitors they bring to an area. Likewise, whether the student enrollment figures for a local college reflect resident or commuter students has implications for the number of potential restaurant customers. Military installations may have large numbers of civilian employees and military personnel, but these individuals sometimes have restricted mobility and buying power. In each instance, one is faced with the difficulty of developing a sensitivity measurement of the key features of a customer activity generator. It is seldom sufficient simply to total the reported number of employees, students, or visitors in the area without considering their different characteristics or orientation. In place of sensitive measures (weightings) of generative facilities, location models often rely on surrogate indicators of activity, such as average daily traffic counts, reported gallonage of nearby service stations, or even commercial property values. Of these various indicators, current traffic counts collected by governmental agencies are perhaps the most reliable. Nevertheless, hourly traffic counts related to the hours of operation are far more pertinent than the overall counts because they reflect the wide peaks and valleys of traffic that may occur throughout the day and evening and, more particularly, during periods of extreme traffic congestion. Essentially, it is important to identify the critical indicators for each specific operation.

Competition

The impact of competitive outlets on a proposed food service unit depends to a large extent on the market strength of the particular unit or operator. Hence, it is one of the most important aspects of a location to quantify. An attempt is often made by counting the total number of competing outlets within a specific distance of a site, or the number of direct or indirect competitors. The problem is further compounded because the appeal of competitors is not uniform, but is directly related to *their* respective site characteristics and *their* varying degrees of market acceptance. The market strength of a food service operator versus competition can best be determined by consumer research. In the absence of such information, location models must often employ only gross competitive indices, (number of competitors) which can represent a significant failure in any model. One way to overcome some of the deficiencies is to determine the specific sales levels of the competitors or better yet the sales by daypart. This usually takes time, and therefore it is not carried out.

Site Characteristics

For any potential location, numerous physical features influence the sites of customer attraction: adequate ingress and egress; clear and unrestricted visibility as measured by time and, perhaps, distance; traffic flow conditions; traffic light locations and time cycle; median strips, turning provisions, speed limit, number of lanes; and the placement of the facility with respect to major traffic arteries. Much of what represents the "quality" of the site depends on the judgment of the observer. A case can probably be made for the potential of almost any reasonable property. The difficult question, however, is assessing *the degree of potential*. For a market and location model to be effective, a system must be developed for consistently measuring and recording the important physical features of a site.

EVALUATING THE METHOD

The benefits to be derived from a well-constructed location model can be well worth the research time and expense necessary to develop it. To do it correctly, however, is extremely time consuming and costly. The costs and time are significant for developing the sensitive program-weighting elements; debugging the system once it is in place; establishing the procedures and processes necessary to maintain consistency; and, finally, constantly updating the sensitivity by inputting actual results from the model output to improve the accuracy of the prediction formula. This includes entering figures to reflect the impact of new units on the sales of existing units. Not only is the process of site evaluation made more systematic, consistent, and efficient, but the resulting analysis should yield a more accurate bottom-line estimate of potential sales. That in itself is a significant achievement, since so many food chains and individual operators do not systematically estimate sales, but rather back into it. The statistical method provides an estimate of the sales range, or standard error, associated with the final figure.

Unfortunately, models often fail because the process is turned over to real estate people who are unenthusiastic about the program. The real estate department must accept and uniformly implement the process and procedures. If the real estate people respect the program, they will respond to it by completing the forms with adequate and accurate data. It does help if their response is tied to their annual salary review. I have seen numerous situations where the real estate people's replies on the evaluation forms were totally inconsistent, and thus the program did not perform well. Management, thinking that the problem was the program, shelved it. Another responsibility of management is to be consistent in reviewing the data and applying the results.

The requirements for building a reliable computer-assisted location model are stringent; foremost is the need to clearly define and specify the type of food service operation and the type of location for which sales are being estimated. Closely related to this is the need for an adequate sample of cases that meet the definitional criteria. Naturally, both requirements favor large multi-unit operators of standardized units. Both small and large operators, however, can turn to consulting organizations for assistance, especially if their methodology for forecasting sales takes into consideration compatible sample restaurants.

The need for consistent measurement of key locational character-istics and for uniform data collection procedures is paramount. It is crucial that the methodologies used for demographics, traffic, com-petition, and the like follow a standard procedure to maintain that consistency. Similarly, it is essential to exercise care when selecting a computer demographic service and determining the accuracy of their data. Where local source data are used, such as traffic counts, the form of the data must be the same as that for data collected in other locales. If not, the results of the location model will be dis-torted among individual market areas.

The task of maintaining consistent data collection methods is more demanding than most model builders realize. This is especially true for data that cannot be taken from public sources but must be gathered by field inspection, such as the assessment of site charac-teristics, competition, employees, major activity generators, and oth-ers. Even though careful control can be exercised over field personnel to maintain uniform reporting standards, it is impossible to eliminate subjectivity from the recorded data. This unavoidable common source of error affects even the best location models. In fact, to maintain consistency, the same people should collect and evaluate the data whether it be for individual sites or for multiple markets. It can be a serious mistake to spend literally tens of thou-sands of dollars developing a computer model if you then dump the process and the form on real estate representatives, who are com-monly judged on their deal-making performance and not on data collection or evaluation. More importantly, very few receive ade-quate training in precisely what needs to be done and the method-ologies and procedures required to accomplish the objective. Simply stated, the process fails unless the representatives "buy into the pro-gram" and learn how to carry it out. In my seminars for private companies and associations, I emphasize the need to understand the entire process and how it can benefit the real estate department or the franchisee. If you are seriously thinking about developing a model, then make the commitment to create a data team who bear the responsibility for collecting and evaluating the information and maintaining consistency of the process. Then gradually shift the re-sponsibility to the real estate representatives.

Without question, computer-assisted locational techniques in the food business industry are best suited for large multiple-unit compa-nies. Major chains have a clear advantage in establishing a data base for a location model because of their past experience and supporting customer research. Nevertheless, without an adequate commitment, size does not guarantee that the model will work. If you decide to develop a computer market and location model, think about the following before proceeding:

- Understand exactly what is involved in the program in terms of cost, timing, and resources.
- Clearly define your objectives and goals.
- Establish a realistic budget. Check with other companies that have developed models to benefit from their experience.
- Make sure that the individual in charge truly understands your business.
- Establish an advisory committee of persons now involved in the process at all levels.
- Thoroughly test all the variables against how they are currently assessed in the field.
- Establish consistent, sensible, and practical procedures and policies. Also, develop and introduce the new Locational and Market Submission Kit to selected real estate representatives for comment and review.
- Bring the field real estate staff into headquarters so that you can present, discuss, and promote the methodology, procedures, and demands of the program. Do not assume that they know where to get all the required data. Make the meetings both informative and educational. Also, explain how it will affect their work, the number of deals that they are expected to complete, and any other important facts.
- Remember, that the commitment does not end with the implementation of the program. It begins. You should continually update the process and input the actual sales results of the model into the program to update its accuracy and predictability.

There will be discouraging times. The original timing estimates are rarely met and the cost overruns are usually significant. Resistance from the real estate field people will be considerable unless they are a part of the process and come to respect both the model builder and the process. Finally, senior management must support the process and not bypass it for their convenience. I remember one situation where a senior executive wanted a new unit placed in an area where his sweetheart lived. Unfortunately, the real estate people knew that the market was thin and the location secondary. Nonetheless, he pressed (real estate reported to him), and he demanded a set of forms. With the assistance of a new member of the department, he "successfully" filled out the forms so that the location looked like a go, and the company eventually built the unit. It was a "dog" before it was built, and it is a dog today. As you might expect, the executive is no longer with the company and the unit has been closed. The impact on the real estate department and the process was devastating. The program lost its credibility, not to mention the million dollars that the company lost to the poor location. Incidentally, the woman is no longer his sweetheart, so there is no longer a need for that unit. Chalk one up for executive privilege.

Presently, a variety of consulting services offer computer base methods, to aid in market review and site selection for small and medium food service operations. These services may afford a convenient, relatively inexpensive approach to evaluating potential sites.

In determining whether to use such a computerized service, keep the following suggestions in mind:

- How was the food service location model developed? What specific types of food operations, types of locations, and number of cases were included in the model? Make sure that the sample is limited to food service units similar to your own. Sales forecasts derived from the experience of noncomparable units will be spurious.

- There should be a definitive set of guidelines and instructions. Be wary of methods that rely too heavily on subjective measures in forecasting sales. There should be clear-cut guidelines for determining any rankings.

- Be suspicious of methods that attempt to include factors not related to market and location. Data on advertising budgets, management practices, operating ratios, or employee turnover have no place in a location model.

- In general, the more pertinent and accurate the information that can be brought to bear on the problem, the better the solution.

- The demographic and socioeconomic composition of the trade area population is important to the model, but only if the relevant background customer characteristic data are known from previous consumer research. Data generated only by reviewing resident population, household characteristics, and income characteristics to establish similarities of so-called customers provide for a wide variety of error. Operators who are already in the food business, should do customer profiling first to identify the significant customer characteristics, which then can be matched to the resident population characteristics and be included in the prediction model.

SUMMARY

The most important element to keep in mind is that a computer-assisted location model is only one of several management tools, and it should be used with other inputs in the decision-making process. There is no substitute for experience, insight, and sound business judgment. Collectively, they should be utilized to develop the best market and location selection process.

Nineteen

Prioritization of Markets and Saturation Strategy

F ood operators, large and small, are often faced with deciding which city or which segment of the metropolitan area to enter. All too often the decision is made because real estate is available, "somebody knows somebody," or it is "on the way to the lake." Fortunately, there is a better method for choosing opportunities. Prioritizing markets is like selecting locations; it can be accomplished scientifically, unscientifically, or foolishly. Moreover, it can be done simply or in a detailed fashion. Therefore, the time and cost of prioritizing markets is within the reach of any food operator who is smart enough to recognize the need to limit risk and maximize opportunity.

Market saturation means different things to food operators. To the individual restaurateur, it may mean that he cannot open another unit in a particular city. To a multi-unit coffee shop operator, it may mean that he or she has reached the maximum number of units that the market can handle. To a major fast food operator, it may indicate that the maximum sales have been squeezed from the market, without experiencing sales cannibalism. This chapter addresses both priority and saturation.

245

PRIORITIZING MARKETS

For the major food operator, priortizing markets, correctly, results in higher sales, profits and a better return on investment capital. Often, priortizing is fairly simple. A food operator, for example, may be considering two cities or towns, trying to decide which to enter. The decision may be influenced in part by the recognition that many people in one of the cities may be familiar with the restaurant because of having visited it, or perhaps because of radio or television coverage overlap between the two market areas. Regardless of the reasons, the operator must consider numerous factors. As previously indicated, it is possible to take either the *detailed approach* or the *simplistic approach*. Both approaches have validity; resources and objectives should determine the degree of application. For the chain operator, I recommend the detailed approach, because resources are usually available and return on investment is generally a crucial element. The small operator usually has no choice but to use the simplistic approach.

SIMPLISTIC APPROACH

The simple process involves obtaining data for markets under consideration inexpensively and quickly. This can usually be accomplished through the local library. The various elements are described in the following subsections.

Comparison of Similar Data

The objective is to develop data similar to your customer profile. Through the use of *Sales and Marketing Management, Editors and Publishers Market Guide,* or a computer demographic data service, you can review current estimates of population and age distribution. The two former guides are published annually, while the latter must be purchased on a market or site basis. The publications are usually available in major libraries. All of the sources have an estimate of income. A word of caution—please read their individual definitions of income, to be sure that what you are comparing is similar to the data that you have developed in your own market. Once you have comparative data, what do you find? Are there more people in the age category that you are considering or less? How do the incomes compare? Also, find out what drives the economy of each city or town under consideration. How are they affected by recessions? What is their future?

Comparative Retail per Capita Figures

Using any of the previously mentioned data sources, identify their estimate of total retail sales, eating and drinking sales, and food sales (grocery stores and supermarkets). Also take their population data and divide it into the sales numbers that you have identified. This will provide per capita figures. Follow the same process for your own markets, and compare the information. Does it appear that the new markets under consideration are generative in attracting dollars to the community? What is happening with food sales (grocery stores and supermarkets)? You may want to do a comparison of several years to see sales trends.

Local Business Conditions

Call the Chamber of Commerce in the community under consideration and ask for their investment and development package, which normally includes bank deposits, employment, unemployment, names of the primary industries, retail sales, and other economic indicators. Compare the indicators with the community in which you currently have a restaurant or fast food operation. How do they compare? Does the new market appear to be stronger or weaker?

Competitive Evaluation

There are no shortcuts for competitive evaluation. If you are considering entry into a market, you need to go into the market, shop the competitors, and evaluate their facilities (see Chapter 11). How strong are your competitors? How do they compare with your proposed operation (honesty)?

Employment

Employment concentrations and the type of employment affect many restaurants and fast food facilities. Therefore, it is imperative to review any available information regarding the type of employers, number of employees, types of jobs, changes in job totals by types of jobs, their locations, and salary and wage rates. Remember that communities with heavy industry have been declining, while those with office developments, light industry, and distribution facilities have been growing. How do the markets under consideration compare?

Real Estate Costs

While checking the competition, you should check with local realtors to find out the real estate costs in the area, any available existing facilities, real estate taxes, the approval process, and environmental issues.

Entry and Priority

After going through the process, it usually is obvious whether you should consider the new market. If it appears marginal, then the degree of risk has increased significantly. Do not fall in love with an area and then try to force an opportunity when all the market factors point against such a move. Given the volatile nature of many segments of the restaurant and fast food business today, it might be wiser to pass and consider a different alternative. The following example shows the methodology used to reach a decision. A restaurateur has a successful restaurant in a city of 800,000 people and is interested in locating another in one of two smaller satellite cities of about 500,000 people. The restaurant is a family-oriented facility open for lunch and dinner. The unit has 90 seats, and a check average of $9.80. Lunch is mainly sandwiches, salads, and plate specials. The lunch check average amounts to $6.10. Dinner is family style and casual. Complete dinner specials are usually $9.95, including soup, salad, and entree. The menu is fairly wide, featuring dinner specials, as well as the standard fare, including chicken, fish, and a special steak sandwich, which is quite popular. The bar in the restaurant is a place where friends often meet. Meals are served in the bar, mainly at the booths that line the walls, and sporting events are featured on the bar's numerous television sets. Annual sales amount to $1,500,000, bar sales represent approximately 20% of the total.

The most frequent customer is predominantly 35 to 45 years of age, with an income ranging from $35,000 to $45,000. The next strongest customer groups are 45 to 59 years of age, with incomes over $50,000. They visit the restaurant about every two weeks. They especially like the good food, service, and relaxed atmosphere. The customer's employment is predominantly white- and tan-collar (high-tech service). The median driving time is nine minutes.

The existing facility is located on a major traffic artery in a densely populated portion of the city. There is considerable manufacturing and employment nearby. The location is squarely in the pattern of the residents of the nearby neighborhoods, and the socioeconomic characteristics of the residents are similar to the most frequent customers. There is another restaurant across the street that serves a much higher income market, with a check average of $17. Neither considers the other directly competitive. However, numerous family-oriented restaurants are located throughout the area, along with a large number of popularly price Italian restaurants and pizzerias.

The two cities, Alpha and Bravo, are presented for comparison in Table 19.1. Notice the differences between the two cities. Alpha is slightly larger, with a strong concentration of population in the age categories of 20 to 29 years and 30 to 44 years. Conversely, Bravo has fewer people in those categories. Application of the restaurant's age profile compares more favorably with Alpha than Bravo.

Bravo actually has more households because of a smaller number of persons per household (2.53 persons compared with Alpha's 2.75 persons). Alpha has a much higher median household income— $43,450 versus Bravo's $36,768. However, because Bravo has a smaller household size (2.53 persons), its per capita income, $14,532, is only slightly less than Alpha's, which is $15,800. A further look at the distribution of income, however, indicates that Alpha has a much closer distribution of income in relation to the restaurant's customer characteristics. For example, although Bravo has 25.8% in the $35,000-to-$49,999 income category compared with Alpha at 25.4%, Alpha has a better distribution toward the stronger white-collar income ranges of $50,000 and above.

Next, a review of retail dynamics indicates that Alpha enjoys a per capita retail sales (all retail dollars currently spent in the community) of $7,443 versus Bravo's $5,478. It appears that Alpha is importing retail sales dollars from the surrounding areas. In contrast, Bravo apparently is exporting sales dollars to another city. Finally, per capita eating and drinking sales amount to $948 for Alpha; in contrast, Bravo has per capita eating and drinking expenditures of $726. Assuming that the competition is about the same, Alpha would be a better market in which to develop new units.

TABLE 19.1

Comparison of Socioeconomic Characteristics
Alpha and Bravo Cities

	Alpha	Bravo
Population	587,000	542,000
Population by age (%):		
14 to 19 years	11.2	12.3
20 to 29 years	22.8	21.0
30 to 44 years	23.4	18.9
45 to 59 years	14.4	13.2
60 years and older	9.0	13.1
Households	213,454	214,229
Persons per household	2.75	2.53
Income—median household	$43,450	$36,768
Per capita income	$15,800	$14,532
Income distribution (%):		
$15,000–$24,999	14.6	23.0
$25,000–$34,999	17.9	19.1
$35,000–$49,999	25.4	25.8
$50,000–$74,999	22.5	14.4
$75,000 and over	18.9	12.2
Employment (%):		
White-collar	55.9	47.3
Tan-collar*	23.6	9.7
Blue-collar	20.5	43.0
Per capita retail sales	$7,443	$5,478
Per capita food sales	$1,896	$1,743
Per capita eating and drinking expenditures	$948	$726

*Tan-collar refers to high-tech service jobs.

DETAILED APPROACH

A complete priority analysis requires developing comparable data for each market under consideration in a definitive manner by evaluating the data within a logical framework and arriving at a sensible conclusion. The following elements are included in this analysis.

Develop Applicable Demographic Data

The first step is to take the customer profile data and, more specifically, the characteristics of the most frequent visitors and develop a similar data structure for each city or market under consideration. The objective is to compare compatibility of age, income, and other important elements to the new markets to see if they have sufficient compatible resources. How compatible are the incomes and the number of households within each income category? What is the age structure? How compatible are the number of people within each age category? What is the economic base of the community and how likely is it to be sustained?

Application of Your Customer Data to the New Market

Obtain the data from the 1990 census, current estimates, special censuses, income studies, the latest Census of Business estimates of retail sales, and other important sources, as described in previous chapters. The application of your customer profile to the market or markets under consideration will help to identify the extent to which adequate resources are available in those sensitive elements. Developing comparable data and matching it to the resources available in other cities or neighborhoods provides a clear picture of any potential opportunity. This becomes especially important if competition is strong for similar types of customers with compatible ages and incomes. Given today's frugal diner, if the situation is marginal—do not consider it!

Competitive Evaluation

Competitive evaluation requires identifying those restaurants or fast food facilities that will both directly and indirectly compete with any unit located in the city or town under consideration. Competition involves reviewing the locations, performance, pricing, seating, daypart activity, customer acceptance, weekend activity, any menu variations, and the overall sales of the existing competitors. Are they well located? Are they performing up to expectations? What is your analysis of their performance, service, product, presentation, and pricing? How will your restaurant or fast food operation compare?

Evaluation of Eating-Out Food Expenditures

Determine and evaluate the eating and drinking expenditures within a market area (see Chapter 14) and contrast the velocity of activity to that of the competitors in the marketplace. Furthermore, it can help pinpoint whether the community is importing or exporting retail dollars and food dollars. A simple trick in determining the extent of dollars available is either to utilize one of the computerized demographic data sources to provide overall data on the community or to use *Sales and Marketing Management* or *Editors and Publishers Market Guide*.

The former service can quickly provide a printout reflecting the demographics as well as their estimated expenditures. The latter books are published annually, giving estimates of population, income, age structure, and the like for most markets in the United States. Reviewing, not simply eating-out food expenditures, but also total retail sales and food (eaten at home) sales provides insight into whether the community is importing dollars or exporting dollars. Another trick is to divide the sales by the population to develop per capita figures; then compare the per capitas to the market in which you are currently competing. Any wide variations will indicate some rather considerable differences.

Advertising

Advertising denotes two things: the extent of advertising dollars spent by the major competitors in the marketplace, and the cost and the coverage of advertising within the new market or markets. Assessing these items will indicate who is spending money and how effectively; it will also suggest the amount of "bang" that you might get from your advertising dollars in the new market.

Existing Market Coverage

Often in considering new cities or towns, you may discover that some overlapping coverage exists. It is important to determine the extent of that coverage. Often, I have heard restaurant and fast food people say, "We have customers who come from [a specific area] who are constantly saying we should open a unit." That may be a reason for reviewing a market opportunity, but it certainly is not a reason for opening a unit without thoroughly evaluating the situation.

Market Share Comparison

If you have done your homework, you know the market share that you are currently capturing within your trade areas. If you were to apply similar market shares to the new market, what volume of sales dollars would be generated? Are they adequate?

Awareness

Often because of the proximity of cities and towns, there is a certain amount of interchange between them and, thus, frequently a reasonable level of awareness. The more awareness, the greater the opportunity to move into the community and do business very quickly. One way to test awareness is to see if the local newspapers in the community or communities under consideration have done any research that would indicate awareness. Some newspapers will carry out research at no cost to you, in order to add you to their list of advertisers. Nonetheless, getting a handle on any awareness that may exist is certainly important.

Product Consumption

If your particular menu is predominantly beef, fish, poultry, or other strongly identifiable items, it would be worthwhile to get as much information as possible on the level of consumption for those items in the local market. Supermarkets may be able to provide information about their sales or number of units sold, which you can then compare with your current market. Again, any wide variations would signal a need to be cautious.

Real Estate

If everything appears to be a "go," then it is important to look at real estate costs and possible available opportunities. You can then compare the cost of land (and/or buildings) to your current market.

Along with real estate costs, real estate taxes and assessments (where applicable) should be compared. By obtaining this kind of information, you can run a rather rough *pro forma* of sales to real estate costs to return on investment for the new market areas. This process not only can indicate whether it makes sense at this point to go any further but also can help to prioritize the opportunities, particularly if you are examining more than one market.

Licenses

License availability can queer a deal instantly, especially if a liquor license is needed and none are available. Certainly, the availability and, perhaps, cost of licensing should be added to the equation.

Environmental Issues

The hottest and most troublesome items in the process of developing new restaurants today are environmental issues. Many corner locations, much sought after by the fast food industry, were previously gasoline service stations. The Environmental Protection Agency is coming down hard on cleaning up former gasoline service station sites. Therefore, anyone considering the development of such a site must move cautiously. The theory of "deep pockets" appears to be consistent with the EPA; namely, the company with the most money pays for the clean up and must necessarily sue the others to recover. Environmental issues are adding a considerable amount of time to the site development process. In many areas, it can delay construction by at least a year. It is necessary, therefore, to protect yourself by examining this issue at the outset and understanding the implications for any specific site acquisition.

Approvals and Timing

Other approvals are required, such as building and zoning permits, health permits, and curb cuts. The timing of these approvals can be critical. By doing a little spadework, you can quickly discover the likely problems and identify the necessary timing to overcome such obstacles. These conclusions need to be part of the input into any priority analysis, since the added cost or time to develop a new unit or units may very well change the priority of one market area in favor of another.

Distance

I always ask, "Is distance a factor?" Some will say "yes," and some will say "no." Distance *is* a factor. From a management perspective in supervising the unit or units, the further the distance, the greater the amount of lost time. It is critical to take management resources into consideration in any decision to enter a new market, particularly if the market is somewhat distant.

Priority

Finally, after all the data has been gathered and evaluated and put into a logical sequence, conflicts will exist. For example, one site may reflect a low level of competition, a high opportunity score, and yet a long process of approvals. Conversely, another may show a fairly competitive market, expensive real estate, and immediate opportunity. The differences could require a reevaluation of priority, and simple "availability without problems" might move to the first position, an opportunity that ordinarily would not deserve such attention. The process is an eye-opener because it permits companies and individuals clearly to understand opportunities and their concomitant problems before jumping into what may be a tremendous opportunity or an incredible blooming disaster.

SATURATION PLANNING

Saturation of a market assumes that adequate resources are available to implement a restaurant or fast food development program. Whereas saturation can be accomplished over a long period, competition tends to prevent maximum penetration. Nonetheless, most companies, particularly fast food companies, will create a presence in all segments of the market and then attempt to "in-fill" between the exiting units to create saturation.

Individuals starting out in the restaurant or fast food business usually are not thinking about market saturation. Instead, their efforts are focused, as they should be, on making that first unit successful. Nevertheless, as additional units are added, management must consider the number of units that the marketplace can support. Usually the problem is not defined as saturation, but instead is expressed in a simple form such as, "We need one on the north side, the south side, the east side, and the west side." By reaching that objective, the operator may accomplish saturation. For some restaurateurs, saturation is a single unit within the market, while for others it might be 100 units. Much depends on the uniqueness and the type of restaurant facility. Also, the number of units that it takes to maximize the opportunity for, say, a single fast food operator, whose trade areas are relatively small, determines need. Whether the trade area is saturated with 1 or 100 units, a time will come when an additional operation will have an adverse impact on the existing unit or units.

In my experience, saturation usually occurs with multiple units. Sometimes the desire to add a unit is the result of a restaurateur's growing family, marriage of his children, or the need to expand to "meet the payroll." It may also simply be the desire to take advantage of an opportunity that exists. There can be any number of reasons for wanting to expand within a market area.

OBJECTIVES OF SATURATION

It is important in any business to establish a set of objectives. Unfortunately, in small businesses, goals are often not clearly stated. There are, for example, a number of reasons for considering expansion. The operator might want to:

- Serve maximum number of "my" customers.
- Capitalize on an existing opportunity.
- Develop a market as rapidly as possible.
- Optimize the advertising umbrella.
- Deter competition.
- Maximize sales, profits, and return on investment.

IMPLEMENTATION

There are several ways to accomplish objectives, depending on the available capital and the success of the existing food units. Regardless of the approach, the sought-after result is success in the market.

Rapid Development of Units in the Marketplace

Where money is no object, a food operator can *blitz* the development of new units. This approach will, hopefully, provide sufficient market presence to impact the market and overcome competitive consumer orientation.

Acquisition of Existing Food Operations

Companies often will acquire an operation with market representation to achieve an initial level of penetration, such as Hardee's acquisition of Roy Rogers' in the northeastern states. As a result Hardee's achieved market share immediately within difficult markets; they picked up a major product, chicken, which they could put in their other units nationwide; and they acquired locations that they most likely could not have obtained in the marketplace. Absorption can be difficult in the short run. However usually, after such a purchase, the company goes on to fill out the market area with additional units.

Franchising Market Area

Franchising can be a fast way to develop an area, if the existing units are apparently successful. Also, food concepts that require a limited amount of initial capital and a forecasted chance for good profits usually will sell well. Naturally, an aggressive advertising and promotion program is needed to sell franchises and increase customer awareness. Some have done extremely well, while many others have either not performed up to expectations or have failed. When operators have handled franchising correctly, with the right food concepts, good locations, adequate capital, and the necessary management, they have achieved success.

A Combination of Factors

Most aggressive companies adopt some combination of approaches, usually involving both company unit development and franchising. At a later date, some of the franchises are acquired to add to company operations.

A STRATEGIC APPROACH TO MARKET SATURATION

There is a priority approach to market development saturation. The primary objective is to develop the potentially highest sales units first, thereby increasing the amount of capital available to develop additional sites. Admittedly, unavailability of sites in an area, cost of land,

and other factors often change priorities. However, any good program must have flexible priorities to address changing situations. The procedure is accomplished by *priority levels*. The highest priority should produce the highest sales, profits, and return of capital, thus, driving additional development. The lowest priority is for long range planning. The following sections describe the various priority levels.

Priority 1—Locations with the Highest Potential Sales

Sites with the highest sales potential are often the most expensive and sometimes the least available. However, given the recent problems in the food industry, smart operators are solving this problem by taking existing facilities that have failed for other than locational reasons and converting them to their concept. This level should also have a strong concentration of residents with compatible characteristics. Where the likely locations are primarily in developed commercial areas, this level is often torpedoed by real estate representatives who do not want to deal with the difficulty or time required to obtain this type of site. Locationally, such sites are either in the dense urban environment, in areas with significant employment concentrations, or in proximity to major retail complexes. The priority often changes because of the time and frustration resulting from the attempt to accomplish the objectives. Nevertheless, Priority 1 locations usually will generate significant cash flow and capital to greatly assist the development of other locations at a faster rate. Furthermore, I have heard time and time again that it is impossible to get a location within a given area. Yet, when I review the area at a later time, I often find that others have succeeded. Timing is everything. I usually suggest that before throwing away an excellent locational strategy, the operator should take a little more time to accomplish the best. It will pay significant dividends in the long run.

Priority 2—Major Roadway Locations Serving a Wide Area

Major highway or roadway locations are often selected next. These are sites on, at, or near the interchanges of heavily traveled expressways, or sites located on highly visible and accessible local highways that carry a constant flow of heavy traffic throughout day and evening hours. For most types of food service facilities, this type of location represents high sales levels, assuming that competition is not overwhelming.

Priority 3—Strong Residential, Commercial, and Employment Market Areas

These locations normally represent the majority of sites for a metropolitan market area strategy. Locations developed in or near areas of commercial and employment concentrations generally will have a large residential population base, a generative commercial or employment node, adequate traffic at the proper times, and a position within the local driving patterns.

Priority 4—In-Fill or Secondary Locations

Once the best locations have been developed, the in-fill process usually proceeds. This involves reviewing the performances of the existing units against areas where the food operator's units are not represented. Smart operators will determine the customer distributions for their most frequent visitors, prior to beginning the in-fill process. Usually, these locations only reach adequate sales levels because of significant advertising resulting in consumer awareness and product acceptance. Priority 4 units provide maximum market saturation. Sometimes, given all the customer acceptance and success of the food concept in the marketplace, secondary locations simply do not work because they are situated in residential areas where no significant generator exists, and where traffic is only moderate. Without this type of strategy, these locations would never be selected, and most often, should not be.

Priority 5—Special Locations

Special locations include either regular units or kiosks in downtown areas, beaches, airports, in-line locations, inside malls, near schools, and inside university student unions, railroad stations, and tops of buildings. Often they are developed along with other units. However, because they are special, they require more attention than more typical locations. Also, their orientation sometimes is the result of trends (i.e., another food operator opens a unique unit that invites imitation).

Priority 6—Intermediate and Long-Range Locations

During a market analysis locations are usually identified that are premature for development. Nevertheless, they can be targeted for future acquisition. For firms with adequate resources, some land banking might be in order, especially if it is obvious that land values are going to explode. It is usually wise to acquire a site several times larger than needed. When the site is developed at a later date, the appreciation in land value not only will pay for the carrying costs but often will pay for the location itself. Unfortunately, most food operators do not have the capital to "bank" land. Knowing where future units should be placed allows for flexibility, planning, better negotiating, and a much more efficient use of executive time.

SUMMARY

Prioritizing opportunities is useful for both the small entrepreneur planning a second location and the chain operating hundreds of locations. The secret is to match the characteristics of your most frequent visitor with market areas that have similar or even larger concentrations of people with the same profile. In doing so, it is necessary to measure consumer attitudes and the acceptance of the food operator's products. Also, the impact of advertising on sales and market penetration needs to be measured, to determine the impact on prioritized locations. Finally, a strategy should be developed for implementing development. Objectives should be established, priorities determined, resources measured, and strategic programs designed to accomplish the plan. Programs need to be flexible because they will change. Sometimes the changes are the result of new competition, while other times the board of directors will change the direction for no adequately explainable reason. Regardless, plans rarely end up working as they were originally designed. Nonetheless, the process will have occurred and the company will be better for it.

A final word on advertising from a locational point of view. Advertising can rarely make a poor location good. Instead, advertising provides awareness and a mental picture of what a food operation is (or would like to be). That awareness can have a dramatic impact on sales, if properly done. In the 1960s when Kentucky Fried Chicken first started, a national advertising campaign, the results, in markets where there were enough units, were dramatic. Sales doubled in most good locations. However, mediocre locations did not experience the same impact. Advertising supports sales but does not create enough of them to support a poor location.

Part Three

Implementation

Twenty

General Site Selection Criteria

I am sure that you have noticed that this chapter is near the end of the book. That is for a very specific reason; namely, it is important to read and understand the importance of all of the preceding principles and applications before rushing to select a site. If you have skipped to this chapter without reading the others, please, for your own sake, go back and start at the beginning.

The following sections describe general site criteria guidelines. *They are not absolute!* Each existing or potential food operator must thoroughly evaluate the market for opportunities before selecting a site. Failure to adequately do so may lead to poor results. Moreover, without good food, service, and management, the facility will probably not meet expectations and may be destined for failure.

Site selection for most people is neither an art nor a science. Instead, it is a process of matching available dollars to available locations in the marketplace. For those who select locations regularly, the process becomes a science, while to others it remains an art. Whether the decision is made by the numbers or through intuition, a fairly standardized set of considerations come into play. This chapter, reviews the important considerations for various restaurant and fast food facilities and also provides some general guidelines for site selection. There are no shortcuts for choosing sites. The discussions in the other chapters have been designed to arrive at this point in the site selection process armed with the proper tools. The more tools that you have available, the better your ability to select a good location.

All locations have many similarities and dissimilarities, so it is important to understand the emphasis and the sensitivity of each market and locational principle. For example, the difference between success and failure in a small town can be the ability of the restaurant to attract customers on a highly frequent basis, usually from a wide area. This is often a function of location, good food, personality, menu, price, quantity of food, and perhaps environment. In a large community, these factors are equally important; even though the market is much larger, the requirements are the same.

Rightly or wrongly, there are often psychological reasons for selecting an area. The attempt to justify an area or a location is actually one of the most common locational approach mistakes. An operator might like an area for one of many reasons such as, its being near home, work, or the beach, or because a good real estate deal can be made. The primary reason for failure in the restaurant business (other than poor food and inferior management) is usually trying to force a restaurant or fast food facility into an area where it does not belong. An operator's desire to be in a specific area regardless of the market stands high on the list of mistakes. Ego causes many mistakes, as does the lack of adequate funds.

A better approach is to choose an area because the market and customer knowledge indicate that it has the potential for success. *The area should be selected because the market forces indicate that a new unit can be supported at an acceptable sales level.* This decision is only possible after analyzing the demographics, market structure, competition, patterns, accessibility, income, age, structure, household size, household structure, occupational status, topography, eating-out habits, spending and saving patterns, and price or rental rates. Once that has been done, the next step is to identify locational opportunities within the area delineated. The most common choice is the major traffic artery bisecting an area or where the greatest concentration of activity exists. Some restaurant operators will avoid those locales in favor of a less congested and more placid setting. Both decisions can be right for an individual restaurant, if all the other ingredients are in place.

STEPS IN SITE SELECTION

1. Gather the relevant data regarding the overall market leading to the selection of a specific area.
2. Prepare the demographic and income data for the appropriate trade area.
3. Apply customer profile data or data developed from evaluating competitive facilities.
4. Compute the expenditure dynamics applicable to your type of food operation.
5. Thoroughly evaluate the competition. Determine competitors' sales, dayparts, menu, pricing, strengths, customer attraction, service, general customer characteristics, and other considerations discussed throughout this book.
6. Estimate potential sales within the area that you identify.
7. Estimate sales for your potential restaurant or fast food unit.
8. Apply locational principles to identify good alternative locations.
9. Evaluate site location criteria to identify individual opportunities.
10. Determine land costs and rental rates.
11. Test the economics in relation to sales potential.
12. Develop a pro forma on the location, reflecting anticipated sales, cost of goods, controllables, uncontrollables, and net income before taxes.
13. Proceed only if your market and locational evaluation is positive.

The following pages present general market and locational guidelines to assist in the selection of locations. Again, it is essential to evaluate your customers' characteristics thoroughly (and perhaps those of your prospective competitors or the food operation that you may be copying). It is important to understand and define your specific objectives, type of food operation, your niche in the marketplace, menu, pricing, atmosphere, customer targets, daypart percentages, economics, locational needs, parking, costs, rental affordability, capitalization, and anticipated return on sales and investment. Next, you must be sure that the customers that you expect can actually find the unit, gain access, park, dine enjoyably, leave the unit, egress the location, and return on another day because of satisfaction.

TABLE 20.1

Fast Food Site Selection Guidelines

These guidelines represent customer and site analysis findings gathered over the past 30 years. They are subject to variations depending on the community, type of facility, type of location, and the operator's skill. The information should be used simply as a guide and not as the basis for final decisions. You must assess your own trade area, market potential, locations, and financial capability and then draw your own conclusions.

Categories	Downtown	Suburban Highway	Commercial Area	Major Street, Dense Urban	Business District, In-line	Near Major Mall	Resort Area	Major College Campus	Highway Interchange	Small Towns	Country Crossroad
Frequent customers	Workers	Residents, workers	Residents, shoppers, workers	Residents, workers	Shoppers, workers	Shoppers, residents, workers	Visitors, workers, residents	Students, staff, residents	Travelers, residents	Residents, visitors	Area residents, transients
Primary trade area	1–2 blocks	3–4 miles	3–4 miles	2–3 miles	3–5 miles	1–5 miles	1–3 miles	1–2 miles	1–10 miles	3–10 miles	3–10 miles
Business within the primary trade area (%)	80–90	50–60	60–70	80–90	60–65	30–40	80–90	80–90	50–60	75–90	50–60
Business from outside primary trade area (%)	10–20	40–50	30–40	10–20	35–40	60–70	10–20	10–20	40–50	10–25	40–50
Market penetration within the primary trade area (%)	4–5	1–2	1–2	0.5–1	1–2	1–3	1–3	1–4	1–5	2–7	N/A
Demographics—Dominant age categories	18–45	5–45	16–45	16–45	16–45	16–45	16–35	16–35	16–50	16–50	16–50
Driving time—average mins.	N/A	8–12	6–9	5–8	7–11	10–15	5–9	5–9	10–15	8–12	10–15
Traffic requirements—cars	Lunchtime pedestrians	20,000+	12,000+	8,000+	6,000+	15,000+	7,000+	8,000+	15,000+	7,000+	10,000+
Side of street											
Lunch, dinner, some breakfast	Lunch side	Homeward	Either	Either	Either	Homeward	Activity side	Heavy walking	Activity side	Either	Activity side
Strong breakfast, lunch, and minor dinner	Morning side	Work side	Work side	Work side	Work side	Work side	Activity side	Toward class	Work side	Either	Work side

Site access	Principal street	Highway	Principal street	On street	Principal street	Primary artery	Main drag	Primary commercial street	Primary road	Main street	Primary highway
Traffic light	No	Very desirable	Beneficial	Helpful	Helpful	Beneficial	Helpful	Helpful	Helpful	Helpful	Helpful
Major traffic backup	N/A	Avoid	Beware	Avoid	Beware	Avoid	Beware	Beware	Avoid	Beware	Beware
Median strips	N/A	At break	At break	At break	N/A	At break	At break	At break	Avoid	At break	Avoid
Hills and curves	N/A	Avoid	Be aware	Caution	OK	Avoid	Be aware	OK	Avoid	OK	Avoid
Nearby generative complexes	Yes	Beneficial	Essential	Helpful	No	Essential	Helpful	Helpful	Helpful	Helpful	Helpful
Visibility—directions	Yes	Both	One minimum	One minimum	One minimum	Both	Both	One minimum	Both	Both	Both

TABLE 20.2

Restaurant Site Selection Guidelines

These guidelines represent findings gathered over the past 30 years. They are subject to many variations depending on the community, type of location, restaurant facility, management, and financial strength. The information should be used cautiously and not as the basis for final decisions. It is designed simply to present examples of different types of typical restaurants and their locational needs. You must assess your own trade area, market potential, location, management, and financial capability and then draw your own conclusions.

Categories	Coffee Shop	Major Suburban Restaurant	Fine Dining, Dinner Only	Family Restaurant, Suburban	Theme Restaurant	Bar and Grill	Ethnic Restaurant, Suburban	Downtown, Unique	Special Occasion Restaurant	Major Mall Restaurant	University Restaurant and Bar
Annual sales	$1,200,000	$2,500,000	$950,000	$1,750,000	$4,500,000	$450,000	$550,000	$5,000,000	$2,400,000	$2,500,000	$3,000,000
Type of location	Major street	Major street	Dense urban	Commercial area	Commercial area	Business district	Commercial area	Downtown	Highway	Shopping mall	Campus, street
Frequent customers	Workers, residents	Managers, residents	Residents	Residents, workers	Workers, residents	Workers, residents	Residents	Workers, visitors, residents	Residents	Residents, shoppers	Students, staff
Primary trade area (in miles)	3	5	10	5	7	3	5	20	10	10	3
Business within (%)	70	60	40	80	55	90	70	85	75	75	80
Business from outside (%)	30	40	60	20	45	10	30	15	25	25	20
Market penetration within the primary trade area (%)	2	5	1	4	5	0.98	2	0.5	2	3	6
Demographics— dominant age categories	35–55	40–55	34–45	25–45	21–35	45–65	25–45	45–65	35–60	18–44	18–25
Driving time— average minutes	12	15	24	11	17	5	12	25	40	25	Walking 10

Traffic requirements	15,000+	25,000+	14,000+	9,000+	30,000	5,000+	12,000	N/A	40,000+	33,000+	N/A
Side of street											
Lunch, dinner	N/A	Toward home	Not important	Not important	Toward home	Not important	Toward activity	In activity	Inboard side	Facing primary street	Facing campus buildings
Strong breakfast, lunch and minor dinner	Toward work	N/A	N/A	N/A	N/A	N/A	N/A	N/A	N/A	N/A	N/A
Site access	Major street	Major street	Major street	Primary street	Primary street	Primary street	Primary street	Historic street	Near highway ramp	Parking lot	Off street
Traffic light	No	Yes	No	No	Yes	No	No	Yes	Yes	Yes	No
Major traffic backup	No	No	Yes	Yes	Rush hour	No	No	No	No	No	No
Median strips	No	Break	No	No	No	No	Yes	No	No	No	No
Hills and curves	No	No	No	No	No	No	No	No	No	No	No
Nearby generative complexes	Yes	Strong	Yes	Yes	Major	No	Yes	Yes	No	Yes	Yes
Visibility—directions	Both	Both	One	One	Both	One	One	One	Both	One	Both

SITE SELECTION GUIDELINES

Tables 20.1 and 20.2 provide some guidelines for both fast food facilities and restaurants. The following comments supplement the information in the tables:

- There are numerous types of fast food facilities. Some are national chains, such as McDonald's, Kentucky Fried Chicken, Long John Silver's, and Hardee's. There are also national sandwich shops, such as Subway. Each has its own idiosyncrasies. Nonetheless, they share certain market characteristics that help to ensure success. Market penetration and trade area sizes are affected by the number of units, how close the units are to each other, consumer acceptance, consumption trends, advertising, promotion, operations, management, and, last but certainly not least, location. There are numerous variations in all these factors.
- The market penetration figures presented in Table 20.1 for fast food units represent strong, successful units. While a 1% penetration is quite normal for a three-mile radius, to achieve anything above that requires a good location, a strong product mix, total consumer acceptance, adequate promotion, good management, and financial stability.
- Traffic counts, as I have previously indicated, do not tell the entire story. Therefore, it is important to determine when the traffic occurs, along with any impediments to access.
- Generally, median strips and traffic backups in front of a prospective location are deadly. Each location must be analyzed individually.
- Hills and curves usually obstruct visibility and make it difficult for customers to get into and out of sites. Although such sites are sometimes successful, exiting can be hazardous, especially for older customers. Cafeterias should never be located on a hill or curves, nor should the speed limit be faster than 45 miles per hour.
- Restaurants, in contrast to fast food units, are often very much affected by management. Good food people have been able to overcome poor locations by building a strong clientele through good food, unique surroundings, and excellent service. Price also often plays a role. It usually takes years to accomplish this.

Twenty-One

Site Economics and the Deal

S ite economics is a fancy way of saying, "What can I afford?" or, "What kind of deal can I make for a site?" Regardless of the question, the issue is "What *should* I pay either for rent or to buy a site and build a building?" Site economics procedures help to establish parameters. "What can I afford to pay and what amount should I not exceed?" Beyond that, the nuance of negotiation and the "deal" become the major factors (assuming the building fits the site, adequate parking is available, proper permits can be obtained, and on and on). All too often, the stimulus to consider going into the food business is the availability of an existing restaurant or fast food facility, combined with ego. Thus, the economics are worked in reverse to determine the sales requirements that will support the rent. While this approach often works, the many failures in the restaurant industry speak for themselves.

THE ECONOMICS OF RESTAURANT OR FAST FOOD OPPORTUNITY

In determining "economic parameters," it may be logical to work the numbers from several directions, including the Sales Approach, the Investment Approach, and the "What Can I Afford?" Approach.

The Sales Approach

Historically, the food industry has come to recognize that certain levels or percentages of sales should be maintained to be successful. These are comparative guidelines that a restaurateur or fast food facility can follow. Most food people are aware of levels of food cost, labor costs, controllables, uncontrollables, and net profit before income taxes. Rent has levels as well. For the restaurant or fast-food operator who is not considering a "watering hole," rent, as a percentage of sales, should usually be about 6%, although occasionally it may be as high as 8%. Total occupancy cost (rent plus maintenance and taxes) should not be more than 10 to 12%. In the initial years, the percentage of rent to sales may be between 8% and 10% because of the high cost of setting up a new business. However, by the third year, the percentage to sales should be between 5% and 6%. With rent, real estate taxes, insurance, maintenance, and any local use taxes, the total percentage to sales should not exceed 10% to 12%. For example, if a restaurant (we will call it "Joe's Place") were to have sales of $500,000 annually, the rent should not exceed about $30,000 annually. Total occupancy costs should be between $50,000 and $60,000 annually.

Leasehold improvements are those improvements made in a facility, exclusive of Furniture, Fixtures, and Equipment (FF&E). If the leasehold improvements were $100,000, and they are amortized over 10 years, then $10,000 annually is applied. Thus, the rent that the operator can afford is $30,000 annually, plus the $10,000 for leasehold improvement amortization. Combined, the percentage to gross sales amounts to 8%. With taxes, insurance, and maintenance, the percentage will be between 10% and 12% of sales.

Food costs, at 35%, and labor costs (including management salary), at 24%, together amount to 59%. If the controllables amount to 15%, and the operator expects to have a net profit before income tax of 15%, the uncontrollables, including rent, cannot exceed 11%. Table 21.1 reflects these figures.

In this example, the reader may have concluded that any provision for FF&E has not been identified. It *should not* be included as part of the rent calculation. Only the interest cost on FF&E and the annual amortization is included in the Profit and Loss Statement. The Net Profit before Taxes is also before debt service. If the equipment cost were $125,000, amortized over five years, the annual

TABLE 21.1

Joe's Place
Profit and Loss Statement
12-Month Period

		Dollars	Percent
Gross sales		$500,000	100
Food costs	$175,000		35
Labor costs	120,000		24
Cost of sales		295,000	59
Gross margin		205,000	41
Controllables		75,000	15
Uncontrollables		55,000	11
Net Profit before Taxes		$ 75,000	15

FF&E amortization would amount to $25,000 a year. If the investment and working capital had amounted to $100,000, it would take less than two years to recover the investment. If the $100,000 were financed, then the return would be higher, but the interest cost would also be higher.

In another example, a restaurateur has a 250-seat restaurant with cocktail lounge. The facility is about 8,000 square feet and costs approximately $960,000, not including the FF&E, which adds an additional $225,000. The restaurant sits on 60,000 square feet of land, at a cost of $500,000. The FF&E is financed over seven years. The restaurant is successful, at least by sales standards, capturing $3,000,000 annually. Table 21.2 depicts the sales, expenses, and profit.

If the restaurant were rented, an investor would probably want a return of 12%, net, net, net. This simply means that the landlord wants the restaurant operator to pay all the real estate taxes, maintenance, and insurance. In this example, the landlord's investment, including the land and building, amounts to $1,460,000. Thus, the rent would be $175,200 annually, or 5.84% of gross sales. The equipment would be amortized at approximately $32,143 annually (amortized over seven years).

A quick way to figure the required sales level is to take the rent and divide it by 6%. For example, if the rent were $60,000 annually,

TABLE 21.2

Jack's Place
Profit and Loss Statement
12-Month Period

	Dollars		Percent
Sales		$3,000,000	
Food costs	$1,140,000		38
Labor costs	720,000		24
Cost of goods sold		1,860,000	62
Gross margin		1,140,000	38
Controllables	450,000		15
Uncontrollables	360,000	810,000	12
Net Profit before Taxes		$ 330,000	11

then the sales required to successfully meet the payments would be $1,000,000, (divide the rent of $60,000 by 6%, which will result in sales of $1,000,000). A 10% rent would require sales of $600,000, given the same $60,000 in rent. However, the additional 4% must come from either improved performance or net profit (usually from net profit). Through this procedure, you can determine the sales level required to operate a restaurant successfully. If the rent is too high, then the situation should be reevaluated. Perhaps you may decide to forgo "the agony of defeat."

Many go into this business without really calculating what they expect to make to support themselves. Whatever that amount, it should be included in the computation to determine a realistic level of sales. If profits and return on your investment look marginal, stop the process before you bleed to death!

Some individuals approach the rent situation somewhat differently. They pick out a restaurant that they would like to copy, obtain its operating figures, and assume that they can do as well. If they choose wisely and remain within the rental parameters, they will probably be successful. However, if they are below the anticipated sales level, the rent may kill them. Remember, for many in the food business, success is not instant; it is achieved through years of surviving against additional competition and changing patterns and trends.

The Investment Approach

The Investment Approach recognizes that a risk investment requires a risk reward. Therefore, return on investment is the key to the decision process. When correctly undertaken, it does not interfere with the concept, but rather with the economics, of a location. Most restaurant and fast food chains insist that the Sales Approach must yield a rent not to exceed 6% and that an investment must provide an adequate return on invested capital.

What is a fair return on invested capital? That determination usually rests with the current availability and cost of money. The larger chain operators also consider the internal rate of return; however, there may be other elements. One of the most common computations is the "12% return on investment" usually sought by an investor. Other investors may require 10% on the land and 12% on the improvements, or even a 20% return on equity. Naturally, the current rent interest rate, the amount invested, and the existence of financing plays an important role in establishing an investor's expected rate of return.

In this example, there is a requirement for a 20% return on capital; I will work backward toward the sales required to justify this kind of a return. Assume that the investment in a new restaurant facility amounts to $1,000,000. A 20% return on invested capital would require a minimum net profit of $200,000. If that return were to be designated as rent, then it would be necessary for the restaurant to have sales of at least $3,333,333 to provide a $200,000 return to the real estate. However, if the actual dollar investment was 25% of the total land and building cost ($1,000,000) and 75% of it was financed, then the actual equity in the deal would amount to $250,000. The annual return before debt service would amount to 80%. By comparison, a 12% return on the overall $1,000,000 investment would create a rent of $120,000. Given an actual $250,000 investment, the return is 48%. It is, therefore, important to understand the basis for the computation. Nevertheless, it is necessary to approach the concept of economics from both directions.

Often the restaurant industry does not accurately compute return on investment. This is particularly true when the property is owned by the restaurant, and is listed on the balance sheet; however, no actual rent is charged, other than mortgage payments. This arrangement does not adequately reflect the value of the real estate or the value of the business. The real estate should be able to support a rent comparable to that of a real estate investor. In fact, it is often much better to hold the real estate in a separate corporation or partnership and rent the facility to the restaurant corporation or partnership. The business should make an adequate return on its invested capital, while the real estate should provide an investor's return, so that if it should become necessary in the future to sell the real estate and lease it back (sale/leaseback), the business could support the new rent. Many operators find this a great way to finance additional restaurants without disturbing their existing operations.

The "What Can I Afford?" Approach

Many restaurants and fast food operations fail because someone believes that he or she can succeed where others have failed. While this has been proven true quite often, success can be dependent on a real estate deal. The important elements include having the right product and concept in the right location to meet the demand of potential customers.

How many times have we all heard of food operators who had concepts similar to McDonald's but failed miserably in the latter 1950s and early 1960s? In examining many of these operations, I have found that they were definitely in the wrong location. The operators have explained that they were motivated by being able to get into business at an extremely low cost, and they figured that they could overcome the locational deficiencies with an unusual or superior product. Sometimes, though infrequently, this works. Usually, however, it takes years to create customer loyalty. Unfortunately, most people who go into these kinds of situations are undercapitalized, and, as a result, need success immediately. Success, in the food business, can be very elusive.

I fully recognize that most new food operators have limited resources and must stretch every dollar as much as possible. Nevertheless, real estate, over the long term, is a relatively inexpensive part of a business's success. Moreover, with a little investigation, you can often find a location in a good area that will help to ensure profits.

"Panic" site selection, created by a real estate agent's indicating that the location will be lost if it is not taken immediately, accentuates what will ultimately be the problem. Having limited resources does not necessarily confine the spectrum of opportunities. It takes time to investigate the concept and the potential customer, and to identify the area that will best combine concept and customer.

Usually when you have done so, you will find a plethora of real estate locational opportunities from which to choose.

THE DEAL

Basic Principles

Making a real estate deal often makes a person feel intimidated, worried that the property will get away, and inclined to believe the happy real estate broker. There are numerous other considerations, but that pretty well sums it up. People feel intimated because of a lack of knowledge. The more knowledge you can gain on the subject, the wiser you will become and the better deal you will be able to negotiate.

The most basic principle to remember is that *there are no rules in making a deal*, other than what may be dictated by financing or income tax considerations. Many real estate people may tell you that the only way you will make a deal is by paying a base rent, plus an annual adjustment in that rent based on the Consumer Price Index (CPI), along with a percentage of gross sales, on net, net, net terms. While a considerable number of deals may be made along those guidelines, they are not absolute; therefore, they are almost always subject to change. For every so-called absolute, ten deals are made that have anywhere from major to minor variations in the guidelines.

Definitions

Lessor

The lessor is the owner or landlord of a property who agrees to allow someone to use his or her property, usually for a specific period of time, at an agreed-upon rental rate.

Lessee

A lessee is one who leases property from an owner for a given period of time. For this privilege, the lessee pays rent to the property owner. Sometimes leases are for long periods of time, while other times they are for a very short term.

Lease

A lease is a legal instrument in which a property owner permits a user (lessee) to take possession of his or her property for a specific period of time, subject to the covenants and conditions contained in the document. These conditions usually include the amount of annual rent, when it is to be paid, how it is to be paid (monthly), any adjustments in the base rent over the term, and any options to extend the lease term. Also included are conditions that govern should a default of the agreement occur, or should the unit be partially or totally destroyed by fire, tornado, or other disaster. Leases range from simple agreements to extremely complicated documents. Regardless of size and complexity, the agreement still relates to the same possession of property.

Purchase

A purchase is an agreement, entered into by consenting parties, to acquire the "fee simple title of ownership" for a piece of property, usually including all rights pertaining thereto. The purchase should give the purchaser the right to operate the property as he or she sees fit. In some geographic areas, mineral rights are excluded, as are air rights. A purchase contract usually has specific dates for actions and is subject to certain conditions.

In the food industry, those conditions usually pertain to the necessary governmental approvals and permits including operating, zoning, building, health department, and environmental permits. When the conditions are met, a closing date is set up for conveying the title to the purchaser and the purchase price to the seller. This could also be a trade instead of cash, by which the buyer and seller exchange acceptable equivalent properties.

There are times when purchases take place under contract, and a closing does not occur immediately. This could be a rental agreement with a purchase option, including a small payment at closing and installment payments for a specified period. The contract usually provides that, at a certain point in the payment schedule, title will be transferred to the purchaser, subject to conditions and covenants.

Closing

A closing usually occurs when all of the contingencies and obligations in an agreement have been met. At that time, the title to the property is conveyed to the purchaser and the funds are disbursed. Often, the closing is handled by a real estate title company, which holds the agreement and the necessary documents in escrow until all of the conditions are fulfilled.

Ground or Land Lease

A ground or land lease is an agreement between a property owner and an individual, partnership, or corporation that is interested in using the property for a specified period. The ground lease gives the user specified rights to the property over an agreed-upon term, usually for a specific annual rent. Ground leases are often used when the property owners do not wish to sell their property. The user is usually not interested in owning the real estate. Sometimes the lessee simply is trying to minimize capital outlay by leasing rather than buying the land. Also, there are numerous real estate developers throughout North America who are interested in leasing rather than selling, land. In a ground lease, the ownership of any improvements to the property usually reverts to the property owner at the end of the lease term.

Ground Lease Subordinated

A subordinated ground or land lease permits the lessee not only to use the property but also to subordinate the lessor's interest in the land to a mortgage or some other type of financing. Thus, the property owner subordinates his rights to the property to a financial institution's first right-of-lien. Therefore, should the lessee default on the agreement, the lending institution has the first right of recovery, and may, in fact, sell the real estate to satisfy the indebtedness. Should that occur, it is quite conceivable that the property owner will end up with nothing. As previously indicated, at the end of the lease term and any agreed-upon options, the improvements on the property (buildings and the like) usually revert to the property owner (this is, of course, fully negotiable). Sometimes the appraised fair market value of the improvements is determined, and the lessee has several options available regarding recovery of some of the improvements.

Ground Lease Unsubordinated

An unsubordinated ground lease permits a lessee to use a parcel or tract of real estate. It does not, however, permit the lessee to use the land or its value in arranging financing. Instead, any improvements to the property must be accomplished with the lessee's cash, credit line, or some other means. In the event of a default (the lessee not paying the rent, or some other violation of the rental agreement), the property owner has a right to recover the property, including any improvements that have been made. This is a simplification of a usually complex arrangement. Normally, there are remedies to rectify the situation, all of which are negotiable and range over a wide spectrum.

Term of the Agreement

The term is the period of time over which property, and/or the buildings are leased. In the restaurant and fast food industry, lease lengths are between 15 and 20 years, with anywhere from two to five 5-year options. For smaller space users, it is not unusual to have leases of either 5 or 10 years, sometimes with options as well.

Options

An option is an agreement (or part of a lease or purchase agreement) that usually allows the lessee certain future rights. For a lessee, it may permit an extension of the original term over which the property will be used. Thus, if a restaurant has a lease with two 5-year options, at the end of the original lease term the restaurant operator can exercise the first 5-year option, extending the term for use of the demised premises. Normally, there is a rental adjustment at the commencement of the option. Usually, the agreement spells out the amount of rent; there are situations, however, where an option is given, but the rent is determined when the option is exercised, based on market conditions and the appraised value.

Mortgage or Mortgage Deed

A mortgage is a secured loan; the security is usually a specific piece or parcels of real estate. It is also a legal document in which the property owner pledges the value of his or her property to ensure payment of a loan or mortgage placed on the property, usually to construct improvements on the property. If, however, the owner defaults on the mortgage, the lending institution normally has the right to recover the loan through the lease or sale of the property.

Earnest Money Deposit

Earnest money, sometimes referred to as escrow money, represents funds placed in the hands of a third party (often the title company), pending the satisfaction of all contingencies stipulated in the contract. Earnest money is a reflection of the buyer's good faith desire to consummate a contract.

Build-to-Suit

A build-to-suit agreement normally requires that a landlord build a new restaurant or fast food facility to the operator's specifications. Usually, the landlord must place an agreed-upon amount of money in an account to pay for the construction of the building and parking lot. In turn, the operator agrees to pay a specific monthly or quarterly rental to the landlord. Usually, there is a "cap," or an agreed-upon amount for the construction. Also, the construction of the building is often the responsibility of the food operator. Should the cost of construction exceed the agreed-upon amount placed in the construction fund, the excess charges are the responsibility of the food operator. Naturally, there are numerous variations to this type of arrangement. Also, when the building is finished, or at an agreed-upon time, the food operator must begin paying rent. The date for commencing rent payments is often tied to financing or the beginning of mortgage payments by the landlord.

Consumer Price Index (CPI)

The Consumer Price Index is a measure of economic change that was established by the U. S. Department of Commerce to track changes taking place in value. By charting specific economic data (such as the cost of money and changes in the price of durable and nondurable goods), the Commerce Department has charted changes in economic levels since 1959. Because of the long-standing nature of the index, it is often used as a measure of change in our society. Therefore, it has become a much used gauge of changes in real estate values and rents. Landlords now try to make leases subject to frequent adjustments, based on changes in the CPI. Some try to insert a CPI change on an annual basis, while others attempt to have the base rent adjusted every three to five years on the basis of the CPI.

From a food operator's perspective, I am opposed to using the CPI in real estate deals because the tenant has no control over it. In periods of excessive inflation, the CPI adjustment can cause bankruptcy. Instead of permitting the use of the CPI, I suggest negotiating for specific dollar changes in the base rent, so that the rent obligation is known and can be planned for accordingly. If that is impossible, then try to put a "stop" on the extent to which the rent can be raised in a single or multiple years. This qualifier will protect against excessive changes.

Percentage Lease Clause

A percentage lease adjustment clause is the landlord's way of participating in inflation and sales increases. While rent is the primary consideration, the percentage lease clause often provides a significant addition to the landlord's return. It works as follows: The base rent is paid monthly. In the negotiations, the parties determine a "breakpoint," which is the point at which the percentage of sales (say 6%) is greater than the rent obligation. At that point, the landlord is entitled to the agreed-upon percentage of sales (the difference between the agreed-upon rent and the percentage of sales). This arrangement will be discussed in greater detail later in this chapter.

Sometimes the percentage breakpoint is set higher, so that it does not come into play unless sales are actually considerably higher than that point. A percentage lease clause is better than a CPI adjustment; avoid both, however, if possible. (Naturally, this is from the restaurateur's perspective.)

The Real Estate Broker

The real estate broker is the individual who claims to know your business and, in 95% of the cases, does not. He or she is in the real estate business and derives income from selling or leasing real estate to food people. Selling some land to a major chain or another successful restaurant does not make a person expert in restaurant site selection. The broker generally receives a commission from the seller. Furthermore, the higher the sale price of the property, the more commission the individual earns. Can you see the motivation? It is not in favor of the buyer. In my experience, for every 1,000 real estate agents, there may be one or two who truly understand the food business, have integrity, and work to be sure that the deal succeeds.

Approvals

All deals should be subject to the approvals required to operate a restaurant or fast food unit on a specific site or location. Approvals include zoning and building permits, health requirements, Environmental Protection Agency (EPA) permits, liquor license (if needed), driveway permits, and landscaping. In more than 30 years, I have seen only two situations where a deal need not have been contingent on all approvals, prior to closing or signing the final lease deal. Protect yourself, regardless of what the broker says.

Attorney

An attorney is a licensed individual who should understand and practice real estate law. If a qualified attorney handles your deal, it will not be necessary to rewrite the agreement several times, nor will later changes be necessary. While I may be a bit cynical regarding lawyers, I have known some truly great ones, who saved the buyer or lessee a small fortune by insisting on the proper verbiage in the agreement. Unfortunately, it has often irked me to see a lawyer's hourly meter running continuously, when a simple alteration would have sufficed. The agreement does not have to be pretty; it simply needs to be correct.

Numerous other terms are used in real estate, however, most of them are secondary to the purposes of this book. As previously indicated, the more you know about the real estate aspect of deal making, the less likely you are to get hurt, and the more likely you are to make an acceptable deal or to consummate a contract.

EXAMPLES OF SOME DEALS

Deals are agreements negotiated between two or more parties. There are some guidelines, but no hard and fast rules. The deal depends on the strength of position of both the landlord and the potential lessee or purchaser. The strength of one party's position over another's often determines the extent to which the other party can be "pushed." I had a client who would take only *vacant restaurant facilities in good locations,* offered by owners who were hurting. His rationale was that, given the problems that had occurred, he could drive a hard bargain with the owner. It usually worked! The deal was often a two-year lease, with four to six 5-year options. Also, there was no percentage rental and often no adjustment in the base rental. The food operator wanted a two-year lease because, if he was wrong on the location, he could "walk" after two years. If he was right, he had the property tied up for a very long period. This type of deal mandates only minor changes in the restaurant facility in the first two years. Occasionally, when my client agreed to exercise his option, he required the landlord to provide funds for leasehold improvements. Although this approach did not always work, it worked often enough to ensure a substantial profit to the food operator, whose sales averaged over $3,000,000 per unit annually. The following subsections provide additional examples of various kinds of deals.

Example 1: Lease of an Existing Restaurant

Location	Major commercial traffic artery
Size	3,500 square feet—90 seats
Type	Free-standing
Land and parking	One acre—125 parking spaces
Lease term	20 years, triple-net
Options	Two 5-year options
Building condition	Excellent
Rent	$100,000 annually, payable monthly
Leasehold improvements	Landlord provided $100,000
Percentage rental	5% of sales over $2,000,000
Special conditions	Recapture of real estate tax increases are deductible from one-half of any percentage rental payments

In this example, the restaurant was in a good location; the former operator was simply a bad food operator. Thus, the restaurant went bankrupt. The new operator negotiated a good deal, especially in light of the leasehold improvements provided by the landlord amounting to $100,000 and the recapture of real estate tax increases from one-half of any percentage rental overage payments.

Also, the restaurant operator's percentage rental clause in the agreement was only for 5%. Finally, this unit achieved sales of $2,300,000. The rent then became $115,000 annually, less the increases in real estate taxes.

Example 2: Lease of a Location in a Strip Shopping Center for a Sandwich Shop

Location	Average strip shopping center
Size	1,500 square feet—40 seats
Type	In-line location (not at a corner)
Land and parking	Provided by shopping center
Lease term	10 years, triple-net
Options	None
Building condition	Good
Rent	$10 a square foot, or $15,000 a year
Leasehold improvements	Tenant allowance of $6 a square foot, or $9,000
Percentage rental	6% of gross sales
Special condition	Common area maintenance charges (CAM) are estimated at $3.50 a square foot, including real estate taxes

Locations in shopping centers differ from free-standing locations in the nature of the rent and its composition. In shopping centers, the costs of parking are shared, as well as such expenses as exterior maintenance, security, snow removal, and other tenant needs (common area maintenance). For a free-standing location, such costs are normally the responsibility of the occupant. Shopping centers can provide a way to get into an area where sites are either not available or are very expensive. Also, shopping centers normally have sufficient parking. Finally, they usually have a traffic light or two to ensure adequate ingress and egress. The drawbacks include being overlooked because of inadequate identification, limited visibility, poor signing, poor access, limited parking near the unit, and poor tenant mix. Each shopping center must be looked at separately. They do not guarantee success.

In the subject example, the store was adequate, and the location was good. Visibility was good, the tenant mix was satisfactory, and the identification was good. The area had a large concentration of employment for the luncheon meal, as well as a strong residential population. Also, the shopping center was located on a street with numerous successful commercial facilities and was in the normal travel patterns of the residents of the area. The rent was $10 a square foot, or $15,000 annually. The breakpoint in sales was $250,000. The real estate taxes, maintenance, snow removal, and merchants' contribution to advertising amounted to $3.50 a square foot, or $5,250 annually. In this case, the unit had sales of $270,000. Because the sales exceeded the breakpoint, the base rental was $15,000, plus an overage rental of $1,200, or a total of $16,200 annually (or 6% of gross sales).

It is difficult to negotiate any recapture for a unit this small. If the shopping center is marginally successful; that is, has low sales productivity, sometimes a percent-only deal can be negotiated, such as 5% with no base rent. The tenant would then be obligated to pay 5% of gross sales monthly. Also, most shopping centers require audited sales figures at the end of the year to validate the actual sales achieved. In this instance, the food operation must be generative, since the shopping center probably cannot provide many customers. However, if this type of location is in the right area, it can provide a reasonable entry cost. Nevertheless, make sure that all of the necessary locational factors are positive.

Example 3: Build-to-Suit Fast Food Facility

Location	Strip shopping center pad
Size	2,400 square feet—80 seats
Type	Free-standing with drive-thru
Land and parking	32,000 square feet
Lease term	15 years, triple-net
Options	Two 5-year options
Building cost	$400,000 lid on landlord's contribution
Land value	$450,000
Rent	$100,000 annually, payable monthly
Percentage rental	6% of gross sales
Special condition	Triple-net
Breakpoint	$1,666,667

In this case, the fast food operator actually built the facility with the property owner's funds. That way the operator controlled the building construction and the materials used, as well as the installation of furniture, fixtures and the equipment. Many chain operators prefer to use the build-to-suit method for this reason. Furthermore, they can control the time required to get the unit built.

The unit has to capture sales greater than $1,666,667 annually to activate the 6% clause. This unit enjoyed sales of $2,100,000, resulting in rent to the landlord of $126,000 in the second year of operation. Thus, the landlord was receiving $126,000 on an investment of $950,000, including land and building. His return on a nonleverage basis was 13.3%. If the landlord borrowed 75% of the investment, then he has $237,500 invested and the balance is borrowed. At this point, prior to debt service, his return amounts to 53%. However, he has interest and debt payments to make on the borrowed funds. If his annual payments on the loan amount to $90,000, his return after his payments amounts to 15.5%.

Example 4: Lease for Independent Restaurant; Graduated Rental with Relief in the Initial Years Payable in the Final Five Years of the Lease

Location	Free-standing restaurant
Size	8,000 square feet—160 seats
Type of location	On major road to mall
Land and parking	60,000 square feet
Lease term	20 years
Options	Two 5-year options
Building cost	$800,000
Land value	$600,000
Deal	Build-to-suit
Rent	$168,000 annually, payable monthly in a structured rental program (see following explanation)
Percentage rental	6% of gross sales—natural breakpoint, $2,800,000
Special condition	Triple-net

In this case, the restaurant operator wanted some relief in the first few years. At the outset, the property owner was adamant about the rent. The restaurateur took his time. He also invited the property owner and his family to his other restaurant for dinner. The property owner was able to observe the inner workings of the restaurant, the efficiency of the operator, and the staff's superior performance. Finally, he tasted the food and witnessed the presentation. By inviting the family, instead of simply the property owner, the operator was able to duly impress them all and win them over.

Two days later, the restaurateur met with the property owner, and, at my suggestion, proposed a structured rental program. The restaurateur offered to pay total rent over the term of the lease amounting to $3,360,000 (20 years × $168,000 annually), if the first five years could be staggered, starting with $100,000 for the first year; $115,000, the second year; $130,000, the third year; $145,000 in the fourth year; and $168,000 in the fifth year. The $490,000 savings in the first four years would be added to the rent in years 16 to 20. *This plan would come into play only if the sales were below the breakpoint of $2,800,000.* The total amount to be paid was the same, simply paid differently. The property owner finally agreed, since he was going to put the property in trust for his children and was not in need of immediate income. Also, he had owned the land for a long time. The restaurant was built, and the facility captured more than $4,000,000 in sales in the second year. At 6% of sales the landlord received $240,000 in total rent in the second year of operation. While it turned out that the adjustments were not necessary, they offered some protection for the operator in case he required time to develop a customer base.

Example 5: Lease of Restaurant Space in an Older Building in a Major Downtown Area

Location	Well-located ground floor of office building
Size	7,000 square feet—250 seats, including the bar
Type	Theme bar and restaurant
Lease term	15 years, triple-net
Options	One 5-year option
Building condition	Good

Rent	$40 per square foot, or $280,000 annually, adjusted by 2% annually
Leasehold improvements	Tenant's responsibility
Percentage rental	None
Taxes and maintenance	Pro rata to space in building

This operation is a theme/fern restaurant and bar. The location is excellent for serving a strong luncheon crowd. However, there also are a growing number of young professionals who live near the downtown area. No facility of this nature is located in the area. New high-rise apartments are being constructed that would increase the number of residents of similar ages. The area also is becoming a gathering place for divorced individuals. The restaurant is currently operating at above $5,000,000 annually. Thus, the rent-to-sales percentage amounts to about 5.6%.

Example 6: Unsubordinated Ground Lease on the Pad of a Major Shopping Center

Location	Major mall, pad location with a parking and access easement.
Land area	10,000 square feet
Type	8,000 square feet—160 seats
Lease term	25 years, triple-net
Options	Two 5-year options
Building cost	$1,000,000
Ground rental	$120,000 annually, payable monthly
Special condition	Base rent adjusted upward at $1\frac{1}{2}\%$ annually

This national chain restaurant constructed the building and operates a high-volume restaurant. They need the considerable activity generated by the mall. They also need the mall's basically unlimited parking. In this instance, the restaurant opened with sales of $2,800,000. By the end of the third year, sales had reached $3,500,000.

The deal required a base rent of $120,000 for the land lease. Added to that is the borrowing rate of money for the food chain company, plus amortization of the building and improvements. The building, including carrying cost, is amortized at $140,000 annually.

Thus, the occupancy cost amounts to about $275,000 annually, including real estate taxes and common area charges. It does not require a rocket scientist to see that the unit's sales are below the anticipated level. This restaurant operation erred by not paying attention to the age structure of the mall's trade area, which turned out to be older than anticipated. Thus, the expected sales of over $5,000,000 never materialized.

SUMMARY

The examples can go on and on. Basically, the property owner is trying to maximize either sale price or rental value. The restaurateur is trying either to keep the purchase price low or the rental as low as possible. Between the two is the happy hunting ground of negotiation. Take your time. Haste, in fact, does make waste. Keep your pencil sharp, and take advantage of your opportunities. Be aware of current market conditions and the advantages or disadvantages that they might provide. Calculate the initial level of sales that the restaurant or fast food facility can actually and realistically capture. Stretch, but do not "elasticate" to such an extent that profitability is elusive.

Twenty-Two

Parking Guidelines

Parking is a critical element for most restaurants and fast food units. Its importance varies with the type of unit, type of location, size, seating, sales, turnover, party size, persons per vehicle, parking layout, daypart concentration, waiting periods, type of clientele, check average, take-outs, drive-thrus, walk-ins, delivery service, and perhaps many other factors. Parking needs can also be modified through valet parking. Also, remember employee spaces.

People perceive restaurant parking differently in densely populated areas than they do in suburban areas. In many northeastern and midwestern metropolitan areas, city parking is an expected problem, whereas in the western, southwestern, and southeastern states, parking is usually taken for granted. Fast food operators have similar, but different, parking demands. Variations caused by drive-thrus, take-outs, delivery service, walk-ins, and peak parking overlap all affect the demand for parking in some manner.

The situation is somewhat different for every restaurant; therefore, there are variations in the actual number of parking spaces needed. Fast food chains often have several sized units, and site layouts frequently can be repeated. The suggestions provided here are designed to serve as a guide. They are not absolute! Each situation must be analyzed to determine the number of spaces needed and the hours of peak demand. Also, do not rely on zoning or building code requirements. They often meet minimums, which may be inadequate for many restaurants. Make sure you are not starting with a parking problem. While municipal codes may be correct from their perspective, individual operators should determine their needs and then address the code requirements.

How is parking need determined? There are a number of methods for determining parking needs, ranging from simple computations to the more definitive individual parking calculation. Some of the most popular parking demand approaches follow.

THE SEATING METHOD OF DETERMINING PARKING NEEDS

The seating method is used by both restaurants and municipalities in their zoning ordinances related to parking. A ratio often specifies the number of parking spaces in relation to the number of seats in the dining room. For example, some require one parking space for every two seats. Thus, a dining room with 160 seats requires a minimum of 80 parking spaces. Often there is an additional requirement for the lounge and for employees. Others may require only one parking space for every three seats. While such regulations may satisfy the community, for many restaurants the number of parking spaces would be inadequate.

For example, a restaurateur might decide that he wants 160 seats with 50 seats in the bar. He expects Saturday night to be his peak daypart, with a turnover of three times. If there is an average of three people per car, then he needs 70 spaces to meet parking demand, including the bar. If some waiting is expected (more than the 60 bar seats), then additional spaces will be required. Also, employee parking must be added to determine the total parking required.

RESTAURANT SQUARE FOOTAGE TO PARKING SPACES REQUIRED

This approach is probably the method most often used for determining parking needs. In the commercial real estate world, a ratio of so many parking spaces for each 1,000 square feet of gross leasable area (GLA) is commonplace. For example, shopping centers usually provide between 4.5 to 5.0 parking spaces for each 1,000 square feet of GLA. In fact, it has become so standard that lenders, buyers, retailers, and others expect and demand it. It is a little more complicated in the food service field, primarily because there are so many different kinds of restaurants and fast food facilities. Moreover, sales per unit vary widely.

First, let us consider what some municipalities require. One of the fastest growing suburbs in the Chicago area, with the largest concentrations of office buildings and shopping center space, requires 18 parking spaces per 1,000 square feet of floor area for full-service restaurants. Applying this to a restaurant with 6,000 square feet would require 108 parking spaces. Furthermore, if the restaurant has carry-out service, the community requires 10 additional spaces per 1,000 square feet of floor area, or—in this example—168 parking spaces.

Many communities require a straight 20 spaces per 1,000 square feet of floor area. Others require a more definitive computation depending on waiting area. For example, a community may require one parking space for every two seats, sometimes expressed as a percentage (50%) of seating. Furthermore, an additional parking space is required for each 15 square feet of waiting area. Other communities may simply require 10 spaces per 1,000 square feet of building area. In that case, only 60 parking spaces would be required for a 6,000 square foot restaurant.

Again, while each community has a parking requirement, I recommend that every restaurateur compute parking needs according to the unit's individual requirements.

THE DEFINITIVE PARKING DEMAND COMPUTATION

This approach recognizes the need to evaluate definitively each individual restaurant situation. The key ingredients include anticipated sales, seating, check average, peak days, peak hour or daypart, party size, waiting overlap, bar activity, table turnover, diners per party, diners per car, seating efficiency, take-outs, walk-ins, ingress, egress, parking layout, age of the diners, available parking alternatives, employee needs, and other specialized requirements.

In the *fast food* business, it is usually only necessary to carry out the initial definitive parking computation since the "cookie cutter" approach to parking is used. Once the need is determined, it is repeated in numerous similar sites. Nevertheless, there are always some variations, especially for very expensive locations.

Restaurant—Dinner Only, American Fare (Sales $1,700,000)

Peak sales in this type of restaurant are usually on Saturday. In fact, sales rise throughout the week to peak on Saturday. Sunday starts with a brunch at 12:00 noon, which is well patronized. This particular restaurant is closed on Mondays, Christmas, and the Fourth of July. The restaurant has 160 seats, with an additional 50 seats in the bar. The suburban community does not permit any on-street parking; all parking must be on-site. The restaurant's sales average $141,667 per month, but the peak month's sales amount to $180,000; it is important to meet peak parking demands. During that month, sales amount to $45,000 a week. The unit is open six days a week, resulting in average daily sales of $7,500. The unit's check average is $22. Thus, there are approximately 340 diners per evening. Liquor sales amount to 15%.

Sales on Saturday, the peak day, amount to $13,000, with a check average of $27 and an average group size of 3.3 persons. Saturday customers average 480 persons. The restaurant seats 160 persons, if every chair at every table is full, but that is rarely the case. The actual seating efficiency is about 88%. Therefore, at maximum times about 140 seats are actually occupied. Assuming that the restaurant serves 480 persons on a Saturday evening with about 140 seats occupied at each sitting, the turnover rate is 3.4. With this amount of activity, parking will be required not only for the immediate diners, but also for the people waiting.

As previously indicated, each group averages 3.3 persons. Many groups come in separate cars. In this case, about 60% come together. Therefore, 84 of the diners come in groups of 3+ persons, resulting in about 26 cars. The balance of each sitting (56) come in groups of 2 persons, generating about 28 additional cars. Thus, each sitting will generate approximately 54 cars for which parking will be required. Additionally, the bar is always full of people waiting for tables. The bar holds 50 seated persons and about 10 standing. Furthermore, the lobby seats 10 people. Therefore, the restaurant can have about 70 people waiting. This often occurs on Saturday night. If the same rules apply, namely an average of 3.3 diners per group, then they represent about 21 groups. If 60% come in groups, this will create a demand for about 12 additional parking spaces. Moreover, the additional, 9 groups will require about 18 parking spaces. Therefore, the people waiting require about 30 parking spaces. Thus, the total peak parking demand will be about 85 cars.

Fast Food Unit with a Drive-Thru (Sales $1,200,000)

A fast food unit, capturing sales of $1,200,000 with 40% of sales orig-
inating from the drive-thru window, has a different set of parking
requirements. Assume the following: the check average is $3.50; the
unit is open seven days a week, except for Christmas; the busiest
days occur on the weekends; the unit serves about 342,857 customers annually; the busiest months are the summer months; the
average number of customers per month is 28,571 persons. In the
summer months, the average is about 44,000 customers monthly. Average weekdays generate 1,214 customers. However, weekend days
generate more than 1,833 customers. Since the unit has two primary dayparts—lunch and dinner—that account for 80% of sales,
approximately 8,800 customers are accommodated weekly during
the two dayparts. Lunch captures about 60%, with the balance at
dinner. Therefore, lunch generates 5,280 customers weekly, or 754
luncheon daypart customers daily. This unit has no walk-in business; everyone comes by car. If the luncheon daypart covers 90 minutes, then the peak hour must serve a minimum of 502 customers. If
the average car has 1.7 persons, then a total of 296 cars are generated during the peak hour. If the average seating time is 15 minutes,
then about 74 parking spaces are required to meet the luncheon
peak. However, the unit has a drive-thru that can handle one car per
minute, and about 60 customers are served through the drive-thru
window during the peak luncheon hour, or 15 cars per segment.
Thus, the total peak parking demand amounts to 59 parking spaces
for lunch (74 minus 15), plus employee parking. Naturally, adequate
land area must be provided to facilitate the drive-thru.

Seafood Restaurant—Lunch and Dinner, On-Street Parking Available, Check Average $19 (Sales $5,000,000)

This 15-year-old restaurant is in an urban setting, where some on-
street parking is available. On Saturday night, however, other restaurants are vying for the same parking. The restaurant has 220 seats in
the dining room and 60 seats in the lounge. Lunch accounts for 30%
of weekday sales, while dinner generates 70%. The same menu is
used for both dayparts, but specials are available for both meals. The
restaurant is closed on Mondays and on Christmas, or about 53 days.

The restaurateur has a dilemma; namely, he only has 40 parking
spaces and his customers are complaining. He owns the restaurant.

His first alternative might be to buy the adjacent property for $140,000, which will provide another 40 parking spaces, bringing the total controlled parking to 80 spaces. He could also expand his restaurant simultaneously, adding 40 seats without affecting the parking area. This will cost an additional $80,000. His second alternative is to install valet parking to maximize the existing lot's utilization. This will mean that his customers will need to tip the valet people. He expects some resistance to this solution. His next alternative is to do both—expand both his parking and the restaurant, while adding valet parking. His last alternative is to do nothing. He will probably lose some customers who are complaining; he is highly regarded, however, and might be able to replace the lost customers with new patrons. On Saturday evening, most customers have a 20-minute wait, regardless of their reservations.

The restaurant is averaging about $96,000 a week in sales, or about $16,000 per day. On Saturdays, the unit averages about $22,000 in dinner sales. The check average is $19, overall; on Saturday, however, the check average amounts to $25. Therefore, Saturday evenings generate about 880 customers. About 80 customers come by taxi, leaving 800 customers who come by private automobile. The average Saturday night party size is 3.4 persons, and the average number of people per car is 2.5. The restaurant turns over about four times on a Saturday night. Therefore, each seating requires approximately 80 parking spaces (200 customers per seating divided by 2.5 persons per car). Additionally, there are usually about 90 people waiting, about 80 of whom come by private automobile. Thus, an additional 32 parking spaces are required. The total peak parking demand amounts to 112 parking spaces. His current 40 spaces are only providing for about 36% of his customers' needs. Even if he adds 40 additional spaces, he will still be short 32 spaces, or the equivalent of those customers waiting for tables. Nevertheless, he will probably solve 90% of his parking problem. What would you do?

I would buy the adjacent site and expand the parking, see the extent of the impact, and then probably expand the restaurant. However, I would do it in phases. I would also try valet parking on Saturday night and monitor the amount of resistance. Are the customers who are complaining, frequent visitors? The additional 40 seats in the dining room would add about $4,000 in sales on Friday and Saturday nights alone, or $8,000 for the weekend. If the restaurateur could make a profit of 20% on the $8,000, then it would take about 2.6 years to recover the cost of the additional seating and the adjacent parking lot.

ADDITIONAL GUIDELINES

Table 22.1 presents examples of other restaurants, their situations, and their parking needs. Table 22.2 presents the same information for fast food units. In each case, the objective was to determine peak daypart segment demand. To determine the maximum parking required, you must add any "parking demand overlap," parking spaces for the disabled (usually specified if the zoning code), and employee parking needs. Variations in parking supply include on-street parking spaces, the use of parking on adjacent properties, the size of the vehicles (campers and recreational vans), and the percentage of your parking spaces used by nearby occupants and others.

The parking computation formula is as follows:

- Take total peak month sales, less any take-out or drive-thru sales.
- Net sales eaten in the unit divided by the average check provides the number of customers per month.
- Next, review the anticipated or actual daily peaks. Allocate the sales by day to reflect the peak day or days.
- Multiply the daypart's peak percentage by the peak daily sales; this will indicate the number of customers generated in the peak daypart.
- Divide the number of peak daypart customers by the number of hours covering the peak daypart. For example, if lunch runs two hours, divide the peak daypart customers by two, thus arriving at the number of peak daypart customers per hour.
- Divide the number of peak hour customers by the average party size. This will determine the number of groups that you will have.
- Then, divide the resulting number by the anticipated or actual turnover per daypart hour. This will provide the number of customers per daypart segment.
- Finally, divide the anticipated or actual number of customers per car into the anticipated or actual number of customers for the daypart segment. This will indicate the number of parking

TABLE 22.1
General Parking Guidelines—Restaurants

Type of Location	Anticipated Sales	Check Average	Peak Customers Month	Peak Customers Day	Total Seating	Daypart Activity Peak (%) Breakfast	Lunch	Dinner	People per Car	Waiting Overlap (%)	Seating Turnover per Hour	Peak Hour Demand	Parking Spaces Allocated
Major artery	$2,200,000	$15.00	May	Sat.	160	No	20	80	2.5	30	1.2	113	143
Major comm. area	1,750,000	12.00	Nov.	Sat.	120	No	40	60	2.0	20	2.0	70	90
Dense urban	3,300,000	22.00	Dec.	Sat.	180	No	20	80	2.2	30	1.3	130	160
Secondary street	800,000	10.80	Sept.	Sat.	50	No	30	70	3.0	0	1.5	31	40
Neighborhood	600,000	6.00	July	Sat.	50	No	10	80	2.0	0	3.0	31	35
Near a mall	2,000,000	12.00	Dec.	Sat.	110	No	40	60	2.0	0	2.0	72	80
Interchange	1,300,000	8.50	May	Fri.	85	30	40	20	1.2	0	3.0	57	65
Mixed use project	3,500,000	12.00	May	Sat.	160	No	18	85	2.2	0	1.0	300	350
Major highway	2,600,000	70.00	Nov.	Sat.	87	No	No	100	2.7	50	1.0	36	50
Rural highway	1,850,000	9.00	June	Fri.	80	20	30	30	1.7	0	3.0	36	45

TABLE 22.2

General Parking Guidelines—Fast Food Facilities

Type of Location	Anticipated Sales	Drive Thru (%)	Check Average	Peak Customers Month	Peak Customers Day	Total Seating	Daypart Activity Peak (%) Breakfast	Lunch	Dinner	People per Car	Seating Turnover per Hour	Peak Hour Demand	Parking Spaces Allocated
Dense urban	$1,200,000	50	$3.75	July	Fri.	60	No	60	30	2.0	4.0	50	60
Hwy. interchange	800,000	50	4.25	June	Sun.	80	10	50	30	3.0	3.5	32	35
Commercial street	600,000	None	4.00	July	Sat.	63	No	50	50	1.7	4.0	35	35
Major road	900,000	50	4.00	June	Fri.	70	No	60	35	2.0	4.0	30	40
Near a mall	850,000	40	3.75	Dec.	Sat.	75	No	50	40	2.3	3.75	27	30
Mixed use project	2,300,000	45	4.10	Aug.	Fri.	110	20	50	30	2.5	3.0	122	140
University area*	1,400,000	30	3.85	April	Sat.	120	20	45	30	2.2	3.0	8	8
Industrial Area	900,000	60	3.95	May	Fri.	60	No	70	30	2.0	4.2	24	26

*50% walk-in business.

spaces required to meet peak daypart segments. Add to this figure disability requirements and employee parking needs.

SUMMARY

Go into a new situation with your eyes wide open. Know what your parking demand will be. Many restaurants have been able to live with limited parking because the customers like the facilities so much that they will find a place to park somewhere. *However, these are exceptions.* Moreover, in the fast food business, you either have the parking or you do not. When you do not, the customers will normally go somewhere else.

Twenty-Three

Zoning and the Approval Process

Zoning and the necessary permits to run a food business have become, and will continue to be, a difficult and timely process. With better zoning communications, zoning consultants, newsletters, and zoning seminars, today's average board is much better informed than in the past. Moreover, almost all have heard every tall story and promise regarding the "benefits to the community." Also, fast food units particularly, and restaurants to a lesser degree, have become the enemy in many communities. Restaurant failure, turnover, noise, and litter have caused many municipalities to turn against the food service business. This is true to a lesser degree in Canada, where zoning is more absolute. Nevertheless, Canadians too have experienced the food turnover problem. "Fast food" can be a dirty phrase. "Family restaurant" is a much more acceptable description in the zoning hearing vernacular. Avoid any reference to fast food when submitting an application for zoning, or when presenting the case for approval before building and zoning boards. The following are some suggestions for expediting the process.

UNDERSTAND THE COMMUNITY REQUIREMENTS AND PROCESS

A considerable part of the approval process is understanding how it is accomplished, who sees to its implementation, and who are the primary players. If you do not *fully* understand the process or the players, get someone to help you who does. This might be an attorney, a real estate person, or a zoning specialist. Often, it is appropriate to find out who is the best connected attorney, or the one, at least, who handles the most zoning petitions. This individual will know his or her way around. Regardless, reconnoiter the situation and understand the players.

BE PREPARED

Because most zoning officials are wary of food service facilities, it is necessary to be prepared for questions. Know the financial impact on the community's tax base and the number and type of jobs the operation will create. The revenue created may be from real estate taxes, sales taxes, liquor taxes, use taxes, or some other assessment. Compute the taxes that the community will receive as result of the new facility and generally make a big issue about it. Often the community will request a tax impact study, which requires that you estimate the revenue to be generated by your new facility. Also, the study must address the costs that the community will incur to serve your new facility. This includes inspections, fire and police service, and other services, as determined locally. Sometimes it is necessary to show what the impact will be over 10 or 20 years. Remember, also, to add up all the permit fees, tap charges, impact fees, inspection fees and any others. While these are usually one-time charges, nevertheless they are revenue to the community.

Next, compute the number of jobs that will be generated by the new unit. Jobs are a significant factor for almost all communities today. Present the facts. Be prepared to respond to the issue that most of the jobs are at the minimum wage or near to it. Emphasize that while they may not be the kind of jobs that the community would like to see, they are jobs. As a general rule of thumb, *each dollar of income has a multiple impact of about 2.2, or $2.20.* A $5.00-an-hour job has a multiplier income effect of $12.00 because the employee spends part or all of his or her income in the community for goods and services, and these funds in turn, are spent by the retailer or service shop for additional goods and services.

Have pretty pictures! A picture is worth a thousand words. A rendering or sketch of the proposed facility will help with the zoning process. Remember, the zoning board, city council, or village trustees need justification for making a decision. They are political animals who need facts to support a decision for you. Help them to do their job.

UNDERSTAND THE AGENDA FOR THE ENTIRE APPROVAL PROCESS

It is very important to understand the building and zoning process, along with the approval process of the full city council or trustees. Also, you should know what the building and zoning ordinances require for conformance as well as any special use requirements. If you do not wish to bother, then hire a local zoning attorney who not only understands but also knows the players. It is common for the process to become botched up. However, if you understand the process and the people, you can quickly respond to problems while keeping the process on track. Do not rely on the planning or zoning process to take care of you.

I have been a witness at numerous zoning and city council presentations where I have watched simple matters get defeated for want of understanding on the part of the petitioner. Furthermore, I have seen difficult matters fly through the process because the presentation was smooth and well-organized and the petitioner provided the council members with the answers before they could ask for them. Usually, it is up to you.

In some parts of the country, permit expediters are necessary to get approvals within a reasonable period. Their job is to "ride herd" on the application, to see that it does not end up buried on someone's desk, for who knows how long. While it may be expensive, it may be the best way to get the job done before you are old and gray.

FOLLOW THROUGH

If you agree to do something at one of the hearings, be sure that you do it. You will be operating a business in the community for a long time. It is in your best interest to be a good citizen. Furthermore, in the future you might want to expand, which will require your return for additional approvals. Do not burn your bridges; you will undoubtedly need them.

MAKE THE PROCESS WORK FOR YOU

Remember Murphy's Law: "What ever can go wrong, will." This seems especially true in the planning and zoning process, but if you understand the system and the players, you can make them work for you. First, make sure that all your submittals are correct, on the proper forms, and in accustomed official format. Next, recognize that many planners and zoning officials are harassed, or at least, think that they are. Sympathize with them; let them know you realize how underpaid and how overworked they are. Ask them if you can help them to expedite the situation. If they indicate that you can help by meeting with some of the board members to explain your project, then do so.

ENVIRONMENTAL ISSUES

In recent years, the focus on the environment has come to the forefront. Soil, water, and air are now issues that are addressed in most zoning or building permit requests. I do not pretend to be an expert in this area. However, I know that when the issue is raised, it is important to address it properly with expert assistance. As I mentioned earlier in this book, soil contamination, especially from former gasoline service stations, can be found on most corners of major and minor intersections throughout our metropolitan areas. In some areas, the problem has been caused by industries that either operated in the area in the past or are currently operating there. In many instances, ground water contamination has resulted, in addition to soil contamination. The EPA is enforcing the cleanup, much to the chagrin of many present and former property owners, especially the oil companies. Regardless, the cleanup process is expensive and time consuming, generally adding about a year to the development of a property with the problem.

The unfortunate part of the required process is that many of the regulations are confusing and are not applied consistently. Also, in some cases, the regulators are overly hard-handed. Without question, the cleanup is needed; at times, however, the demands are truly excessive. Finally, the EPA officials are overworked and understaffed, thus creating a push-and-shove process that is exasperating for all. Should you select a property with the possibility of soil or ground water contamination, you will be required to have a qualified engineering firm conduct soil tests to determine the extent of the problem. The report, along with the necessary forms, must be prepared and sent to the EPA for study and decision. You should also be aware that even if your prospective property was not a service station site, an adjacent or nearby site may have leaked contamination into the groundwater, thereby affecting your land. Soil tests are a must for the buyer, and contamination clauses should be in your purchase or lease contract where any construction is planned. This situation can also occur when planning major renovations to an existing building, if there is the possibility of a problem. Pay attention to the past and previous uses, and talk to the local water and zoning people regarding groundwater flows and prospective problem areas. A little homework will go a long way.

Possible necessary approvals include the following:

Zoning approval
Topography and drainage approval
Ingress and egress—curb cuts
Environmental permits
Building permit
Parking requirements approval
Health department permits
Soil conditions approval
Landscaping acceptance
Utility approvals
Site plan acceptance
Demolition permits
Remodeling permits
Liquor license
Current survey of the property

Each item of the list is important, in varying degrees, to the community and the individual food operators.

SUMMARY

Most of us are not experts in all these areas. Therefore, we should either hire the proper experts to protect our interests, or we should take the time to research the situation before we commit money to a possible site. For some food operators, who are not in a hurry, making a deal on a contaminated site can be a bargain. However, you should not undertake such an acquisition unless you are sure that an oil company is responsible for removal of the contaminated soil to the satisfaction of the EPA and local authorities. Usually, even if the property is a good buy, the legal fees more than exceed the alleged savings.

Part Four

Special Considerations

Twenty-Four

Downtown Locations

The evaluation of downtown areas and selection of locations follows basically the same approach used in selecting other locations. The fundamental differences lie in the data, customer concentrations, expenditures, and the distances being considered. Most downtown fast food facilities, and many restaurants, serve very narrow trade areas. The predominant customers usually are the downtown daytime workers, visitors to the city, or residents of the immediate vicinity. Very few downtowns attract consumers back into the area at night for dinner, other than on weekends or for special occasions. Obviously, there are exceptions—certainly some of the older, unique restaurants that have effectively become institutions can maintain that kind of attraction. In recent years, there have been examples of new restaurants in downtown areas that have successfully generated evening business. The customers are usually young professionals employed nearby. It is difficult, if not impossible, to get the traditional "gray hairs" to come back into the downtown area with their spouses in the evening, unless they live nearby. Moreover, with the growth of sprawling suburbia, the distances involved have grown significantly. As a result, driving back downtown on a weeknight can be a major venture. Also, many fine restaurants have been developed in suburbia, making it unnecessary to travel downtown for a good meal.

I do not have to tell long-term downtown restaurateurs how volatile the evening business has been. Conversely, many fast food operators may look gleefully at the sales performance of their downtown units and feel that they have perhaps discovered the Mother Lode. Others may have experienced tragic results regardless of the type of facility, while some operators in very selective downtown areas have experienced unending success. For the most part, downtown areas have been buffeted and, in many cases, devastated by the decentralization of retail, office, and institutional facilities to outlying areas. Simply stated then, the changing functions of downtown areas have often resulted in less activity than previously.

On the positive side, through long-range urban renewal and urban redevelopment, many downtown areas throughout the United States and Canada are or have been experiencing a renaissance. It is important, however, to discern whether the revitalization is of sufficient magnitude to justify food service entry, or whether it would be more prudent to wait until the patterns are established and the new project's degree of success can be determined. Although this caution may cost a few rental dollars in waiting, it may also save you significant risk capital.

HISTORICAL PERSPECTIVE

Downtown areas, differ significantly by size, shape, age, origin, and geographic characteristics. For example, downtown areas in the northeastern part of the United States are extremely old, and tend to have narrow streets that often are bisected by angular traffic arteries further compounding the traffic flow. Population density in proximity to the northeastern downtowns is usually very high; however, as is the case with midwestern cities, these concentrations are primarily low income minority groups. At one time, all the principal highways converged in the downtown area, but this is no longer the case with the development of by-pass expressways and the interstate system.

Midwestern cities have had to face many of the same problems that their counterparts in the Northeast experienced earlier. Perhaps the largest single difference is that many midwestern cities are more spread out and, as a result, do not have the same population densities near their downtown areas. Thus, the development of outlying facilities had a significant adverse impact on most downtown areas in the Midwest. Some exceptions include Chicago, Milwaukee, and Minneapolis.

The growth of many cities in the Far West did not occur until after the advent and proliferation of the automobile and, as a result, the downtown areas, though extremely important, were not the large concentrations of commercial facilities. Thus, major shopping and office complexes developed in outlying areas rather than in the downtown area. In many western cities, then, the downtowns either grew along with the outlying areas, or the outlying areas captured the bulk of the new facilities, leaving downtown as a secondary commercial concentration.

Although many communities in the southeastern states were small, their downtowns were still important commercial centers. With mobility and decentralization, some of the southeastern cities have been able to capitalize on the downtown's primary strengths, while others have failed. Atlanta, for example, did not have a significant downtown office and hotel center until the late 1960s and early 1970s when the face of downtown Atlanta changed. During this period, major outlying facilities were developed, particularly North–South Interstates 75 and 85 and the loop expressways around Atlanta (I-475 and I-485). Nonetheless, the growth in Atlanta was so significant that it was able to accommodate both office and hotel development within the downtown area, while major retail, office, and industrial complexes were developed in proximity to the loop interstate system. Downtown Atlanta is no longer a major retail center because of the significant shopping center development in outlying areas.

Some, but not all, southwestern cities of the United States had significant downtown areas. Dallas, for example, had a sizable downtown, while Houston did not. During the past 20 years, Dallas has experienced major growth in that downtown area as well as massive development of outlying retail and office complexes. In contrast, Houston witnessed the explosion of its downtown area, the construction of the Westheimer–Interstate 610 corridor, and the impact of the new airport to the north. Nonetheless, Houston retailing is not concentrated downtown; instead, that area is a concentration of office and hotel facilities.

DOWNTOWN AREA TRENDS

Significant changes have occurred in downtown areas over the past 20 to 30 years, and for many downtowns even more significant changes will occur during the next 10 to 20 years.

Retail Sales Trends

Most downtowns throughout the United States experienced a significant decline in retail sales from the 1950s through the 1980s, and perhaps even the 1990s. Nevertheless, a few downtown areas in the United States have enjoyed continual sales increases. Some have seen increases in the past 20 years; the increases, however, are usually from a base that had earlier declined.

The decline in retail sales is meaningful because it reflects the downtown area's changing function. Originally the focal place in a community, downtown was the center for major retail facilities. With the advent of the automobile and the significant increase in consumer mobility, outlying shopping center facilities were developed that siphoned off customers previously oriented toward downtown. In many cases, the result was devastating. Shopping centers provided modern new retail facilities in a pleasant environment with free parking relatively easy ingress and egress. In contrast, downtown provided older retail facilities in a congested environment often with expensive parking, resulting in a rather time-consuming shopping chore. The shopping center provided retailing with a carnival atmosphere and made shopping fun again. Furthermore, it created a casual shopping environment. Additionally, the expansion of suburbia moved people further and further away from downtown retail facilities. The one saving grace of downtown stores was their normally immense size and tremendous breadth of merchandise selection, not usually available in the suburban shopping centers.

In the past 15 to 20 years, even that situation has changed. Major malls, including two, three, four, and as many as six or seven department stores, have been built, featuring mammoth facilities to overcome the attraction of downtown. Moreover, major fashion stores have joined the mall parade adversely affecting downtown retailing.

Improvement has occurred in some downtown areas because of tourists and visitors to the area, an increase in the downtown working population, and the development of nearby residential facilities. Thus, downtown stores have become more of a convenience to the local residents and workers and less of a major regional shopping attraction for the metropolitan area. There are, of course, exceptions to this trend.

In Chicago, State Street, known as the "Loop," has experienced a considerable sales decline and store loss. In contrast, the "New Downtown" on North Michigan Avenue, focusing on Water Tower Place (Marshall Field and Company and Lord & Taylor), 900 North (Bloomingdale's), the new Neiman Marcus store, and Chicago Place (Sak's Fifth Avenue and numerous other fashion-oriented specialty stores) has become a significant fashion center. Not to be overlooked is the large number of new and expanded restaurants serving this growing shopping and activity concentration. Similar types of development have also occurred in other cities with concentrations of up-scale shoppers.

Eating and Drinking Sales Trends

In the 1940s and 1950s, the primary concentration of "white tablecloth" restaurants was downtown. People deciding where to dine out on a weeknight or on Saturday night, usually included downtown restaurants among their options. Again, with increased automobile mobility and the development of numerous outlying restaurants and fast food facilities, the orientation changed and consumers no longer chose to travel downtown to eat. As a result, the number of fine restaurants located in downtown areas declined significantly. Obviously, the northeastern and midwestern portions of the United States were more adversely affected than the West and Southwest.

Nevertheless, the change has occurred. The void in restaurants was replaced by fast food operations that discovered gold in "them thar hills." It was, and is, not unusual for a fast food facility to open downtown and immediately experience sales in excess of $1,000,000 or $2,000,000. Fast food chains sometimes were slow to seize the opportunity; once recognized, however, the proliferation has been significant. Interestingly, it has been a real education for many who failed to realize that downtown patterns are similar to the patterns in suburbia. The primary difference is that the customer is walking, rather than driving. Initially, many of those patterns were ignored, but now they are being given their proper due.

For those who are prepared to evaluate the opportunity thoroughly, there are growing opportunities for new downtown restaurants. In fact, in some areas, new facilities are even attracting people downtown at night. The location of such operations is absolutely *critical* as is the need for nearby activity generators.

ANALYZING DOWNTOWN'S OPPORTUNITIES

Today, the two most important components in downtown areas are office concentrations and financial institutions. Subcategories of important concentrations include hotels, convention facilities, cultural activities, and the legitimate theater. Again, this varies, depending on the size of the community and the strength of the area. Thus, today, most downtowns are hotbeds of activity during the day, only to be vacated after 5:00 P.M. Moreover, on weekends most downtowns are essentially dead. This is changing in some areas where new hotel, office, retail, and convention complexes have been developed in concert with new public attractions, such as stadiums, museums, theaters, and festival markets. The primary activity is then created by visitors, conventioneers, and the downtown employees.

Changing Cities

Unfortunately, in many cities today, the "haves" moved to the suburbs, whereas the "have-nots" remained in the cities. Combined with the decline of retailing, the downtown area has seen a reduction in the number of full-service restaurant facilities. In other downtowns, however, major retail development projects have taken place (usually over at least a 15-to-20-year time span) and are now a reality. Large new developments may represent opportunities for restaurant and fast food operators, but each must be looked at very carefully to determine the extent of its likely impact. For example, Horton plaza in downtown San Diego has been a significant addition in the retailing area. Although this major mall complex has been very successful from a retail point view, it has had difficulty in generating significant nighttime restaurant activity. Other downtown San Diego restaurants have been having the same difficulty for many years. Conversely, the development of the Grand Avenue Mall in downtown Milwaukee, which has had a positive impact on retailing, has also helped the famous German restaurants in downtown Milwaukee, although some believe that the new downtown housing is partially responsible. Several new complexes that have been built in downtown Washington, D.C., combining hotels, offices, and retailing, have offered interesting possibilities for restaurant and fast food facilities. In New York City, numerous new office buildings and residential developments have provided opportunities for both restaurant and fast food development.

The main factor to remember is simply that strong financial backing of a redevelopment project does not necessarily ensure its success. It is the consumers who make the success, not the financiers.

Safety and Security

If we were to stop 50 people on the street in Chicago's Loop and ask them their perception of downtown Chicago after five o'clock, most would voice their concern for safety and security. Ironically, a check of the crime statistics would prove that downtown Chicago is one of the safest places to be in the city (perhaps because few people are there after 6:00 P.M.). This is an excellent example of a case where *perception is far more important than reality*. A consumer who does not feel safe in an area will avoid it at night, regardless of the statistics.

Activity Concentrations

Activity concentrations are similar to generative areas. They tend to represent areas within the downtown with large concentrations of people. In evaluating a downtown, it is important to recognize where the major facilities are concentrated, including governmental complexes, financial institutions, existing and new office buildings, hotels, retail facilities, the convention center, restaurants, and cultural buildings. It is also important to recognize the directional developmental trends. Sometimes the various major uses are spread apart making it difficult to combine the concentrations in considering restaurant potential. In those cases, it is necessary to determine if one or more of the concentrations can justify the development of a new dining facility. In other markets, they are close together, and the activities' combined generation creates large market for restaurants and fast food facilities. Again, it is necessary to evaluate the activity concentrations and to determine the extent of their potential restaurant customer generation.

Locational Considerations

A number of locational elements need to be considered when evaluating downtown locations. For example, where are the new office buildings located? Which direction is development moving and why? Where are the hotels, and is there a convention center? What are the luncheon walking patterns? Is the principal walking pattern north to south or east to west? Where are the principal parking lots located? Where does public transportation deposit people in the downtown area and which are the principal bus or subway stations? Do major downtown employers have dining facilities for their employees? There are other questions that must be considered as well. Selecting a downtown location requires a critical awareness of these factors and an understanding of their significance relative to individual sites.

Daytime Working Population

The daytime working population refers to those people who work downtown and are generally concentrated during the daytime hours. They usually represent the largest single group of people oriented toward that area. The following are some important considerations: What is the status of the daytime working population? Is it increasing or decreasing? Where are they primarily concentrated? How much time do they have for lunch? Do many "brown bag" it? What is the size of the executive core of the community and where do they eat now?

The daytime working population should also be looked at both quantitatively and qualitatively. Quantitative study requires looking at the numbers and where the workers are located. Qualitative analysis involves reviewing the types, employment levels, expenditures, and concentrations of this population. For example, the location of professionals in contrast to the corporate employers should be identified. Furthermore, governmental concentrations and other predominant employers of clerical workers should be located. A review of both the quantitative and qualitative changes can help identify where the concentrations are and the extent to which an opportunity may or may not exist. Many cities conduct cordon counts for the downtown area, which depict the number of passengers entering and exiting the Central Business District by mode of travel between 7:00 A.M. and 6:00 P.M. Obtaining data with a cordon count essentially means creating a cordon, or ring, of people around the downtown area to count the vehicles and people entering and exiting the downtown area.

Downtown Resident Population

In the past 10 to 15 years, many large American cities have experienced residential development in proximity to downtown areas. For these residents, downtown is their shopping center. Moreover, they are strongly oriented toward the downtown area for their meals because of both their employment and their residence. Often opportunities for restaurant development occur within a residential complex in or near the downtown area, while in other situations, the potential is not sufficient to support a facility. Thus, eating establishments that are developed in the downtown area may expect part of their support to come from the resident population.

Pedestrian Routes

Habits and patterns are as significant in downtown areas as they are elsewhere, but they are pedestrian patterns, as opposed to automobile patterns. It is important to observe these patterns. The locations of the parking lots where office workers leave their cars during working hours establish walking patterns to and from the parking lots, and there certainly are clues to other walking patterns. For example, if public transportation is a significant factor, then it becomes critical to identify the location of the train depots, subway stations, principal bus embarking and debarking locations, and transfer points. Knowing where the professional offices, corporate complexes, banks, governmental offices, retail facilities, restaurants, fast food facilities, and other institutions are concentrated will also provide clues to the luncheon patterns. For the dinner patterns, it is necessary to pinpoint the proximity to hotels, convention complexes, theaters, and cultural concentrations, as well as the number of activities held in these facilities.

In Chicago's downtown Loop area, the predominant pedestrian patterns are east to west. Why? Because the primary suburban railroad stations are located west of the Loop, and the elevated Rapid Transit tracks form a "loop" around the downtown area, with the primary stations on the east–west streets. Thus, pedestrians walking to and from work are concentrated more heavily on the east–west arteries than on the north–south streets. In addition, State Street, the primary retail concentration in the Loop, is east of the office concentrations.

A sometimes overlooked factor is that persons walking to and from work are very difficult to stop. Many a food operator has failed because of believing that all that pedestrian traffic could generate significant sales. People heading to work or home after work are like cattle; once the stampede is on, there is no stopping them. It has always amazed me to hear people complain about life at home, and then race out of the office into the sea of humanity to get home as quickly as possible. Perhaps, you can figure it out; I cannot.

In Chicago, the predominant walking pattern at lunchtime also is east and west. Why? Again, we are creatures of habit; we tend to follow rather rigid patterns. Certainly at lunchtime there are disruptions of the east and west orientation through the attraction of food facilities and meetings with business associates who are not necessarily in the east–west pattern. Nevertheless, the overall pattern does hold true. In general, restaurants located in the east–west patterns achieve greater sales than those located on the north–south streets. It is important to make the pedestrian pattern evaluation in any downtown area that you might be considering for a restaurant or fast food facility. Being in the pattern and in an intercepting position to the pedestrian traffic will normally result in greater sales. Large cities conduct pedestrian counts at strategic locations throughout downtown areas. These are usually available from the city's planning department.

Activity Areas

Activity concentrations or generative nodes include retail, financial, office, government, institutional, hotel, convention, museum, cultural, theater, and entertainment concentrations. In Chicago, for example, many of the downtown plazas have live lunchtime entertainment during the summer, and there are normally significant concentrations of daytime workers in and around those plazas. As a result, nearby fast food operations have done exceptionally well, particularly in the summertime. Other cities have provided similar and yet different attractions.

Legitimate theaters can be strong evening generators. The amount of annual activity must be analyzed to determine if it can support a nearby restaurant's evening patron needs. Recent studies conducted by our firm and others indicate that Broadway-type plays and musicals can have a significant impact on downtown restaurant business although there are often long "dark" periods when no shows are playing and no benefit is received.

Planned Changes

While many downtown areas appear to be static, changes do take place slowly and usually in waves. Office development occurs in cycles that usually reflect spurts in construction, followed by years during which the office space is absorbed into the market. The late 1980s and early 1990s have represented a period of excessive office development in many downtown areas. Sometimes, downtowns remain virtually dormant for years, only to come alive suddenly because some outsider (usually) sees an opportunity that the locals had not envisioned. Planned changes can be determined by discussing the situation with the planning people, the downtown committee (or some name pertaining thereto), the Chamber of Commerce, and other agencies that are interested in the area's improvement. Some government-instigated changes are designed to be catalytic, that is, to provide the infrastructure or environment that will encourage private development and investment.

As previously indicated, generally things move slowly in downtown areas and thus, a 20-year cycle is quite common. Opportunities today are a mixed bag. Some offer strong opportunities for success, while others will not have potential for 5 or 10 years into the future. Nevertheless, today there is a much greater orientation toward downtown redevelopment and improvement than there has been for the past 20 to 30 years. Nonetheless, the groundwork for this improvement was most often established more than 20 years ago and was nurtured until private investment recognized its opportunity.

Competition

Competition certainly is a crucial factor in considering the opportunities for new restaurant or fast food development within the downtown area. First, however, it is necessary to understand the activity concentrations, the habits and patterns, the pedestrian routes, the daytime working population, the shifting office developmental patterns, and the existing or planned convention and meeting facilities, along with the locations of hotels and other significant generators.

Evaluating competition quantitatively and qualitatively requires understanding the area's history of restaurant change and fast food proliferation. The sales being captured by the existing competitive facilities need to be determined in terms of turnover, pricing, menu selection, food sales versus alcoholic beverage sales (where applicable), lunch versus dinner (perhaps breakfast), seating, check average, and other factors relevant to competitive analysis.

To evaluate competition and the potential for additional downtown facilities, it is necessary to recognize that a number of institutions and corporate offices have in-house food facilities. As a result, a much lower percentage of office occupants eat outside. Moreover, the facilities are often subsidized, making them less expensive than other restaurants. In such situations, a percentage of the relevant employees must be eliminated from the luncheon sales potential.

The restaurant and fast food facilities in downtown hotels also capture a portion of the potential, depending on the effectiveness of the restaurant and fast food facilities in the hotels. Only by thorough evaluation can an operator make that determination.

Eating and Drinking Expenditures

The eating and drinking expenditure potential for which most new downtown restaurants are competing is generated by the daytime working population at the luncheon daypart. On a broader spectrum, it includes the downtown resident population, visitors to the area, conventioneers, businesspeople, theatergoers, and others attracted to the area in the evening hours.

The daily eating and drinking expenditure of large city office occupants ordinarily averages $2.00 to $25.00 per capita. Obviously, the number of $2.00 expenditures is significantly greater than $25.00 expenditures. Usually in office concentrations with professional people, the number with expenditures above $10.00 per day will be higher. By evaluating the number of professionals versus the number of clerical personnel, an operator can get a feeling for the difference between the higher and lower daily expenditure. In small cities, people who eat lunch downtown may spend an average of $3.00 to $4.00, with a very few people spending more than $10.00.

Business visitors to a downtown generally spend more than the area businesspeople because they are visiting downtown primarily to dine with specific clients for business purposes and thus are usually on an expense account. Downtown shoppers generally tend to be frugal in their eating-out expenditures. While it is true that women meeting for shopping and lunch tend to spend more than the solitary shopper, historically the *average* shopper spends less than $3.00 per downtown visit for a meal.

Tourists, in most cities, are the most difficult to predict. Washington, D.C., tourists generally spend more eating-out dollars, primarily because so many of the facilities that they visit are in, or near, downtown. In San Antonio, although tourists tend to spend more money downtown than the office workers, they are usually frugal overall. Florida tourists may spend a considerable amount of money because of their length of stay, but on average, they also are quite frugal. Most tourists in New York City, San Francisco, Chicago, and Boston are freer with their dollars, and thus, the average expenditure for tourists is very high in those cities. Tourists in Hawaii and, more particularly, Honolulu, tend to out spend both San Francisco and New York.

In considering the potential for restaurants or fast food operations in a downtown area, it is important to obtain employment on a block-by-block basis. In larger cities, the planning department, often has data on employment on a block-by-block basis. Convention bureaus can often provide tourist and visitor information, while data on the downtown or near-downtown resident population are also usually available from the planning people. Again, it is important to remember that, for fast food facilities, a downtown trade area usually does not exceed two blocks. In fact, with a thorough understanding of the patterns, it is quite possible to place a unit within one block of another. A study might show that there is not any interchange between the areas because of the pedestrian patterns.

Estimating expenditures on a block-by-block basis starts with a determination of the expenditures by employees within the block. The data can often be obtained from the city's planning department which sometimes may have estimates of eating-out expenditures, but more often will not. To estimate the potential for dinner business requires considering a broader spectrum of both the lunch and dinner daypart. Thus, while lunch is very important for such restaurants, dinner is usually equally important. The dinner audience includes conventioneers, visitors, businesspeople with downtown offices, downtown and near-downtown residents, and those people who are generated into the area for dinner (usually the smallest group). The trade areas for lunch and dinner can be quite different.

The latest available Census of Business, 1987, contains sales for many downtown areas. Moreover, changes in sales and the number of establishments are available for every previous five years making it possible to see the permutations that have taken place. An operator can compute the sales per establishment to see the sales levels that have been achieved. Most importantly, the data indicate the eating and drinking sales trends in the downtown area.

Estimating sales requires weighing all the significant factors affecting a particular facility in relation to competition, patterns, luncheon activities, breakfast opportunities, and likely evening diners. Also, it requires considering the potential for business in levels or groups. For expensive fine dining facilities, it is necessary to consider estimating sales by levels of business to account adequately for what can be achieved.

SUMMARY

Downtowns can offer an interesting and growing potential, as well as an opportunity for new restaurant and fast food facilities. These areas are not, however, without risk. Moreover, they are far more difficult to evaluate than suburban locations because many of the variables are difficult to quantify. In general, it is considerably more important to gather adequate and accurate data prior to making a decision on a downtown location than on a suburban area.

A word of caution! Do not let downtown developers pressure you into making that decision. There are numerous development and redevelopment projects in downtown areas that need food facilities to meet their debt service. That need does not make them right for you. In fact, many of the projects will not reach their potential for years. Instead, measure the information, look at the activities, study the placement within the downtown area, examine the existing patterns, seriously evaluate the location being offered, recognize the importance of pedestrian traffic, consider the proximity of hotels and convention facilities, take the developer's estimate of sales potential and divide it by four, take your expenses and multiple them by two—and then see if there is sufficient potential for you to locate within the proposed complex.

It is my belief that most restaurant and fast food operations entering new development projects in downtown areas should be given some initial relief in the form of a rent abatement for the first one or two years, and certainly some recapture from any percentage lease "overages." The developers may tell you that it is impossible; experience, however, says that it is not. In fact, more and more "turnkey" deals are being made in downtown areas. For a turnkey deal, the developer provides not only the space but also all the leasehold improvements and, at the time of completion, hands over the key to the lessee. This arrangement allows the restaurateur to commence business without any real significant capital outlay.

Downtown areas are complex. Nevertheless, with our changing urban environment, they will continue to offer unique opportunities for those who are clever enough to distinguish between the positive elements and the dangerous ones. Nevertheless, these sites will usually require significant capital and dynamic entrepreneurship.

Twenty-Five

Shopping Centers and Major Malls

M any food operators have considered placing a unit in a shopping center or mall. Others who are planning to enter the food business have also considered such an opportunity. Furthermore, taking a location in a strip center often represents an excellent way to find a location in an area with limited site opportunities. This chapter focuses on the opportunities in centers of all sizes—what to consider and what to avoid.

HISTORICAL BACKGROUND

The automobile and consumer mobility were the cause and effect in shaping the development of our metropolitan areas in this century. The proliferation of the initial major shopping centers and subsequent malls has changed the daily patterns and lifestyles of at least two generations. Malls, today, are the focus of the attention of tens of millions of people throughout North America, not to mention the world.

Initially called shopping centers or shopping plazas, these collections of stores of all sizes and shapes eventually become behemoths. In the 1950s, the shopping center often had but a single small branch department store to generate traffic, along with the cumulative attraction of multiple stores. In the 1960s, merchants quickly realized that if one is good, then two are better. The shopping centers were generally what we call "strips" with an "anchor" at either end. The concept of a mall was truly developed in the 1960s, as two rows of stores facing each other across an open area, with department stores at either end (thus, a mall), with a sea of parking to accommodate Americans' love affair with the automobile. Improvements to the concept resulted in enclosed, heated, and air conditioned facilities with as many as five or six department stores. Continuing improvements resulted in multilevel malls, featuring escalators, indoor plantings, waterfalls, sculptures, other types of artwork, and ultimately even food courts.

In the evolution of events, there were, at first, very few restaurants or fast food units in shopping centers. In fact, initially most of them did not do well or failed. Operations that were located in centers almost always were placed in store space with their own seating. These sites, unfortunately, were usually near an obscure entrance, often close to the mall theater. Restaurants in shopping centers were seldom successful unless they were free-standing in the parking lot.

In the 1970s and 1980s, many changes continued, some for the better, and others for the worse. Mall developers suddenly became food experts and decided *where* restaurants should be placed for "their own good." From the developers' perspective, they were doing the restaurant operator a favor by letting him or her into the complex. Thus, the possible success or failure of the restaurant was removed from the operator's destiny, and, regrettably, quite a few establishments failed. Also, at that time many entrepreneurs believed that simply being in a mall with all those people ensured success. That fallacy, too, caused numerous failures.

The newest food phenomenon is the food court, where anywhere from 4 to as many as 20 small food shops are gathered together with shared or common seating. Initially, the food court was located in an obscure spot, as a stepchild. More recently, food courts are being placed where they should be, namely, near the center court with heavy pedestrian traffic.

In another trend, popular theme restaurants have located in malls to capitalize on the large concentrations of people and the plentiful available parking. Some restaurant operators have opted for a pad location in the parking lot, near a major entrance. On the pad, they not only benefit from the parking but also they have control of visibility, exposure, and often hours. Many find that their in-mall units generate a limited amount of business from the main mall entrance.

What does all of this mean to the restaurant and fast food operator? Well, it means that you need to capitalize on the major positive elements and avoid the negatives.

TYPES OF SHOPPING CENTERS AND MALLS

There are numerous types of shopping centers and malls including strip shopping centers; L-shaped, U-shaped, T-shaped, arc-shaped, and open malls; enclosed malls; single-level and multilevel malls; suburban, urban, downtown malls; weekend malls; underground malls; low-end mass merchandise, and off-price malls; factory outlet malls; fashion malls; and specialty malls. There may be others; for the moment, however, this list seems adequate.

Each kind of mall has a distinctive trade area, customer profile, strength of attraction, and varying sales performance. Moreover, malls are appreciated by the consumer in varying degrees. Similarities may exist in overall sizes, store sizes, types of stores, and square foot sales performance, but there are also wide degrees of variance.

Should you be seriously considering a restaurant location either in or on the pad of a shopping center or mall, you should obtain a copy of the latest publication of the *Dollars and Cents of Shopping Centers,* published by Urban Land Institute in Washington, D.C., in conjunction with the International Council of Shopping Centers. It is a compendium of performance statistics for shopping centers and malls of all sizes, with store performances by geographic areas. For those looking at food courts, you might want also to obtain the annual issue on food courts published in the *CARLSONREPORT.* This issue (usually the month of June) features sales performances by types of food units, along with square foot performances. Articles pertaining to food courts are also included. The report can be obtained by writing or calling the CARLSONREPORT (P.O. Box 80209, Indianapolis, Indiana 66280). This monthly periodical is directed almost entirely to shopping center managers throughout the world. I have written numerous articles for the publication.

Shopping centers are usually classified into four types: neighborhood, community, regional, and super regional. There are also some specialized categories such as fashion, outlet, power center, and entertainment malls. Each has a somewhat typical set of tenants and overall size. The most significant enigma is that few regional shopping centers actually serve a region. Rather, they usually serve only parts of a metropolitan area, and are, therefore, better defined as "submetropolitan shopping centers or malls." Regardless, usage usually determines definition. We shall follow tradition and refer to them by the industry's accepted label, "regional shopping centers and malls."

Neighborhood Shopping Centers

A neighborhood shopping center is usually oriented to the sale of convenience goods; it contains at least one major store as a magnet and a series of smaller stores. Strip centers, which form a subcategory of neighborhood shopping centers, generally do not have a major traffic generator. Neighborhood shopping centers usually contain frequently visited convenience goods stores, such as supermarkets, self-service multiline drugstores, liquor shops, and hardware stores. Additionally, they usually have several service stores: cleaners, beauty and barber shops, laundromats, and shoe repair stores. Often fast food, lunchrooms, and sandwich shops are located in these facilities.

A neighborhood shopping center varies in size from about 30,000 square feet to 150,000 square feet. They have grown in size lately because of the increasing dimensions of supermarkets which today average from 40,000 to 80,000 square feet. These stores must capture sales of at least $400,000 to $800,000 per week, initially. Most expect to see sales above $600,000 a week, and some larger supermarkets (80,000 to 100,000 square feet) generate from $800,000 to $3,000,000 per week. If you are inclined to locate near a major supermarket, be aware that another shakeout is coming in the supermarket industry, as these behemoths batter each other for sales dollars. Because of their size, their breakeven points are extremely high. Thus, there will be a number of vacant supermarkets, which could adversely affect nearby fast food units because of the reduction in traffic. This does not mean that you should avoid such locations. Rather, you should be aware of the possible pitfalls and act accordingly. Look at the strength of the supermarket chain, its performance elsewhere in the marketplace, and especially the supermarket's performance at the site under consideration.

Smaller neighborhood shopping centers may contain as little as 10,000 square feet, without a major tenant. These strip centers usually contain a collection of small stores. To be successful, they must be on a major traffic artery leading to a significant activity center. Often pizzerias, delicatessens, and sandwich shops are located in these strips. They have a mixed success, depending on the location, the driving patterns, the amount of activity, and the competition. Often, the food serve facilities in these locations must be generative to survive.

Community Shopping Centers

The major tenant in a community shopping center usually is a discount department store. Possibly, there may be a major supermarket and some promotional stores, such as Marshall's, T. J. Maxx, Mervyn's, or Silo Appliances. In addition, most have a collection of both convenience goods and shoppers' goods stores. Shoppers' goods, which are purchased less frequently than convenience goods, include apparel, shoes, accessories, department store items, appliances, furniture, and household furnishings. Community shopping centers are usually between 100,000 and 300,000 square feet in size. These centers usually have some in-line restaurants and sandwich shops, as well as some fast food facilities or restaurants on the pad near the entrances and exits.

Regional Shopping Centers and Malls

Regional malls usually contain two, three, or more department stores. They can be open or enclosed, although almost all new malls are enclosed. Eventually most of the older malls will be enclosed because of variations in weather conditions and the better competitive position of enclosed facilities. Regional malls usually range in size between 350,000 and 1,400,000 square feet. Many are two-level facilities, capitalizing on the two-level department stores. Thus, customers can enter the mall from either an upper or lower level parking lot. These facilities often contain restaurants and fast food units both in and on the pad of the mall. Most have food courts.

Super Regional Malls

Super regional malls are very large retail complexes, usually containing from three to eight department stores or other major retailers. They are also multilevel structures, ranging from about 1,000,000 to

2,500,000 square feet. Most include food courts and have restaurants both inside the mall and on the pad. Because these malls attract customers from very wide areas, they rely less on frequency of visit and depend heavily on large numbers of customers.

Fashion Centers

Fashion centers, part of the mall family, range between 400,000 and 900,000 square feet. They are usually anchored by stores such as Neiman Marcus, Sak's Fifth Avenue, Lord & Taylor, Bloomingdale's, Marshall Field and Company, Nordstrom's, and Jacobson's. They are merchandised toward upper-middle to upper income customers. In recent years, many fashion centers have had problems because major department stores have gone out of business. Often, the fashion department stores were purchased by shopping center developers who found themselves overburdened with debt and unable to sustain their financial needs.

Factory Outlet and Off-Price Shopping Centers and Malls

The new factory outlet and off-price centers around the nation are often considered to be in the community shopping center category. However, it is not unusual for them to be larger. In fact, some of the new ones are over 1,000,000 square feet, and larger. Like community shopping centers, they have some in-line food units and some pad restaurant and fast food locations. The most successful centers are away from major metropolitan areas, usually on major expressways leading to and from recreational or vacation areas. Restaurants in these complexes have had mixed results. Successful units are generally free-standing, either on the pad or nearby. Food courts in these complexes are usually poor performers because of their weekend orientation. During the week, these centers are dead. As most food operators know, it is very difficult to operate a unit on weekend-only business.

Power Centers

Power centers are generally about 150,000 to 350,000 square feet. The primary tenants, commonly referred to as "category killers," are highly promotional, feature price, provide limited customer service, and are generally quite large. Stores in this category include Cub Foods, Sam's Wholesale Club, Wal-Mart, Silo, Circuit City, Phar-Mor, F & M, Warehouse membership clubs, T. J. Maxx, and Marshall's. Generally, small stores in these centers do not fare very well because so much parking is consumed by patrons of the major stores. Food operators have had mixed results in these centers, principally because their locations are often either far away from the action, or too close. They also can be adversely affected by parking problems. Pad locations can be very good, assuming that the traffic generated fits the operation's customer profile.

SALES PERFORMANCE

The size of a shopping center or a mall is not a measure of success. Rather, the true measure is sales and, more specifically, sales per square foot. The *Dollars and Cents of Shopping Centers* (Urban Land Institute, Washington, D.C.) is published about every three years. It lists the sizes and performances of various types of stores in shopping centers and malls, as well as the sales per square foot. The data, which are provided by shopping center owners and managers, are almost always at least one year old. Table 25.1 presents the ranges of sales per square foot for successful shopping complexes based upon

TABLE 25.1

Sales per Square Foot in Shopping Centers and Malls
(Excluding Department Stores)

Type	Range
Neighborhood shopping centers	$100–$1,500
Strip centers	$80–$250
Community shopping centers	$100–$400
Off-price/factory outlet centers	$150–$1,500
Regional shopping malls	$100–$600
Super regional malls	$100–$800
Fashion malls	$200–$600
Power centers	$500–$900

Source: Adapted from *The Dollars and Cents of Shopping Centers* (Urban Land Institute, Washington, D.C.).

my experience. Some small shops, known as kiosks, may capture higher sales than those shown in the table; however, they are not significant to the mall's overall performance. They do indicate customer traffic in certain parts of a mall.

Since a primary reason for going into a shopping center or mall location is "action or pedestrian traffic," it pays to find out how the facility is doing. The next critical item is the location within the mall. There are numerous examples around North America of highly successful shopping centers and malls where the food facilities have fared poorly or failed. Location within the complex, the profile of the shopping customer, and the amount of action or pedestrians are the determining factors.

Some food operators are interested in shopping centers and malls because of the ample parking. Nonetheless, they also need a certain level of action for success. It pays to find out how well the facility is doing. How can you find out? There are a number of ways. First, ask the leasing agent to see a sample of store sales, especially those near the location under consideration. Next, talk to the merchants in the complex and find out their reactions. Have sales met with their expectations? Additionally, check with the research department at the local newspaper. They usually have information about the mall and its sales.

State sales tax receipts for the community in which the complex is located may provide an indication of the sales level. If the ownership is a public company, the data may be in either the annual report or a recent prospectus. Keep in mind that the sales by the stores in a complex are usually not uniform. Some locations are better than others, while some stores and food operations capture more business than others.

MALL LEVELS

Selecting the correct mall level is very important to a restaurant's success. Most fast food units do not have this option, since they either go into the food court or they are not allowed into the mall. Leasing agents will tell you that activity in a multilevel mall is the same on all levels, but that is usually incorrect. I have known very few malls with equal activity on each level. How can you tell which level might be right for you (assuming that you have the opportunity to choose)? First, look at the entrances to the shopping center or mall and the number of cars parked nearby. Look before the stores open to see where the employees are parking. Next, observe the entrances during peak shopping periods. Usually, people tend to select the parking lot "in front" of the complex, even when the road planners try to direct traffic to the rear. Study the actual or anticipated traffic flow including evenings toward the end of the week and the weekends. Weekend malls, which generate almost all their business on Saturday and Sunday can be difficult for restaurants and fast food operations. If the mall has yet to be built or is currently under construction, study the road patterns, the traffic counts, and the roads that the mall will face. Also, talk to local traffic officials regarding the traffic flow and the entrances that will be used. When in doubt, try to select a location that favors an entrance capitalizing on the major street that the mall will face.

I recently analyzed a mall that had a perceived parking problem. By "perceived," I mean that the customers believed that the mall had a parking problem while management did not. Actually, from ratio standpoint, adequate parking was available; the problem was its placement. Everyone wanted to park in front of the mall although the majority of the parking spaces were located in the rear. Thus, a perceived parking problem can become a real one.

The department stores can provide clues of activity by level. For example, Sears' greatest strength is in hard goods (appliances, washers, dryers, tools, equipment, furniture, and other durable goods). The level at which Sears merchandises those items will generate the greatest amount of traffic for Sears. A word of caution! In my experience, Sears' customers, much more often than others, go to the store with their charge card, make a purchase, and leave the mall. Therefore, pedestrian traffic is often lighter near the Sears mall entrance. It is not unusual to find the stores on either side of the Sears mall entrance either vacant or occupied by low intensity uses.

Other department stores have different patterns. For example, at Marshall Field and Company, the action takes place primarily on the level with the ladies' ready-to-wear, especially sportswear. This also holds true with most conventional department stores. With J. C. Penney, the predominant activity is on the level with the greatest amount of apparel, mainly in women's and children's wear. These concentrations can provide a clue to the activity level of the mall.

RENTS

Rents in shopping centers range from about $8 per square foot to more than $100 per square foot. The rent level should depend on the degree of success of the shopping center and the sales potential for the food operator. Rents are usually net, net, net, which means that the tenant pays his or her share of real estate taxes, maintenance, security, snow removal, promotion, and merchants' association fees. The lower rents are usually found in strip centers, whereas the highest are found in major downtown atriums and unique fashion developments.

The *Dollars and Cents of Shopping Centers* provides a guide to last year's rental fees. Remember that everything is negotiable. The degree to which the landlord will bend depends on how valuable you might be to the center. Restaurants have the edge over fast food units in negotiating reasonable rentals, since they are considered more desirable. Nevertheless, it pays to negotiate carefully, since any savings will be significant in the long run.

COMMON AREA MAINTENANCE CHARGES

In addition to rent, tenants in shopping centers and malls pay what is known as "common area maintenance" (CAM) charges to cover their share of operating and maintenance costs for common areas. These charges include maintenance of common areas, snow removal, contributions to the merchants' association, security, real estate taxes, and, in some cases, other charges as well. CAM charges often run between $2.50 and $40 a square foot, depending on the size of the complex and the geographic part of the country. The highest CAM charges are usually found in downtown atrium developments. Most shopping centers attempt to have the tenants pay their pro rata share of these charges without any maximum. Larger tenants can negotiate variations, while small tenants usually have little choice in the matter. Nevertheless, it never hurts to try.

PERCENTAGE RENTAL LEASE CLAUSES

Most shopping centers and malls require, in addition to base rent and CAM charges, a percentage rental clause, which requires that, in addition to base rent, the landlord will receive a percentage of a unit's sales, if those sales exceed certain levels. What is paid is over and above the base rent and is usually known as "sales overage." For example, if a food operator has a 6% lease agreement and, say, a base rent of $60,000 per year, then the breakpoint in the rent is $1,000,000 in sales annually ($60,000 rent divided by 6% equals annual sales at the breakpoint). If sales rise to $1,200,000, the rent would then be $72,000 (base rent of $60,000, plus an "overage" of $12,000, for a total of $72,000). The total rent would be 6% of sales. Of course, remember that the CAM charges are in addition to the base rent plus any overages. To make matters even more confusing, the breakpoint is usually negotiable and can be raised or lowered to achieve higher or lower total rents. From the food operator's perspective, no percentage lease clause is the best. However, when it is either have one or go elsewhere, then it is best to keep the percentage low or raise the breakpoint. The percentage most often seen in the restaurant and fast food business is 6%.

SHOPPING CENTER AND MALL ACTIVITY

Locations within malls are usually very different for restaurants than for fast food facilities. Restaurants with outside entrances (you should have an outside entrance), often generate a high percentage of their sales on the basis of their own good food and reputation. Fast food facilities are almost wholly dependent on the pedestrian traffic generated within the mall. That is why the performance of the mall and the location within it are so important. Remember that the largest amount of activity will be found around the greatest generators. That may seem so obvious as not to require mention. Again, remember it, since successful food people need to be where the action is.

The first step in determining the amount of activity in a shopping center or mall is to estimate the number of people who are likely to visit the complex. This is much easier to do for an existing shopping facility than for one that is planned. An existing complex can be visited, observed, and studied, whereas a planned complex can only be envisioned with the aid of plans and drawings. Moreover, the food operator is at the mercy of "estimated sales" and "anticipated success." *Do not believe everything that the leasing agent tells you; if you have doubts, ask for it in writing.* You may be surprised to learn that much of what you are told, you will not be able to get in writing. The reasons given might include "There is a law against it," "We have a policy that prevents us from doing that," or even, "If we did it for you, we would have to do it for everyone." For the record, it is not illegal to restrict another food operator in the food court from selling your product, nor is the lease agreement sacred and unchangeable. Basically, the agent will not put it in writing because you would have evidence for a lawsuit later on if what was promised did not materialize.

Shopping centers and malls with at least two department stores vary in the amount spent by customers on an average day. Daily per capita expenditures in a center usually range between $25 and $100 per customer. The lower the total, usually the less dynamic the center. Also, the store mix of the center and the income of the area play a role in the amount spent. For example, a center with a major Sears store will usually have an average sale per customer per day of more than $40, because the majority of Sears sales are generated from large ticket items such as washers, dryers, refrigerators, and tools. Also, centers with several fashion stores usually have much higher average purchases. Truly high-fashion complexes will have average purchases of more than $100.

Assume that we have a mall with sales of $100,000,000 annually. Moreover, the average purchases of each customer per day amount to $30. Incidentally, mall managers usually know this number because most shopping centers and malls exceeding 600,000 square feet interview in the complexes every two to three years to determine changes in their customers. That notwithstanding, $100,000,000 in sales at an average sale of $30 per day results in a total annual number of 3,333,333 purchasing customers. The actual total number is larger, because everyone does not make a purchase. Most malls are open 364 days a year. Assuming that the facility is open 364 days, there are an average of 9,158 customers per day. That means that between 9,000 and 10,000 customers visit the mall on an average day. While that is the average, the center captures a majority of its sales in the last half of the year and, in fact, has its highest sales during December. Thus, the sales pattern for a food operations in the mall would be different from the pattern of food facilities outside the complex. Also, with reference to a location nearby on a major road leading to the mall, in this example 9,000 to 10,000 customers per day means that there are probably double that many trip generations. If all the traffic to and from the mall is on one road, then the mall will generate a traffic count of at least 18,000 to 20,000 daily. Naturally, the road will have some other traffic. As a food operator, you essentially will have two interception opportunities for each car; one when it passes your location enroute to the mall, and one on the return trip.

Now that you know the averages, you can do several things. First, you can ask the mall manager for the customer traffic figures. The manager may respond with automobile traffic in the parking lot or the total number of customers served within the past year. Regardless, the data are helpful in determining the *number of customers* as well as *when they come to the mall*. Second, you can count the customers passing a specific location within the shopping complex, to check the extent of the pedestrian traffic. This is very important because a great mall can have poor locations within it. Thus, unless you have the right location, do not expect your operation to succeed simply because the mall is successful.

Usually, the best opportunity for mall restaurants is within upscale centers, where customers have more time available, so they spend more time and, generally, more money. Such customers will go to the mall to spend the day, meet friends, have lunch, and make a social function out of the trip.

ADDITIONAL OBSERVATIONS

For full-service restaurants, the parking lot pad location is usually better for sales, identity, and individuality than a location in the mall (even with an outside entrance). Moreover, a location across the street or down the street with good access is often a better solution because you can avoid the common area maintenance charges and perhaps a percentage lease. Furthermore, the benefits from the mall's generative activities are usually only slightly less than with the pad location. Additionally, pad locations are often unsubordinated ground leases, which must be financed with a line of credit or cash. A lien or a mortgage cannot be placed upon the land.

Fast food operators who do not want to be in food courts but want to be represented in a mall might make a deal with major department stores to rent space as a subtenant. This represents a way to get around the food court concept and yet be in the mall. The location may not be quite as desirable, but if the department store is a high sales generator, it may be acceptable. Obviously, the location should be at an entrance, preferably adjacent to the mall entrance to the department store.

The best locations for restaurants within malls are situated at or near the major entrances. In fact, the best location is usually right at the major entrance. Most often, the entrance facing the most significant traffic artery gets the most play.

Malls, especially newer ones located in suburban fringe development areas, are highly oriented toward women. As a restaurateur, you must examine your customer characteristics to determine if the consumers attracted to the mall have similar characteristics. Men resist change and are usually the last ones to become frequent customers of a new mall.

For many fast food operators, food courts are often a *compromise* solution, representing the only way to get into the mall. On the other hand, all pad locations (freestanding locations in the shopping center parking lot) are not winners. Again, traffic patterns need to be studied to determine the amount of traffic passing a particular location. I have seen numerous pad locations that have failed because they were on the wrong side of the complex, or facing the wrong street.

Strip centers must have all the other required market support factors before being considered. Nonetheless, strip shopping centers that have good access, adequate parking, and convenience goods shops, service stores, and some apparel and secondary retail facilities must be looked at very closely. If the center is located on a good traffic artery with favorable access, it can offer promising locations for pad development. This is especially true if it is an ancillary shopping center to a major mall. However, strip centers that share the same site with a major mall often do not receive the same amount of exposure or activity as the main complex and, thus, are not good places for restaurants. Also, they are usually in the back, or on the less active side of the overall complex. This does not mean that a particular food operation cannot be successful in these secondary complexes. It does mean, however, that they must be approached with more caution. Success or failure rests on your shoulders.

Twenty-Six

Food Courts

Food courts have proliferated since about 1980. Very simply, they are a collection of fast food operations clustered together, with common seating. The theory is that the food operator can rent less space (less rent), since everyone is sharing the same seating. Also, the collective arrangement will allow individual operations to do more business.

Food is an integral part of shopping, although it has taken a long time for shopping center developers to truly understand the need and how to merchandise it. The food court, as opposed to a food operator having an individual store space, was conceived to share common elements such as seating and to focus specific attention on the cumulative attraction of food facilities. It can be a good concept. Each of us feels certain stomach pangs two, three, or more times a day. Consolidating the food operations in a single location encourages the hungry consumer in the shopping center or mall to head for the food court. The fallacy of the theory is that many fast food meals are based on impulse decisions, as a result of seeing a sign, smelling food, or walking by a food unit. The senses should create a mental image of "good things." When that occurs, the consumer will deviate slightly from the existing walking pattern to partake in the "hopefully succulent tidbits." This works when the food court is placed in a convenient and highly accessible location within the mall. Unfortunately, many food courts have been placed in out-of-the-way locations, so that the landlord can fill vacant space, thus, eliminating the concept of impulse.

(Naturally, some customers will find the food court regardless of the location.)

Initially, the concept was to provide the consumer with a "menu spectrum" by attracting multiple operations, with various types of food entrees, including hamburgers; chicken; pizza; deli sandwiches; Oriental, Greek, and Mexican food; salads; cookies; pastries; hot dogs; potatoes; seafood; ice cream and yogurt; and barbecue. Again, in theory, it is desirable. Unfortunately, it is necessary to recognize who the consumer is, and what the consumer's tastes really are. Moreover, this initial concept involved independent food operators with very narrow menus rather than franchise chains, which often have wide and varied menus. Thus, the landlord believed that more food operators could be placed within the food court. Today's more sophisticated mall owners and developers are coming to the realization that the food court, as originally conceived, is ill-fated. Small independents are falling by the wayside; vacancies are increasing; and, from a landlord's point of view, too much time is being spent "nursing" the food court.

Unfortunately, many independent food operators who saw the food court as a panacea, discovered, much to their chagrin, the long hours, the higher than expected common area maintenance charges, the lack of promised sales, and in many cases, the subsequent entry of a major, well-known fast food chain or franchisee. All these elements have created significant problems for the majority of suburban mall food courts.

In contrast, well-located downtown food courts have outperformed their counterparts. The primary reason for this greater degree of success is simply that considerable employment usually exists in proximity, and customers can take the food back to their offices. Therefore, the food courts do not require the same level of seating. Adequate seating goes considerably further in a downtown food court than in a suburban mall. The following sections describe some food court specifics.

SIZE

Food court sizes usually range from approximately 5,000 to 25,000 square feet. Ideally, the size should be sufficient to meet the demand within the mall. Unfortunately, in the process of events, demand does not determine size. Instead, the size of the food court is usually determined either by the developer dictating to the architect, or the architect coming up with a space allocation for what appears to be a likely area. Few landlords understand that the age structure of the population within a mall plays a considerable role in the food court's degree of success. The true measure of success depends on four factors: (1) location, (2) age and income of the consumer, (3) types and effectiveness of food operators, and (4) adequate seating for peak periods.

There is no standard size for all shopping centers. Instead, the size should be determined by the extent of the trade area, the age and income structure of the prospective customers, the potential sales that the facility expects to capture, potential expenditures, and placement and seating provided in the facility.

LOCATION

As previously indicated, initially food courts were placed in secondary locations, such as near the mall theater. Today, more and more shopping center developers and leasing people recognize the importance of placing food courts in the pedestrian pattern. Therefore, food courts are being placed near center court or near the main entrance to the mall. The result is that the food operations will capture higher sales, and the landlord will achieve higher rents. Ironically, food courts located at main entrances have played to mixed reviews. Often, the customers entering and exiting the mall are on a "mission" and, as a result, are difficult to stop, much like commuters going to and from work. Each site needs to be evaluated on its own merit.

In addition, the food courts can provide "excitement" and bring "fun" back into shopping. In today's society, with more working women and fewer housewives, the time for shopping has been compressed into evenings and weekends. Thus, for many consumers, shopping has become a chore. If shopping center operators can make shopping and its environment attractive, consumers will visit the complex more often and will stay longer in the facility. Our studies have shown that people do tend to remain longer in malls with food courts. Additionally, the more time a consumer spends in a mall, the greater the expenditure, on any given day. Therefore, food courts play an important role in increasing dollars spent in the mall.

INDIVIDUAL UNIT SIZES

Individual unit sizes vary from some that are very small to some that are double the typical size. Basically, they are usually between 300 and 2,000 square feet. Occasionally, a full-sized restaurant will be located immediately adjacent to the food court, giving the impression that it is part of the court. In those cases, the full-sized unit might be between 3,500 and 8,000 square feet. A food court unit today is usually between 500 and 600 square feet. In the future the more typical size may be closer to 600 or 800 square feet, as more and more food operators expand their menus and strive for individuality within the food court, to generate higher sales.

THE NUMBER OF FOOD OPERATORS

A food court usually has anywhere from 5 to 20 operators. Smaller shopping centers, obviously have smaller food courts, while the larger courts are usually in downtown areas and super regional malls. Today, food courts with more than 10 units generally have some under-performers or vacant units, and those with 12, 15, or 20 units are experiencing considerable turnover, below square foot performance, and vacancy. Beware of those food courts unless you happen to be a unique independent, chain, or franchise operation with considerable consumer acceptance.

In a typical mall today, the number of food operators is declining. Landlords faced with this problem are now turning to chain and franchise operators as a solution to their vacancy problem. Without question, the well-known food names will generate higher sales per square foot and often will create more excitement and interest within the food court. The chain and franchise operators should bring higher sales, a higher level of awareness, and experienced professionalism. That, unfortunately, is not always the case. Depending on the type of operation, some of the existing food court tenants will be adversely affected. Food units that can often live in a competitive environment include operations that sell hamburgers, Oriental food, pizza, sandwiches, and some others in special situations. Nevertheless, most food courts should have only one of each major food group. The market simply cannot sustain two units in the same category (chicken against chicken) at high sales performance. Although two might survive for a while, one will usually outdistance the other, finally resulting in the loss of the less successful unit. In the future, the optimum number of food operations in a typical mall will probably average about 10 units, representing a mix of chain, franchise, and independent units. The chains and franchise units will be in a majority.

TYPES OF FOOD FACILITIES

The highest sales performers in malls usually include hamburgers, chicken, pizza, Oriental and Mexican food, and sandwiches. These are often followed by pastries, seafood, Greek food, hot dogs, and salads. In some markets, a barbecued food unit may be added to the count. Cookies, ice cream, and yogurt generally complete the array. The sales performance varies by mall, depending on the age structure of the customers and the placement within the mall. As more and more food courts begin to permit chains and franchise units into food courts, a positive change in the performance level will occur. The sales leaders are likely to continue to be hamburgers (chains or franchise operators), Oriental food, pizza, Mexican food, and chicken. The remaining mix of food units is difficult to forecast but will be quite varied by type of mall, depending on its age structure and placement.

SALES PERFORMANCE

Average food court sales are between $400 and $425 per square foot, or between $240,000 and $255,000 per unit. However, sales of food court units vary considerably. High sales units normally include hamburgers, Oriental and Mexican food, chicken, and pizza. Annual sales range from a low of about $150,000 to more than $1,000,000. The million dollar units are often larger than the typical 600-square-foot unit. Most of the strong hot food operators are clustered between $400 and $600 per square foot. The remaining units, both for hot foods and desserts are concentrated between $300 and $400 per square foot; however, numerous food courts have units that perform below this level.

Two transitions in food courts are having an upward impact on sales. Namely, more chain and franchise units are being added, which is generally increasing the sales per square foot performances, and furthermore, some super regional malls are adding more than one unit of a specific type with apparent success. However, the jury is still out on the long-range success of both trends.

Changing eating habits have had a positive impact on sales, especially for Oriental food, chicken, and pasta. To a lesser extent, seafood, yogurt, and salads have enjoyed similar benefits. An excellent source of information on food courts is the *CARLSONREPORT* (available at P.O. Box 80209, Indianapolis, Indiana 46280, or by telephone at 317-844-9024), which publishes an annual survey of food court sales performance by food type. Their findings are reported in one or more of their monthly reports. Also, they have a detailed study, crammed with information on tenant mix, size, sales, types, common area maintenance (CAM) charges, seating, rents, and other pertinent data. Our findings have paralleled theirs.

SEATING AND TABLES

Food court seating is like shopping center parking; when it is inadequate, the deficiency limits sales. The number of seats in food courts can range from 200 to 2,200; typical seating is between 400 and 450 seats. Large seating facilities are usually found in downtown areas, festival marketplaces, and other major concentrations of people. The number of square feet devoted to seating ranges from 15 to 25 square feet. While the industry continues to focus on the number of seats provided, it is the number of available suitable tables that is important.

Our studies in malls have shown that typically the seating turns over between three and four times per hour, with an average sitting time of 17 minutes. (This can vary considerably depending on the food mix, the type of shopping center, the age of the shopper, and whether small children are present.) Additionally, the average party size is approximately two persons. Also, most malls do not allow food to be consumed outside the food court. Therefore, if there are 400 seats and they turn four times per hour, then, on an hourly basis, the food court has 1,600 available seats. *However, they are rarely all available because of limited table sharing and reduced seating efficiency.* Nevertheless, if the check average were $4 and all seats were occupied, the sales per hour for all the food operations in the food court would amount to $6,400 (1600 seats × $4). If there were ten food court units, the average at peak would be $64,000 per hour.

Naturally, some units do not require seating, such as cookies, ice cream, and yogurt bars. You might want to extend this little computation throughout the day, recognizing that peak sales will only occur during peak periods.

A significant part of any seating equation is the type of tables. Many food courts have fixed tables, in contrast to movable tables and chairs. While fixed seating is often easier to maintain, it is often quite inefficient. Many fixed seating food courts are a mix of tables of fours and twos. Some tables of fours are fine, as long as the majority of customers are groups of three or four persons. However, as previously indicated, the average party size is usually two. Thus, movable tables of two are far more efficient than fours and, particularly, fixed fours. Furthermore, with an average party size of two, tables of fours will have a 50% seating efficiency because most tables of fours are occupied by twos. Conversely, tables of twos usually have an efficiency of at least 70%, thereby increasing the available seating. The equations also reflect that all seating is never fully occupied, even if people are waiting for a table. This is extremely important. Seating type, seating efficiency, and seating turnover can make the difference in whether the food court has sufficient seating. In many respects, seating efficiency should be termed table efficiency because rarely do people share tables. Finally, downtown food courts usually turn over more slowly than mall food courts. We find that the average seating time is about 20 minutes. Therefore, the seats turn over about three times per hour.

The types of food operations in an outlying mall affect the need for seating. "Hot foods"—those facilities that are basically sandwich or hot food oriented—require more seating than "dessert foods," which are items such as cookies, ice cream, yogurt, pastries, donuts, popcorn, and other "finger foods." My studies indicate that hot food customers seek seating at least 90% of the time, while dessert food customers require seating about 60% of the time. In downtown food courts the percentages will usually be quite different because many customers take their purchases back to the office and therefore do not require seating.

The typical food court needs at least 500 seats to meet peak demand, if the food court units are to be successful. Many shopping center food courts have inadequate seating. While this problem can be overlooked somewhat in downtown food courts because of strong take-out business, it cannot be ignored in suburban malls. The total number of seats, however, is not the most significant factor. *Instead, the number of tables with available seating is the critical element.* An occupied table, even if three seats are unoccupied, is not available seating. People prefer to sit alone or with friends and rarely share a table with strangers.

How do you determine if a food court has adequate tables and seating? It is easy if the food court already exists, but it can be difficult to look at plans and try to determine if the seating and its placement are sufficient. However, you can ask for the food court layout and seating plan, along with the types of tables. Next, follow along making your own calculations. For existing food courts, the following steps are designed to identify the needs of the food court more accurately than by relying on industry averages. This procedure can also be followed by mall management. Each food court has its own personality and, therefore, must be addressed individually.

1. *Count the Number of Tables and Seats in the Food Court.* Classify them by types of tables (i.e., movable or fixed twos, fours, etc.).

2. *Prepare a Diagram of the Food Court.* Give each table a number and indicate the approximate location of the seating. Also, prepare an inventory form with each table and its seats listed down the left side. The top of the page should have hours listed, with each hour divided into six segments. With this form you will be able to record the number of people occupying each table and the time that each table turns over.

3. *Talk to the Food Operators in the Food Court about Peak Days and Peak Hours.* The food service industry operates to meet peaks. Select the busiest days' peak times. When something (such as inadequate seating) prevents exceeding current peaks, it places a lid on potential sales, affecting both the operator and the landlord.

4. *During the Selected Periods, Count the Utilization of Tables and Seats.* By recording both the vacant tables and the number of people occupying individual tables, you will later be able to compute approximate seating efficiency. Try to observe the number of customers who take food out of the food court. Also, observe group sizes. Does the table configuration work effectively?

5. *Observe Table Turnover.* Watch the turnover and record the time that each table turns over. In larger food courts, it may

be necessary to use two or three people to accomplish this task.

6. *Observe How Quickly the Tables Are Cleaned.* Fast clean up means more tables will be available.

7. *Compute the Table Availability, Seating Turnover, and Seating Efficiency.* The following examples show how to make these computations.

Example 1

A 15-minute average turnover means that you have four times the total number of seats on a per hour basis. For example, if you have 400 seats in the food court and the seats are turning over an average of every 15 minutes, then you literally have four times the number of seats, or 1,600 seats on a per hour basis. However, if the seating efficiency (the average number of seats utilized at each table) is only 70%, then you only have 1,120 seats available, or an average of 280 during each 15-minute interval.

When going into a food court where your objective might be to capture annual sales of $500,000, you should know your seating needs, especially those on either side of you. If you have a $3 check average, then you will require a total number of 166,667 customers annually. On a daily basis, this will require an average of 458 customers, resulting in sales of $1,374 on an average day. Assuming that you are in the "hot food" business, about 90% of your customers will require seating, resulting in a demand for of 412 seats. Moreover, assuming that approximately 60% of your business is done at lunch, you will generate approximately 247 luncheon customers who require seating on an average day. If lunch time spans a two-hour period (this needs to be checked with each individual situation), 123 seats will be required per peak hour. Moreover, if the turnover is three turns per hour, your seating requirement will be 41 seats. If the seating/table efficiency is 70% on average, you will need a total of 58 seats (41 seats divided by 70%) to meet your seating demand.

Example 2

In this example, assume that your expectant sales goal within five years is $750,000. Furthermore, you expect your check average to rise to $4. This will result in total annual customers of 187,500 and an average of about 515 customers daily. The average daily sales will amount to about $2,060. Should you have an 90% seating demand, your customers will require daily seating amounting to 464 seats. Again, assuming that the luncheon seating requirement of 60% will remain the same, this will require 278 seats. Furthermore, given a two-hour lunch period, 139 seats are required per hour. With a turnover of three times per hour, a total of 46 seats are now necessary. However, at 70% efficiency, a total of 66 seats are needed. If there are 10 units in the food court with similar seating demand, a total of 660 seats will be required.

Example 3

The food court in this example contains 10 units, averaging $400,000 per unit, and total sales amount to $4,000,000. With a check average of $3.50, approximately 1,142,857 customers are served annually. Assuming that the center is closed on Christmas, this leaves 364 days a year. Therefore, on a daily basis, there are an average of 3,140 customers in the food court. In many food courts, lunch often generates about 60% of the daily sales or 1,884 customers. If 90% of the customers need seating, then seats must be available for 1,695 persons. Usually, the luncheon demand occurs over a period of one to two hours. Thus, over two hours there would be seating demand for 848 customers. Should it be an hour and a half, then a total of 1,130 would be required. Should the food court activity be concentrated within one hour (highly unlikely), then the food court would require seating for 1,695 persons.

If the turnover of seating is three times an hour (every 20 minutes), the food court must provide 283 seats each hour for a concentration of two hours, 377 seats for one and a half hours, and 565 seats for one hour. However, since all tables are not efficiently occupied, it is necessary to apply a seating efficiency level to the available seats. If the efficiency level is 75%, then the two-hour seating requirement would be 378 seats per segment, the one-and-a-half-hour seating requirement would be 503 seats, and one-hour seating requirement would be 753 seats. The crucial factors here are *peak concentrations*, *seating efficiency levels*, and *table turnover*, which really determine seating availability in a food court.

Additional Considerations

The preceding calculations ignore several important facts that would increase the number of seats needed. All malls have customers who stop in the food court to rest and do not make a purchase. Some surplus seating is required. Also, averages do not reflect the reality of peaks; and peak seating requirements *MUST* be met if the operator is to achieve anticipated sales. There is nothing more frustrating for a food operator than to see a potential customer leave without placing an order because all the food court tables are occupied. Unfortunately, it happens every day all over the country. With some advanced planning, the seating situation can be resolved before it becomes a problem. Without question, if you are or plan to be a food court tenant, aside from the court's location, seating, in terms of available tables, is the next most critical factor to your business.

A final word about seating. From a mall operator's point of view, about 30% to 40% of the seating should be fixed seating, with the balance in movable twos. This suggested mix will help to maximize seating efficiency, while reducing maintenance costs because it takes more time to clean and move twos into their proper position. Also, where inadequate seating exists, stand-up tables or counters will help to alleviate the situation.

It should also be pointed out that an imbalance in seating can be caused by a high-volume operator's customers occupying the seating near other food operators. When reviewing a location in an existing food court, pay attention to where people are sitting. Is all the seating near the available unit currently utilized at peak periods? If so, you may want to take a pass.

TABLE PLACEMENT

Seating placement is also very important. The customers' perception of available seating is directly related to where they buy their food and the general proximity of empty tables. The primary consideration is not necessarily the total number of seats, but rather the placement, especially in large food courts that have either an open space looking over a lower level, or escalators and a fountain in the center. Equally influential is the often-found jungle of trees and bushes, which tends not only to obliterate the available seating but also to obscure the food facility's signs. While the greenery may be beautiful, it often defeats food merchandising.

In a food court, "seating is king." Seating must be designed to meet peak demands, not only at opening, but also 5 to 10 years down the road. In most food courts, space allocations have not allowed for additional seating in the future. Therefore, *the lack of available seating places a "lid on sales."* Numerous food courts have barely adequate seating at peak times, limiting the food operators' business at those times. The only way then to increase sales is during nonpeak periods, at a time when the consumer's stomach is not rumbling.

COMPUTING YOUR INDIVIDUAL SEATING REQUIREMENTS

As I said previously, seating for a food court is similar to parking for a shopping center or retail facility. Both are necessary for success. Most shopping center owners and developers would never consider a site without adequate parking. Thus, today a shopping center or mall should have at least 4.5 spaces per 1,000 square feet of gross leasable area. Is it then practical to say that food court tenants should have some type of similar ratio? Without question, the answer is yes!

My studies indicate that the ratio of gross leasable food tenant space to seating area should be computed. This translates itself into a minimum of 50 seats per unit. Therefore, if there are 10 units in the food court, there should be 500 seats, or 100 seats per 1,000 square feet of gross leasable food space. Assuming 20 square feet per seat, this represents a total of 10,000 square feet of seating, in contrast to say 5,000 square feet of gross leasable area. *The ratio then is 2.0 square feet of seating for each square foot of food operator's space.*

CHECK AVERAGE

The average check in a food court today is under $4. Thus, it takes a considerable number of customers to generate $500,000 or $750,000 or, for that matter, $1,000,000 in gross sales. Unfortunately, the shopping center developer and leasing agent often does not truly understand this need. It is important to educate them to the fact that the food business is as successful as the last customer.

RENTS

Rents in food courts range from $25 to $100 per square foot. Naturally, $100 per square foot is extreme. Nonetheless, typical rents in food courts range between $40 and $60 a square foot. In addition to the base rent, the tenant is usually expected to pay between 10% and 15% gross sales, or whichever is greater. For example, if you operated a 700-square-foot facility and had a base rent commitment of $40 a square foot, your rental obligation would be $28,000 a year. If you were to capture sales of $400,000, and you had a 10% rental, your total rent would amount to $40,000. Thus, the overage, or additional rent, amounts to $12,000.

In addition to the base rental plus a percentage of sales, mall tenants are faced with CAM charges for real estate taxes, mall operating expenses, snow removal (where applicable), merchants' association fees, security charges, and advertising contribution. These represent the more typical charges. Many malls also have a special add-on charge for food court maintenance. Most food people are shocked at CAM charges, which may reach $10, $20, or $30 per square foot, depending on the type of complex in which you are located. It is a factor that the food operator needs to get a handle on *before* entering the food court. The food operator must include the CAM charges in his other financial pro forma. Furthermore, these charges are usually allocated on a pro rata square foot basis, allowing the food operator no control over the costs. While it can be difficult to negotiate some kind of a "lid" or "stop," it is worth attempting to do so. Certainly, some maximum percentage of increase can be negotiated to protect the food operator from excessive CAM charges.

SUBURBAN OFFICE COMPLEXES

There are very few suburban office complexes around North America that, by themselves, have sufficient employees and visitors to support a large food court. In fact, most of them cannot support even a small one. While office developers may design one into the complex, you, as the food operator, must look at the concept with a jaundiced eye and recognize the lack of overall potential. This does not mean that all suburban office complexes are not desirable places for food courts. Actually, some are. Furthermore, some office complexes are desirable locations for restaurants. The one item that food operators in office buildings must consider is that there often is no dinner business. Therefore, the question that must be answered is "Can I live off the luncheon business, and is there enough?"

CLEANLINESS

In observing food courts, the lack of consistent cleanliness is disturbing. Food operators (the good ones) are extremely sensitive to cleanliness and spend a considerable amount of time and money making sure that their facilities reflect an immaculate presence to the consumer. Unfortunately, the cleanliness of the food courts is usually the responsibility of the mall management and its cleaning staff. Equally unfortunate is that, frequently, no one is adequately supervising these employees during peak periods. As a result, it is not uncommon for the food court to look messy and dirty during the peak eating periods. Seats and tables are vacant, but the tables have not been cleaned. Thus, either the consumer or the staff of one of the food operations must clean up, or customers will avoid the court. Shopping center management needs to recognize this problem and work out some type of arrangement with the existing food operators in food courts, so that adequate "policing" of the tables will occur quickly when needed. This may be a food court association that accepts the responsibility for managing the cleanup people in order to meet the basic cleanliness objective.

INDIVIDUALITY

The food business thrives on uniqueness and individuality. In contrast, food courts have a tendency toward sameness. To end this conflict, food operators need to create individuality. Sbarro's started out like many other food court shops, providing the accepted sameness. It almost cost them their business. Subsequently, they redesigned their presentation, creating individuality. Next, they had to convince the landlords that it was good for both of them. Their success speaks for itself. Uniqueness and individuality in the presentation to the consumer consists of many factors, such as the sign, menu board, storefront design, or simply hanging items that reflect the product type being offered by the food operator. Regardless, personality is needed to create consumer awareness.

SUMMARY

Food courts represent continuing opportunities for the food industry. Nevertheless, those opportunities are not without pitfalls. I have often said that the determination of which mall to go into is as important as where to be placed within the food court. Finally, even if all the successful factors are present, the lack of adequate tables with seating can signal the death knell of an otherwise potentially successful food court or food operation.

Appendix

CUSTOMER SURVEY

Cafeteria

Date _____   Ref. No. ___ ___ ___ ___

Unit location _____ ___
                       City or Address

Time of day: _____ (1 = 11:30–12:30) (2 = 12:30–1:30) (3 = 1:30–2:30) ___
    (4 = 2:30–3:30) (5 = 4:30–5:30) (6 = 5:30–6:30) (7 = 6:30–7:30) (8 = 7:30–8:30)

Day of week: _____ (1 = Mon.) (2 = Tues.) (3 = Wed.) (4 = Thurs.) ___
                            (5 = Fri.) (6 = Sat.) (7 = Sun.)

INTRODUCTION: Hello. My name is _____. We are conducting
a survey of our customers in order to serve you better.
Would you mind answering a few questions for us?

1. How often do you visit this _____ Cafeteria   ___
   1. Twice a week or more   6. Six times a year
   2. Once a week   7. Twice a year
   3. Twice a month   8. Once a year or less
   4. Three times a month   9. First visit
   5. Once a month   10. Other (specify) _____

2. How often do you visit the other _____ Cafeteria?   ___
   1. Twice a week or more   6. Six times a year
   2. Once a week   7. Twice a year
   3. Twice a month   8. Once a year or less
   4. Three times a month   9. Never
   5. Once a month   10. Other (specify) _____

3. Where were you *just prior* to your visit to _____?   ___
   1. At work   4. School
   2. Shopping   5. Personal business (bank, doctor)
   3. Home   6. Other (specify)_____

4. How long did it take you to drive here? _____ minutes   ___

5. Where else do you eat out for lunch?   ___
          Name   Location

   _____   _____
   _____   _____
   _____   _____

Where else do you eat out for dinner?
          Name   Location

   _____   _____
   _____   _____
   _____   _____

6. What restaurants do you feel are comparable to _____? ____

        Name   Location

_____   _____

_____   _____

_____   _____

7. Do you reside here year round?   ____
_____ Yes   _____ No
If *No*, how many months do you stay? _____

8. In this area which city or town do you reside? _____ ____

9. What is your zip code? _____   ____

10. What are the closest *major* crossing streets to your place of
residence?   ____
_____ and _____
(Imperative—need two streets)

11. What do you *like* most about _____?   ____
1st mention _____
2nd mention _____
3rd mention _____
                          (PROBE!)

12. What do you *dislike* most about _____?   ____
1st mention _____
2nd mention _____
3rd mention _____
                          (PROBE!)

13. How do you feel _____ could improve?   ____
1st mention _____
2nd mention _____
3rd mention _____
                          (PROBE!)

14. What is the occupation of the head of the household? _____ ____

   1. Executive/Owner/Professional   7. Student
   2. Salesman/Manager/Supervisor   8. Housewife
   3. Nurse   9. Military
   4. Office Worker/Retail Clerk/   10. Retired
       Secretary/School Teacher   11. Unemployed
   5. Construction Worker   12. Other (specify)
   6. Unskilled Laborer   _____

15. What letter on this card represents your approximate age?* _____ ____

*See card facsimile on page 357.

16. What letter on this card represents the total income of all
working members of your household?* _____   _____

17. How many people are in the party? _____   _____

THANK YOU!

Note: Do not ask the following questions, but observe and record accordingly.

18. Sex of respondent   (1) Male   (2) Female   _____
19. Number of young children in the party _____   _____
20. Interview code   (1) White
                            (2) Black
                            (3) Oriental
                            (4) Hispanic

Interviewer's initials _____

*See card below.

CARD FACSIMILE

Age of Respondent in Years		Total Household Income	
J.	15–19	N.	Under $7,500
A.	20–24	D.	$7,500–$14,999
T.	25–29	I.	$15,000–$24,999
W.	30–34	Q.	$25,000–$34,999
X.	35–44	H.	$35,000–$49,999
M.	45–54	K.	$50,000–$74,999
R.	55–64	G.	Over $75,000
F.	65 and over		

CUSTOMER SURVEY

Coffee Shop

| Weather _____ Date _____ | Ref. No. ___ ___ ___ ___ |
| | 01 02 03 04 |

Unit Location
(City) _____ | ___ |
                      | 05 |

(1 = A.M. to Noon) (2 = Noon to 5:00 P.M.)   Time   ___
  (3 = After 5)   06

(1 = Sun.), (2 = Mon.), (3 = Tues.),   Day of week   ___
  (4 = Wed.), etc.   07

We are conducting a survey of _____ customers in order to serve you better. Would you mind answering a few questions for me?

1. How often do you visit *this* _____ unit?   ___
                                                         08
   (1) Twice a week or more   (5) Twice a year
   (2) Once a week   (6) Once a year
   (3) Twice a month   (7) Less than once a year
   (4) Once a month   (8) First visit

2. How many people are there in your party?   ___
                                                 09

3. How did you get here?   ___
                                                 10
   (1) Walked   (4) Bicycle
   (2) Automobile   (5) Other (specify) _____
   (3) Public transportation

4. If you came by automobile, how long did it take you?   ___
   _____ minutes   11

5. Where were you before coming _____ today?   ___
                                                            12
   (1) At work   (4) School
   (2) Shopping   (5) Other (specify) _____
   (3) Home

(If answer to Question 5 is "Work," ask Question 6.)

6. What is the closest major intersection near your | ___ ___ |
   place of employment? | 13 14 |
   _____ and _____ | ___ ___ ___ ___ |
                                            | 15 16 17 18 |

7. What do you like most about _____?   ___
                                                      19
   (1) Good service   (5) Fast service
   (2) Food selection   (6) Atmosphere   (9) Portion size
   (3) Convenient   (7) Good food   (0) Informal
   (4) Quantity of food   (8) Price   (X) Other (specify)

---

8. How can _____ improve? (PROBE!)

                                      `___ ___`
                                      20 21

9. Where else do you usually eat out? (PROBE!)

                                        `___ ___`
                                        21 22

10. Have you visited or are you planning to visit any shopping centers as a part of this trip?   (1) Yes   (2) No

    If yes, specify which ones. _____

    _____

    _____

    `24`   `25`   `26`   `27`

11. What is your ZIP code?

    `___ ___ ___ ___ ___`
    28 29 30 31 32

12. What are the closest major crossing streets to your place of residence?

    _____ and

    _____

    `___ ___ ___`
    33 34 35
    `___ ___ ___ ___`
    36 37 38 39

13. What is the occupation of the head of the household?   `___`
                                                              40

    (1) Professional/Owner/Executive   (6) Student
    (2) Salesman/Manager/Supervisor   (7) Housewife
    (3) Office Worker/Retail Clerk/   (8) Retired
           Nurse/School Teacher   (9) Unemployed
    (4) Skilled Worker   (0) Other _____
    (5) Unskilled Worker   (specify)

14. How many people live with you at home?   `___`
    (Insert total number of persons)   41

15. What letter on this card represents your approximate age?*   `___`
                                                               42

16. What letter on this card represents the total income of all working members of your household?*   `___`
                                                                43

Thank you!

Note: Do not ask the following questions, but observe information and mark.

17. Sex of respondent   (1) Male   (2) Female   `___`
                                                                44

18. Number of young children in party _____   `___`
                                                                45

19. Interview code   `___`
                                                                46

                                      Interviewers initials _____

*See card facsimile on page 357.

CUSTOMER SURVEY

Dinner House

Date _____

Time _____

Location _____

We are conducting a survey of our customers in order to serve you better. Would you mind answering some questions for us?

(A) 1. How many are in your party today? _____

(B) 2. Is this your first visit to _____?
                  1. Yes _____
                  2. No _____

(C) 3. How often do you come to _____?
                  _____
                  (number of times a week or month)

(D) 4. Did you come here from work or home?
                  1. Work _____
                  2. Home _____
                  3. Other _____
                  (specify)

        (If answer to above is "work," ask:)

(E) 5. Where is your place of employment? Location _____
_____
        (address or cross streets and city rather than employer's name)

(F) 6. In what city or town do you live? _____
     6a. What are the closest crossing streets to your home?
_____ and _____

(G) 6b. What is your ZIP code? _____

(H) 7. How long did it take you to get here? _____
                  (minutes)

(I) 8. Do you plan to shop on this trip?
                  1. Yes _____
                  2. No _____

     9. In what shopping area do you make most of your nonfood purchases?
        Name _____ Location _____

(J) 10. What other eating places do *you* frequently visit?

Name	Location	Frequency	Lunch	Dinner
_____	_____	_____	___	___
_____	_____	_____	___	___
_____	_____	_____	___	___

10a. Which eating places do you usually take your family to?

_____	_____	_____	____	____
_____	_____	_____	____	____
_____	_____	_____	____	____

11. What is your main reason for eating at (repeat responses above)?

Name _____ Reason(s) _____

_____ _____

_____ _____

(1) Good food   (2) Quantity   (3) Convenient   (4) Close   (5) Fast   (6) Price
(7) Informal   (8) Cafeteria service   (9) Other (specify)

12. Why did you come to _____ today?

(Do not ask customer following, but check response in appropriate categories)

1. Good food ____   2. Quantity of food ____   3. Convenient ____
4. Close ____   5. Fast ____   6. Price ____   7. Informal ____
8. Cafeteria service ____   9. Other _____
                                                  (specify)

(K) 13. What is your primary reason for patronizing _____?

(Do not ask customer following, but check response in appropriate categories)

1. Good food ____   2. Quantity of food ____   3. Convenient ____
4. Close ____   5. Fast ____   6. Price ____   7. Informal ____
8. Cafeteria service ____   9. Other _____
                                                  (specify)

(L) 14. How can _____ improve?

_____

_____

15. How much do you usually spend for lunch? _____

16. How much do you usually spend for dinner? _____

(M) 17. Do you own or rent your home?   1. Own _____
                                              2. Rent _____

(N) 18. If rent, is it a house or apartment?   1. Apartment ____
                                              2. House _____

(O) 19. Are you married or single?   1. Married _____
                                              2. Single _____
                                              3. Divorced _____

(P) 20. What is your occupation? _____

(Q) 21. What is your husband's/wife's occupation? _____

22. Do you have children?   1. Yes _____

                                              2. No _____

(If answer is "yes," ask:)

22a. How many? ____

(R) 22b. What are the ages of those children living at home? _____

_____

23. Do your children like to eat at _____?   1. Yes _____

                                                    2. No _____

24. Why or why not? _____

_____

25. How many cars do your (living at home) family members own? ____

(S) 26. Would you please look at this card and tell me what letter most closely corresponds to your age? (flash card)*   _____

(T) 27. Would you please look on reverse side of card and tell which letter corresponds to the total income of all working members of your family? (flash card)*   _____

Thank you very much for your help. We will use this information to keep you as a satisfied customer.

Sex: Male _____   Code _____

      Female ____   _____

                                                 _____

_____   Interviewer's initials _____

_____

*See card facsimile on page 357.

CUSTOMER SURVEY

Downtown Breakfast and Lunch Restaurant

INTERVIEWER: PLEASE CHECK TIME AND DAY BELOW

Wednesday ____ 10-1 Thursday ____ -2 Friday ____ -3 Saturday ____

TIME OF DAY: Opening–11:00 A.M. ____ 11-1 11:01 A.M.–closing ____ -2

Hello. My name is _____. We are conducting a survey of our customers. Would you answer a few questions to help _____ serve you in the best possible way?

1. How often do you visit _____ Restaurant?

Every day	____ 12-1	Once a month	____ -5
Three or more times a week	____ -2	Several times a year	____ -6
Once a week	____ -3	Seldom	____ -7
Two–three times a month	____ -4	First visit	____ -8

2. What was your main reason for coming downtown today?

Work	____ 13-1	School	____ -5
Shopping	____ -2	Recreation	____ -6
Work-related business	____ -3	Personal business	____ -7
To eat	____ -4	Other _____	-8

3. How did you get downtown today?

Train	____ 14-1	Car	____ -4
Subway/El	____ -2	Other _____	-5
Bus	____ -3		

4. Do you work downtown?   Yes ____ 15-1   No ____ -2

5. (If "yes" to question 4, ASK) What are the closest crossing streets to where you work?

_____ and _____
            16-   17-

6. What are the things you like most about _____ Restaurant? (PROBE!)

_____ 18-
_____ 19-
_____ 20-

7. What are the things you like least about _____ Restaurant? (PROBE!)

_____ 21-
_____ 22-
_____ 23-

8. How much did you pay for what you yourself ate today? $_____
                                                        24- 25- 26-

9. What city or town do you live in? _____
                                        27-   28-

10. What is your ZIP code? _____
                                  29-   30-   31-   32-   33-

11. How many persons are in your group today?
    One/myself ____ 34-1   Two ____   -2   Three ____   -3
    Four or more ____   -4

12. What restaurants do you consider *similar* to _____ ?
                                              (RECORD "NONE" IF GIVEN)
    _____ 35-
    _____ 36-

13. Which other restaurants in the _____ area do you
    tend to frequent most often for *dinner*? _____
                                              37-   38-

14. What is your occupation? _____ 39-
    (GET KIND OF WORK NOT INDUSTRY, SUCH AS "STEEL," "RAILROAD," ETC.)

15. Please look at this card (HAND CARD)* and tell me which letter on
    this card represents the age category you are in? _____ 40-

16. Please look at this card (HAND CARD)* and tell me which letter
    corresponds to the total income last year of all wage earners in your
    household? _____   41-

17. RECORD SEX OF RESPONDENT: Male ____ 42-1 Female ____   -2

       THANK YOU FOR YOUR COOPERATION. HAVE A GOOD DAY.

Interviewer's initials _____   Date _____

*See card facsimile on page 357.

CUSTOMER SURVEY

Fast Food

Location _____
Date _____
Lunch _____
Afternoon _____
Dinner _____
Evening _____

We are conducting a survey of our customers in order to serve you better. Would you mind answering some questions for us?

1. How often do you visit us here at _____?
   1. First visit
   2. Every day
   3. More than three times a week
   4. More than once a week
   5. Once a week
   6. Once every two weeks
   7. Once every three weeks
   8. Once a month
   9. Once every two months
   10. Once every three months or more

2. Where did you come from?
   1. Home ____
   2. Work ____
   3. Shopping ____
   4. Other _____
      (specify)

3. How many minutes did it take you to get here?   _____

4. In what city or town do you live?   _____

5. What is you ZIP code?   _____

6. What are the closest crossing streets to your home?
   _____ and _____

7. What other drive-ins (take-outs) do you eat at regularly?
   1. _____   4. _____
   2. _____   5. _____
   3. _____   6. _____

8. How often do you eat at (1st mention)?
   1. First visit
   2. Every day
   3. More than three times a week
   4. More than once a week
   5. Once a week
   6. Once every two weeks
   7. Once every three weeks
   8. Once a month
   9. Once every two months
   10. Once every three months or more

9. How much did you spend here today?   _____

10. How many persons live in your household?   _____

11. How many are children under 18 years of age?   _____

12. What is your age? _____

13. What is the occupation of the head of the household?

1. Professional/owner/executive	9. Skilled worker
2. Engineering & technical	10. Unskilled worker
3. Manager–supervisor	11. Nurse
4. Foreman	12. Farmer
5. Salesman	13. Housewife
6. Office worker & clerk	14. School teacher
7. Retail clerk	15. Student
8. Government employee	16. Retired

14. Do you live in an apartment or home?   1. Apartment _____
    2. Home _____

15. Are you married or single?   1. Married _____
    2. Single _____
    3. Divorced _____

16. Why do you eat at _____?

1. Good food	6. Coupons
2. Price	7. Variety
3. Convenient	8. Good drinks
4. Fast	9. Parking
5. Service	10. Other _____
	(specify)

17. Do you own a car?   1. Yes _____
    2. No _____

18. Would you please look at this card and indicate the total yearly income of all adult working members of your family?*   _____

Size of group _____

Code: 1. _____

Sex   1. Male _____   2. _____

2. Female _____   3. _____

Interviewer's initials _____

*See card facsimile on page 357.

CUSTOMER SURVEY

Seafood Restaurant

Day _____   Time _____

INTRODUCTION: Hello! We are conducting a survey of our customers in order to serve you better. Would you mind answering a few questions for me?

1. Did you eat or are you planning to eat at _____?   _____

2. How often do you visit? _____

3. Where did your trip originate today? _____

4. (If at work) What are the closest crossing streets to your place of employment _____ and _____

5. Where are you going after you leave here? _____

6. How did you get here? _____

7. How many minutes did it take you to get here? _____ minutes

8. Why did you decide to eat here today? _____

9. (If at lunch) Would you consider coming back with friends or spouse for dinner?   Yes _____   No _____

10. (If at dinner) Would you come back to _____ for lunch?   Yes _____   No _____   dinner?   Yes _____   No _____

11. Have you ever avoided _____ because of the wait? Yes _____   No _____   If so, how often? _____

12. On a scale of 1 (lowest) to 5 (highest), how would you rate _____ in terms of:

Food quality	1	2	3	4	5
Food quantity	1	2	3	4	5
Price	1	2	3	4	5
Selection/variety	1	2	3	4	5
Service	1	2	3	4	5
Atmosphere	1	2	3	4	5
Location	1	2	3	4	5
Drinks	1	2	3	4	5
Value	1	2	3	4	5

13. What city or town do you currently reside? _____

14. What is your ZIP code?   ___ ___ ___ ___ ___

15. What are the closest crossing streets to your place of residence? _____ and _____

16. What is your:
    Occupation _____
    Marital status _____ (If married, is spouse employed?) Yes _____ No _____
    Age _____ (present card)*
    Income $_____ (present card)*

17. Is there anything that you dislike about _____?
    _____

18. What can _____ do to improve? _____

19. How many people are in your group? _____

20. Is your visit here a special occasion?   Yes _____ No _____
    If yes, what occasion? _____

21. How did you first hear about _____? _____

THANK YOU!

SEX: Male _____   Female _____   RACE: 1. White   3. Hispanic
                                             2. Black   4. Other

                                      Interviewer initials _____
_____

*See card facsimile on page 357.

CUSTOMER SURVEY

Theme Restaurant

Date _____   Ref. No. ___ ___ ___ ___
Day _____
Time _____

Hello! We are conducting a survey of our customers in order to serve you better. Would you mind answering a few questions for us?

1. How often do you come to _____?   ___
   1. Twice a week or more   6. Six times a year
   2. Once a week   7. Twice a year
   3. Three times a month   8. Once a year or less
   4. Twice a month   9. First visit
   5. Once a month   10. Other (specify) _____

2. How many minutes did it take you to get here?   ___

3. Where were you *just prior* to your visit here?   ___
   1. Home   4. School
   2. Work   5. Personal business
   3. Shopping   6. Other (specify) _____

4. What was your primary reason for coming to _____
   today?   ___
   1. Good food/unique   8. Price
   2. Quantity of food   9. Informal
   3. Convenient   10. Good drinks
   4. Good service   11. Atmosphere
   5. Portion size   12. Recommended
   6. Meet friends   13. Other (specify) _____
   7. Oyster bar

5. How many people are in your party?   ___

6. What other restaurants do you patronize frequently?

   _____   _____   _____
   _____   _____   _____
   _____   _____   _____

7. What did you have to eat and drink here today?

   _____
   _____

8. What do you like most about _____?

   _____
   _____
   _____

9. Is there anything that you dislike about _____?

_____

10. How can _____ improve?

_____

11. How much did you spend here today?   ___

12. Is your visit here a special occasion?   ___
    1. Yes   IF YES, WHAT _____
    2. No

13. How did you first hear about _____?   ___
    1. Friends   2. Newspaper
    2. Radio   3. TV
    3. Drove by   6. Other (specify) _____

14. What is your occupation?   ___
    1. Professional/Executive/Owner   6. Unskilled Worker
    2. Salesman/Manager/Supervisor   7. Student
    3. Nurse/School Teacher   8. Housewife
    4. Secretary/Computer Worker/   9. Retired
       Office Worker/Retail Clerk   10. Unemployed
    5. Skilled Worker   11. Other (specify) _____

15. What is your marital status?   ___
    1. Single   2. Married   3. Divorced   4. Widow

16. If married, is your spouse employed?   ___
    1. Yes ___
    2. No ___

17. In what city, town, or suburb do you live?

_____

18. What is your ZIP code?   ___ ___ ___ ___ ___

19. If you came from home, what are the closest crossing streets to your
    place of residence?
    _____ and _____

20. If you came from work, what are the closest crossing streets to that
    location?
    _____ and _____

21. What is your age?   ___

22. Would you please look at this card and tell me which letter most
    closely corresponds to the total income of all working members
    of your household.*   ___

Code: 1. 2. 3. 4.   SEX: <u>M or F</u>

_____   Interviewer's initials _____

*See card facsimile on page 357.

CUSTOMER SURVEY

Telephone Interview

Ref. Number ——— ——— ——— ———
                 01   02   03   04

City _____
                                                   05

Date _____
                                                 06

Phone number _____

(First question)
Is this (telephone number dialed)? _____ If yes, contine:

Good morning (afternoon/evening). My name is _____. I am
with _____ Market Research Company. We are
conducting a survey concerning the preferences of patrons of restaurants
in the _____ area. I wonder if you would mind answering
a few questions for me?

            (Respondent should be 16 years of age or older.)

1. What eating places do you usually take your family to?   ——— ———
   (Record and enter order of response: 1st, 2nd, 3rd, etc.) (If no   07   08
   family, go to question 3.)

                NAME   **LOCATION**

    1st response _____
    2nd response _____
    3rd response _____
    4th response _____
    5th response _____

2. Why do you go to _____?
                        (1st response)   09

   DO NOT READ LIST!

(1) Good food	———	(6) Price	———
(2) Quantity of food	———	(7) Informal	———
(3) Convenient	———	(8) Cafeteria service	———
(4) Close to home	———	(9) Atmosphere	———
(5) Fast service	———	(10) Other (specify)	———

   Record each mention in order of response. For example, if "Good food"
   were mentioned first, "1" would be placed to the right of "Good food."

3. How often do you (and your spouse or social acquaintance) go out for lunch?

———
10

1. Twice a week or more	5. Twice a year
2. Once a week	6. Once a year
3. Twice a month	7. Less than once a year
4. Once a month	8. Never

4. Where do you most frequently eat lunch?
   (Record and mark in order of response: 1st, 2nd, 3rd, etc.)

—— ——
11   12

NAME	LOCATION
1st response _____	_____
2nd response _____	_____
3rd response _____	_____
4th response _____	_____
5th response _____	_____

5. Why do you go to _____?
   (1st response)

———
13

DO NOT READ LIST!

(1) Good food	____	(6) Price	____
(2) Quantity of food	____	(7) Informal	____
(3) Convenient	____	(8) Cafeteria service	____
(4) Close to home	____	(9) Atmosphere	____
(5) Fast service	____	(10) Other (specify)	____

_____ (PROBE!)

6. How much do you usually spend for lunch? $_____
   Record the amount spent at first response.) (Total amount spent for all in party.)

—— ——
14   15

7. What restaurant do you most frequently visit for dinner?
   (Record and mark in order of response: 1st, 2nd, 3rd, etc.)

—— ——
16   17

NAME	LOCATION
1st response _____	_____
2nd response _____	_____
3rd response _____	_____
4th response _____	_____
5th response _____	_____

8. Why do you go to _____?
   (1st response)

———
18

DO NOT READ LIST!

(1) Good food	____	(6) Price	____
(2) Quantity of food	____	(7) Informal	____
(3) Convenient	____	(8) Cafeteria service	____
(4) Close to home	____	(9) Atmosphere	____
(5) Fast service	____	(10) Other (specify)	____	(PROBE!)

_____

9. How much do you usually spend at dinner? $_____ __ __
                                                            19 20

10. When you select a sit-down restaurant, what would be your   __
    first choice?   21
    Name _____
    Location _____
    Why?   __
                                                                 22

DO NOT READ LIST!

(1) Good food	____	(6) Price	____
(2) Quantity of food	____	(7) Informal	____
(3) Convenient	____	(8) Cafeteria service	____
(4) Close to home	____	(9) Atmosphere	____
(5) Fast service	____	(10) Other (specify)	____
			(PROBE!)

Record each mention in order of response. For example, if "Good food"
were mentioned first, "1" would be placed to the right of "Good food."

_____
_____

_____

Second choice?   __
Name _____   23
Location _____
Why?   __
                                                             24

DO NOT READ LIST!

(1) Good food	____	(6) Price	____
(2) Quantity of food	____	(7) Informal	____
(3) Convenient	____	(8) Cafeteria service	____
(4) Close to home	____	(9) Atmosphere	____
(5) Fast service	____	(10) Other (specify)	____
			(PROBE!)

_____

11. When was the last time you were at a _____ restaurant?   __
                                                                  25
    1. Twice a week or more   5. Twice a year
    2. Once a week   6. Once a year
    3. Twice a month   7. Less than once a year
    4. Once a month   8. Never

12. With or without your family?   (1) with family _____   __
                                    (2) without family _____   26

13. What did you like about it?

    DO NOT READ LIST!

(1) Good food	___	(6) Price	___		
(2) Quantity of food	___	(7) Informal	___		
(3) Convenient	___	(8) Cafeteria service	___		
(4) Close to home	___	(9) Atmosphere	___		
(5) Fast service	___	(10) Other (specify)	___		

    (PROBE!)

    _____

    _____

    _____

    $\overline{27}$

13a. If never at _____, why not!

    _____

    _____

    $\overline{28}$ $\overline{29}$

14. What didn't you like about it? (PROBE!)

    _____

    _____

    _____

    _____

    $\overline{30}$ $\overline{31}$

15. How can _____ improve? (PROBE!)

    _____

    _____

    _____

    _____

    $\overline{32}$ $\overline{33}$

16. Do you usually go from home or work to the _____ restaurant?

For lunch	_____	For dinner	_____
Home	_____	Home	_____
Work	_____	Work	_____

    $\overline{34}$

17. Into which category does the head of the hosehold belong?

1. 16 thru 20	6. 55–64
2. 21–24	7. 65 and over
3. 25–34	
4. 35–44	

    $\overline{35}$

18. What is the occupation of the head of household?

(1) Professional/Owner/Executive	(6) Student
(2) Salesman/Manager/Supervisor	(7) Housewife
(3) Office Worker/Retail Clerk/ Nurse/School Teacher	(8) Retired
	(9) Unemployed
(4) Skilled Worker	(10) Other _____
(5) Unskilled Worker	(specify)

    $\overline{36}$

19. Are you married or single?

    (1) Married   (3) Divorced
    (2) Single   (4) Widower

                                                37

20. If married, what is the occupation of your spouse?

    (1) Professional/Owner/Executive   (6) Student
    (2) Salesman/Manager/Supervisor   (7) Housewife
    (3) Office Worker/Retail Clerk/   (8) Retired
          Nurse/School Teacher   (9) Unemployed
    (4) Skilled Worker   (10) Other _____
    (5) Unskilled Worker   (specify)

                                                38

21. What is the approximate yearly income of all adult working members of your family?

                                              39

    T) $1-   4,999   F) $10,000-$11,999   Q) $20,000-$24,999
    V) 5,000- 6,999   S) 12,000- 14,999   A)   25,000- 49,999
    R) 7,000- 9,999   Y) 15,000- 19,999   L)   50,000- over

    1) _____
        Male

    _____
        Female

SHOPPING CENTER INVENTORY

Date _____

Name _____

Location _____

_____

Land area _____

Building area _____

Year opened _____

Anchor Tenants

Name	Size	Estimated Sales
_____	_____	_____
_____	_____	_____
_____	_____	_____
_____	_____	_____
_____	_____	_____

Overall shopping center sales _____

Overall sales per square foot _____

Number of parking spaces _____

Accessibility

Primary Traffic Artery(ies)

Name	Number of Lanes	Traffic Signal	Turning Lanes	Traffic Counts
_____	_____	_____	_____	_____
_____	_____	_____	_____	_____
_____	_____	_____	_____	_____
_____	_____	_____	_____	_____

Secondary Traffic Artery(ies)

Name	Number of Lanes	Traffic Signal	Turning Lanes	Traffic Counts
_____	_____	_____	_____	_____
_____	_____	_____	_____	_____
_____	_____	_____	_____	_____

Trade Area

Directional Attraction	Miles	Barriers	Competitive Impediments
North	_____	_____	_____
South	_____	_____	_____
East	_____	_____	_____
West	_____	_____	_____

Competition

Name	Location	Size	Anchor Tenants	Total Sales	Parking Spaces

Physical Condition

Exterior _____

_____

Interior _____

_____

Current Vacancy

Square Footage _____

Percent _____

Future Expansion

Date _____

Size _____

Entertainment Components

Restaurants _____

Movie Theaters _____

Other _____

Peripheral Uses

Name	Type	Size	Performance

SITE LOCATION INVENTORY

Location

Major artery _____
Secondary artery _____
Address _____
City _____

Site Data

Draw a sketch showing shape, dimension, and any building or significant features below: Mark NORTH on sketch. Indicate access points and adjacent uses.

Attach photos of the site to this submission. Mark the direction of each picture. Bracket the site and the surrounding area.

Proposed Transaction: Cost or Rent

Purchase $ _____
Gound lease $ _____
Lease $ _____

Zoning

Present zoning _____
_____
Restrictions _____
_____
Sign restrictions _____
_____
Other restrictions or requirements
_____
_____

Property Contacts

Owner _____
Address _____
City _____ State _____
Phone (___)_____
Telefax _____
Attorney _____
Address _____
City _____ State _____
Phone (___)_____
Telefax _____
Broker _____
Address _____
City _____ State _____
Phone (___)_____
Telefax _____

Demographics

Primary Trade Area
Current population: _____
5-year forecast: _____
Number within customer profile ___
Current households _____
5-year household forecast _____
Persons per household _____
Average household income $_____
5-year income forecast $_____
Daytime working population _____
Age structure in years:
10–19 _____
20–25 _____
26–30 _____
31–35 _____
36–40 _____
41–45 _____
46–50 _____
51–55 _____
56–60 _____
61–70 _____
71 and older _____

Environmental considerations

Soil condition _____

_____

Air quality _____

_____

Health Department _____

_____

_____

Accessibility

Traffic department _____
Traffic counts _____

_____

Hourly counts _____

_____

Date of the counts _____
Widenings or improvements _____

_____

Speed limit _____
Medians _____

_____

Curb Cuts _____
Number of lanes _____
Accessibility _____

_____

Utilities

Sewer, Sanitary:
Availability _____
Distance _____
Size _____
Hookup permitted _____
Sewer, Storm:
Availability _____
Hook up _____
Distance _____
Water:
Availability _____
Distance _____
Hookup _____
Electric:
Power available _____
Adequate size _____
Distance _____

Secondary Trade Area

Current population _____
5-year forecast _____
Number within age profile _____
Current households _____
5-year household forecast _____
Persons per household _____
Average household income $_____
5-year income forecast $_____
Daytime working population _____
Age structure in years:
    10–19 _____
    20–25 _____
    26–30 _____
    31–35 _____
    36–40 _____
    41–45 _____
    46–50 _____
    51–55 _____
    56–60 _____
    61–70 _____
    71 and older _____

Competition

Direct
Name _____ Location _____ Sales __

_____
_____
_____
_____
_____
_____
_____

Indirect
Name _____ Location _____ Sales __

_____
_____
_____
_____

Visibility

Visibility _____
Right _____
Left _____
Seconds Right _____
Seconds Left _____

Index